Erica ꒱

W9-DDS-834

Mambo Occasional Papers — Missio-Pastoral Series No. 17

QUEST FOR BELONGING

Introduction to a study
of African Independent Churches

by
M.L. Daneel

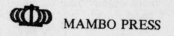 MAMBO PRESS

MAMBO PRESS
Gweru, P.O. Box 779
Harare, P.O. Box 66002, Kopje
Gokomere, P. Bag 9213, Masvingo

QUEST FOR BELONGING

First Print 1987

ISBN 0 86 922 426 3

Printed and published in Zimbabwe
by Mambo Press, Senga Road, Gweru
1987

CONTENTS

CHAPTER 3

CHAPTER 4

CHAPTER 5

CHAPTER 6

Life and faith of the Independent Churches

CHAPTER 7

In memory of the Shona Independent Church leaders, who have gone before:

Bishops Samuel Mutendi, David Masuka (Snr) and Andreas Shoko, the forerunners of Zionism in Zimbabwe;

High-priest Johane Maranke and his two sons, Makebo and Judah, of the African Apostolic Church *(vaPostori);*

Bishop Nheya Gavure and Rev. Musasikwa *(Fambidzano's* composer of songs) of the First Ethiopian Church;

Rev. Mheke Zvekare Sengwayo of the African Congregational Church *(Chibarirwe),* and Rev. Kumani Sibambo of the African Reformed Church *(Shonganiso).*

You, who have died yet live

    who sought and found belonging.

You, sons of Africa

    cloud of witnesses

    stand firm in our dreams

    raise the shooting star.

You, followers of Christ

    see our pilgrimage

    share our suffering, our belonging and love

    where ... His Kingdom comes.

FOREWORD

So far, all monographs which have flowed from Marthinus Daneel's pen have dealt exclusively with the Shona people of Zimbabwe, their traditional religion and, especially, the Shona Independent Churches. Two large volumes on these churches have already been published: *Old and new in Southern Shona Independent Churches:* Vols. I (1971) and II (1974). Three more volumes — unfortunately delayed because of the war situation in Zimbabwe in the 1970s and Daneel's move to the University of South Africa (1981) — are to follow. They are eagerly awaited by the international community of scholars and, no less, by the Shona church leaders themselves. Daneel is acknowledged world-wide as one of the best researchers on Independent Churches. J.F. Holleman once called him " a born fieldworker of rare quality"; this tribute is well deserved and abundantly proved in his studies on the Shona churches.

In *Quest for belonging,* however, Daneel has done what he always hesitated to do: instead of concentrating on the Shona churches — which he has so far studied in almost complete isolation from similar movements elsewhere on the African continent— he has now attempted to survey the Independent church movement as a whole. He always hoped to do that "one day", after he had completed his research on the Shona movements. He now realises, however, that neither he nor anybody else will ever exhaust the wealth of theological material yet to be uncovered among the Shona churches. So he has finally yielded to pressure from several quarters to put his interpretation of the Independent movement as a continent-wide phenomenon on paper.

This interpretation of Daneel's is, in a very real sense, summed up in the title of the book: *Quest for belonging.* It may remind the informed reader of two books on similar religious groups: Lalive D'Epinay's *Haven of the masses,* on the Pentecostal churches of Chile, and *A place to feel at home,* a study on East African Independent Churches by F. Welbourn and B.A. Ogot. There is, however, a subtle difference between these two titles and that of Daneel's book. The Independent Churches, Daneel suggests, offer more than just a haven or a home: they represent, at a profound level, a quest for belonging. It is on this point, more than any other, that they challenge the "mission" churches in

8

Africa and, with them, the entire traditional Western missionary enterprise.

Few students of the African religious scene today would doubt the importance and significance — also for the future of Christianity on this continent — of the African Independent Churches. These churches, together with similar Christian movements among other primal societies in Melanesia, the Americas and elsewhere, may indeed be seen as the fifth major Christian church type, after the Eastern Orthodox churches, the Roman Catholic Church, the Protestant Reformation, and the Pentecostal churches. On our appreciation of the African indigenous churches, we have, moreover, come a long way since the 1940s when Bengt Sundkler, the first person to attempt a serious and comprehensive study of them, wrote the following evaluation in the 1948 edition of his *Bantu Prophets in South Africa:*

> *The syncretistic sect becomes the bridge over which Africans are brought back to heathenism* — a viewpoint which stresses the seriousness of the situation. It can be shown how individuals and groups have passed step by step from a Mission church to an Ethiopian church, and from the Ethiopians to the Zionists, and how at last via the bridge of nativistic Zionism they have returned to the African animism from which they once started. (Sundkler 1948: 297 — Sundkler's italics)

By the time the second edition of *Bantu Prophets* was published (1961), Sundkler was no longer so sure of his earlier judgment. He now said:

> Looking at the situation some fifteen years later we have had to ask ourselves whether this viewpoint was not, in fact, too foreign, too Western, perhaps (Sundkler 1961: 302).

What was only a tentative question in 1961 soon became a firm conviction, as clearly testified by Sundkler's subsequent writings and particularly by his *Zulu Zion* (1976). And what happened to Sundkler happened to many other students of African indigenous churches as well. To mention only one example: in 1964 Marie-

9

Louise Martin came to a decidedly negative conclusion regarding these churches in her *The biblical concept of messianism and messianism in Southern Africa*. Seven years later, however, she published a book on the Kimbanguist Church, *Kirche ohne Weisse* (English translation: *Kimbangu — An African prophet and his church,* 1975) in which she admitted that, in her earlier studies, she had looked at African churches "as it were from outside". Her study of the Kimbanguists was different, however. She was told, even before her arrival in Zaire: "Vous venez vivre le Kimbanguisme" ("You're coming to live Kimbanguism"). This is what she did (and is still doing!). She now knows that "this is the only right way of really coming to a proper understanding of a church which is so historically and culturally different from the churches in the West" (Martin 1975: viii).

Daneel's studies emerge from a similar almost total immersion in African Independent church life. Not that this leads him to an uncritical endorsement of everything Independents say and do. As a matter of fact, to close one's eyes to theological weaknesses in the Independent churches and simply approve uncritically of everything they do, would be a manifestation — albeit a more subtle one — of the same paternalism which could see no good in African Independency. Daneel has not fallen prey to this second, and far more dangerous, form of paternalism. The clearest proof of this is *Fambidzano,* a theological education by extension programme for Independent church leaders which he initiated in 1972 (cf. Peter Makamba, Theological Education by Extension: The Shona Independent Churches experiment, *Missionalia* 12: 3, Nov. 1984, pp. 115-123). Daneel realised that the greatest need of the Independents was to break out of their isolation and to experience an enriching encounter with the wider theological and ecclesiastical world without, however, jeopardising their unique character and contribution. To this *Fambidzano* provided the answer. The fact that he succeeded in obtaining and retaining the leaders' support is a singular tribute to the trust they place in him.

With these words I now recommend *Quest for belonging* to the reader. I am convinced that members of African Independent Churches will be able to recognise themselves in the pages that follow and that they have been both understood and challenged.

I trust that readers from traditions other than the Independents will also be led to a deeper understanding of these churches and be challenged by them.

David J. Bosch
Dean, Faculty of Theology
University of South Africa
Pretoria.

December 1986

ACKNOWLEDGMENTS

As I have made substantial use in this study of the research results of the fieldwork conducted amongst the Shona Independents during the sixties, I wish to acknowledge the financial assistance received at the time from the following Dutch sponsors:

* The *Free University, Amsterdam* which granted me paid leave to engage in field research in the then Rhodesia (1965-1967) and salaried support while I wrote up the results in the Netherlands;
* the *Netherlands Foundation for the Advancement of Tropical Research* (WOTRO) which covered the major costs of the field project; and
* the *Afrika Studiecentrum, Leiden,* under whose auspices I worked and which contributed towards field expenses and assisted with data processing.

Without the generous grants of these institutions I would not have been able to engage in the extensive research programme which gave rise to the publication of the first two volumes in the series *Old* and *New in Southern Shona Independent Churches.*

This study is not a direct result of my current (1984-1986) research work in Zimbabwe, which is a follow-up on the previous project with a view to completing the aforementioned series. Nevertheless, the preparation of the manuscript and negotiations with the publishers took place during this second phase of the research so that there is an integral relationship between this publication and the others that should appear in the not too distant future. I therefore wish to thank the following two institutions:

* The *Human Sciences Research Council* in South Africa for its financial support over a three-year period (1984-1986), which enabled me to devote time to the preparation of this book, in addition to intermittent spells of fieldwork in Zimbabwe; and
* the *University of South Africa,* for granting me several months of paid leave during each of the above-mentioned three years for the follow-up study among the Shona Independents.

I am especially indebted to Prof. Frans van den Bogaerde, vice-principal of Unisa, and Prof. David Bosch, dean of the theological faculty of Unisa, both of whom have generously supported my requests for funds and time in various university committees, thus enabling me to immerse myself once more in Independent Church life as a participant observer. The trust and interest they have shown in my work have not been taken for granted; on the contrary, it was a source of inspiration, particularly during those inevitable spells of fatigue and depression when creative tension appeared to me to be remote. A special word of appreciation is due to my colleague, David Bosch, for not shirking the complications caused in our department (Missiology and Science of Religions) by my protracted spells of absence for allowing me to draw substantially on the Unisa study guide on Independent Churches he had written in 1973, and for writing the foreword to this study. In addition I am grateful to Unisa for permission to publish this work, which is an abridged version of a study guide I produced in 1982 for a third-year course in missiology.

To those colleagues in our department who, by taking over some of my teaching and other responsibilities, have enabled me to pursue the research project I can only express my deepest gratitude. Their sustained support and interest in my work have been a source of inspiration. Without Prof. Willem Saayman's close friendship, loyalty and critical yet stimulating accompaniment of my research I may well have abandoned an often demanding, strenuous and fragmented (owing to endless travel between Pretoria and Masvingo) work programme. Though less directly involved with my academic work, the following colleagues have been of great assistance through their friendship and stimulating conversation: Professors Abraham Viljoen, Johan Wolfaardt, Kobus Kruger, Willem Voster, and the senior lecturers Johan Steyn and Ras van Niekerk.

In a book of this nature I was in a sense also confronted with my own "quest for belonging". Thus I cast my mind back to the years of theological orientation in the Netherlands. Gratefully I remember those men who, less through their intellectual powers and international standing than through their human identification with a "nomad" from Africa, enabled me to discern my own theological roots. Can one forget the enlightened and enthusiastic lectures in systematic theology of Prof. G.C. Berkouwer, the lucid accounts of the history of missions by Prof. Jan van den Berg, and the cool, probing thrusts into the missionary nature of the church by the brilliant Prof. J.C. Hoekendijk?

Shall I forget the inspiring vision of Prof. J.H. Bavinck, mystic missiologist and transparent Christian, as, two days before his death, he blessed me "for a fruitful ministry in Africa", as an Old Testament patriarch would bless a son? Or the off-beat movements of Prof. Johannes Blauw during his visit to rural Africa as we tried, much to the delight of our Zionist friends, to master the Zionist dancing rhythm? Or the long and searching discussions with Prof. Hans Holleman, then director of the *Afrika Studiecentrum*, a demanding yet valued taskmaster who taught me some of the secrets of fieldwork and of writing?

To these men, all of whom in one way or another combined outstanding talent with humility, I am deeply indebted. For they have enriched my life, made me experience a sense of belonging in the Western world of my ancestry and have helped prepare me for my pilgrimage in Africa.

Over the years, as I kept returning to the Netherlands from time to time, there were always friends and colleagues whose lasting friendship, both personal and academic, spelt home to someone coming in from the heat of tropical Africa. To Dr Jan Kaayk (University of Leiden), Dr Jerry Gort and Professors Matt Schoffeleers and Dick Mulder (Free University, Amsterdam) and Arnulf Camps (University of Nijmegen), a special word of thanks. The sharing of mutual academic interests, and with some of you also the adventure of travel and camping in the still wild regions of Africa, this immensely fascinating continent, is a source of treasured memories and inspiration.

Through the years of the liberation of Zimbabwe, I lived and worked amongst the leaders and members of the Shona Independent Churches. Together we built *Fambidzano,* the Conferenc of Independent Churches, and its institute of theological training. It was an experimental venture, often fraught with risk due to exposure in militarily sensitive areas. I can but thank all the bishops of *Fambidzano* (particularly the late Bishop Nheya Gavure and the still living Bishops Forridge, Makamba, Zacheo, Hore and Nemapare, whose courage and persistence in the face of stress and uncertainty I admired), as well as the TEE staff and students, for the sharing of commitment and for sacrifice in the cause of church unity and theological advancement. I treasure the close bond with fellow pilgrim Peter Makamba, whose total dedication to this cause and responsible leadership as principal of the *Fambidzano* TEE College have earned him the respect of all concerned. Thanks to him and numerous friends — the people of *Fambidzano* — my life has acquired meaning: a sense of belonging.

We have all paid a price in the liberation struggle which led to the independence of Zimbabwe. You cannot walk through the valley of shadows, with the agony of suffering and destruction marking your world for so long, and emerge unscathed. You cannot constantly walk the edges of your existence and survive without the experience of trauma and wonder. Behind the laughing faces of today are the inner scars of yesterday, caused by the inevitable fading of ambition and creativity, disrupted relationships with loved ones, broken marriages, loss of livelihood, displacement, maimed bodies, broken minds. . . death. After Independence many of us needed time to adapt to change, to emerge from the inner wilderness of alienation and hurt, to capture a new vision for the tasks of every day.

In my own case the academically unproductive years had to be followed by a renewal of the commitment to write, particularly about the Independent Churches. But the academic ambitions and objectives of the distant past seemed to be crowded out by the experience of the war years in Zimbabwe. Through a protracted phase of reorientation I often visited the Cape for brief spells of writing — away from research demands in Zimbabwe and university chores in Pretoria. It was here that I found the beginning of a return of confidence and willingness once more to commit my thoughts to paper. To my friends in the Cape who cared enough to maintain an understanding presence when it was required, who trusted enough to share their own joys and disappointments with me — despite the heavy demands I made on them — I express my deepest gratitude. You, Bobbie and Helena Liebenberg, Janet Hodgson, Beth and Ann, I thank for the sharing and renewal of purpose in life!

Let me thank Fr Plangger and his fellow workers at Mambo Press for the publication of this book; also Marcelle Manley of Unisa for her rigorous linguistic discipline in editing the manuscript, always accompanied by her keen interest in the contents.

Finally, with loving affection, I mention my family, all of whom I have regrettably not seen or lived with often enough. I am grateful to:

* Nyasa, my eldest sister, for the lengthy and inspirational discussions we have had of late;
* my children of love — Alec, Lydia, Talita and Inus — for their unprejudiced care, understanding and laughter;
* my ex-wife Beulah for her faithful support of my work over many years;
* a respected and honoured father, who in old age has become a close friend, and whose kindly non-judgmental wisdom has always been cause for me to look Beyond for guidance in my own quest for belonging; and
* my mother, who passed away in 1978, and to whose memory — together with that of the deceased Shona Independent Church leaders — I dedicate this book. Hers was a fulfilled life of service and dedication as a missionary in Zimbabwe. When I leaf through the Bibles she used to study I am struck by signs of the intensity and persistence with which she delved for spiritual depth and inspiration. She was rarely depressed. In the back of a Bible she wrote, "Rejoicing is the side of faith that laughs at impossibilities and shouts, 'It shall be done!' No matter what happens — Rejoice!" And this she did. Her rejoicing derived from the joyous surrender of time and talents to the call of our Lord, Jesus Christ. I am indebted to her for having taught me — through her liberating acceptance of the restless adventurer in me — to live with and willingly accept a large measure of the solitude one incurs when conviction flouts convention.

"The Matchbox"
MASVINGO, ZIMBABWE
May 1986

INTRODUCTION

This study deals with the Independent Churches of Africa. The term "Independent" refers to their independence in organization, leadership and religious expression from Western-oriented historical (also called "mainline") or mission churches. Because of the diversity of the thousands of movements we are speaking about, the use of the term "church" does not imply a rigid value-judgment but is mainly a general characterization of religious groups, the representatives of most of which regard their organizations as "churches of Christ". In using the term "church" instead of such derogatory qualifications as "sects" or "separatists" I am also prompted, quite apart from considerations of tact, by the assumption underlying my approach to this phenomenon, namely that, with the exception of a minority of non-Christian groups, we are dealing with the very real and genuine *heartbeat of indigenized African Christianity* and not merely, as has been popularly assumed, with a movement on the periphery of or even outside so-called "mainline" Christianity. The description "peripheral movements" can only be applied in fairness if it is accepted that empirically reality shows *all* Christian churches, conditioned as they are by the incompleteness and frailty of human nature, to be peripheral phenomena — striving as it were towards the centre in recognition of the Lordship of Christ, or trying to achieve a more fulfilled expression of themselves as the body of Christ, which is what doctrinally they are supposed to be. Such a point of departure need not imply a naive levelling of churches, but could lead to more frank, critical discernment of the flaws in the inner circle(s) of each church if there is to be meaningful ecumenical interaction at all between the older historical churches and the Independent Churches in their shared movement towards the centre of Christianity, towards a common destiny — towards recognition of their common pursuit in this existence of the *quest for belonging.*

Quest for belonging indeed! It was the most apt characterization of the Independent Churches that I could think of. It should be noted that this title was not chosen beforehand as a central theme around which the arguments of this book would be built. It dawned on me in retrospect that these words forcefully sum up one of the key assumptions about the very nature of these movements, one that I have held, consciously or unconsciously, over the years of my close involvement with them. Is this then just another formulation of what others have already referred to when they depicted these churches as "a place to feel at home"? In a sense, yes. For in the disruption of social structures caused by the accelerated processes of acculturation and industrialization thousands of alienated individuals have found in the Independent Churches "homes" of spiritual, mental and even material security, truly African *havens of belonging.* It is argued in this book, moreover, that in developing an *intimate corporate life,* the Independents are compensating for the lack of *koinonia* in the historical churches. In contrast to the sober rationalism of the latter, the former express uninhibited emotional joy in response to the African need for religious celebration. Through mutual concern and voluntary service within the tightly knit interpersonal ties of the new community, a new identity is created and something of the lost security of the old order retrieved.

To the attentive reader it will be evident, however, that through the title of this book I am also trying to introduce essentially new perspectives. The most important of these is an attempt to portray the African Independent Churches as *institutions in their own right,* without having to keep qualifying them as movements originating and growing out of *a reaction against missions or an oppressive colonial situation.* This is not to ignore the undeniable motive of reaction, but to liberate our interpretation of these churches somewhat from an overriding preoccupation with this factor, particularly in our analysis of the causes of Independent Church origins and growth. Barrett, for instance, has put forward the hypothesis, basic to his entire research, that 'independency is a societal reaction to mission arising out of a tribal *Zeitgeist* or climate of opinion in which Christian missions were believed to be illegitimately mounting an attack against African traditional society".[1] He finds the root cause of the entire Independent Church movement in the missions' failure to demonstrate consistently the biblical concept of love in the Africa context.[2] Neill, in turn, argued that "at the heart of this whole movement,

1 Barrett, 1968, p. 116
2 Ibid., p. 156

directly or indirectly, will be found the sin of the white man against the black. It is because of the failure of the white man to make the Church a home for the black man that the latter has been fain to have a Church of his own."[3]

On the basis of research findings amongst the Shona Independents, I argue that their quest for belonging is conditioned by much more than a reaction to missions, and that *to concentrate exclusively on the mistakes of missions implies a one-sided view which does not sufficiently acknowledge the creativity and originality to be found within these churches.* Hence I have tried to indicate that much of what the Independents do and experience emerges as their own genius's creative and authentic response to the gospel, a contribution for which they themselves are solely responsible without any conditioning by missions — something which merits positive acclaim.

This study comprises three main parts. The first three chapters provide a broad orientation, the next three offer a close-up perspective on a geographically limited area, and the final chapter is a theological reflection on the whole phenomenon.

Chapter 1 gives a brief outline of relevant literature, a typology of the Independent Churches and an indication of their *missiological significance.* Chapter 2 is a historical sketch of the origin and growth of some of these churches, mainly in Southern Africa and Zaire. Chapter 3 deals with the causes influencing the growth of such churches and the principal theories in this connection. These chapters are based on an adapted and in many ways an expanded version of Prof. D.J. Bosch's study guide on this subject for the BDIII course (1973) at Unisa. His historical survey of the church of Simon Kimbangu in Zaire (chapter 2) and his discussion of nine decisive factors in the growth of churches (chapter 3) have been incorporated in only slightly modified form.

Chapters 4 to 6 are based mainly on my own research among the Shona Independent Churches in Zimbabwe. It provides a close-up perspective on a limited number of churches. On the one hand this is a limitation, but a necessary one in order to avoid the danger of meaningless generalizations in an impossibly wide field. In these chapters I have tried to draw a realistic picture of

3   S.C. Neill, **A History of Church Missions**, London, 1964, p. 164

the functioning of the Independent Churches in rural and urban areas, how they fit into a given socio-economic system and the nature of their political involvement. Leadership in itself is a crucial topic for an understanding of these movements, hence such matters as succession to key positions, "messianic" leadership in relation to schism and ecumenical co-operation are discussed in some detail. I hope to have shown convincingly that the categorical use of the terms "messianic" and "black Messiah" can be highly misleading and should therefore either be totally discarded or used only with great circumspection, lest the most prominent Independent Church leaders of this continent be misrepresented as deliberately usurping the mediatory function of Christ in the lives of their numerous followers. In the chapter on the doctrine and life of the Independent Churches the focus is on the traditional religious background of the Shona, without which it is impossible to understand either the rituals and beliefs of these movements, or the nature of interreligious (Christian and traditional) confrontation and/or dialogue.

Chapters 4 to 6 to a large extent represent a summary of some of my research findings of the 1960s. For the sake of conciseness I deliberately excluded a great deal of illustrative material and the tables of quantified data, most of which have already appeared or are due to appear in other publications. What has emerged as a result is a somewhat skeletal and incomplete outline which will undoubtedly fail to satisfy specialists in this field. I can only justify this approach by pointing out that the original purpose of this study was simply to provide students with an *introductory survey* of the salient features of the movements concerned and of the theological issues confronting missiologists in their efforts to assess and relate meaningfully to the phenomenon. There is no pretence of presenting an exhaustive account of any of the subjects broached, and it is in the light of this statement that this *Introduction to a study of Independent Churches* should be evaluated.

Another limitation on my description of the Shona Churches derives from the fact that it is based mainly on pre-Independence Zimbabwe. An update in the light of recent research has not yet been possible. This in no way implies, however, that the data presented are outdated. The *continuity* after Independence in terms of church structure, leadership, ritual and belief systems is so abundantly obvious from the results of current fieldwork that

I have no hesitation in commending the description of the Shona Independents — at least in their institutionalised religious life — as a sufficiently reliable reflection of the present situation to meet the standards set for empiric study of this nature. What has changed, of course, is the educational system in that denominational control of schools in rural areas has largely been replaced by government control. Since the old patterns of religious instruction are in a state of transition, one can expect the trends of religious recruitment through schooling and the correlation between school-leaving and church affiliation as discussed in this book to change likewise. Because of the post-Independence replacement in rural areas of the old three-tier judicial system (comprising village, ward and chiefs' courts) by socialist committees, as well as the introduction of a wide range of agricultural and other co-operatives, the socio-political involvement of the Independents is also showing new features. Nevertheless, the traditional patterns of tribal authority and behavioural codes determined by kinship are still observed in the new political context, as a result of which the intensive interaction between Independent Church leaders and influential chiefs still remains a significant feature of the church leaders' widespread rural influence. Moreover, the resurgence of traditional religion in recent years and the politically reinforced prominence of the ancestor cult, arising from the liberation struggle, make the discussion in this study of interaction and dialogue between the Independent Churches and the "traditionalists", as well as the various patterns of indigenized church rituals and beliefs against the backdrop of the African world-view, more rather than less relevant.

An insight worth mentioning derived from current research is that the Independents' commitment to the liberation struggle was much stronger and more widespread than I had thought originally. It would still be true to say that officially these churches maintained an aloof, even neutral, stance whereas both their members and leading figures were — at least in the latter years of the war — fully involved in supporting the guerrilla fighters. From the accounts of numerous prophets of the Spirit-type churches it is evident that they took part in the wave of witchcraft accusations which marked that period, that they "prophesied" about many issues to the guerrillas to help them plan their offensives and that some of them were even required to move

21

around with the fighters in the bush to assist the latter with their extrasensory perception. I hope eventually to deal with the role of the Independent Church prophets in the liberation war in a separate publication.

The theological reflection in the final chapter of this study must be seen as preliminary to an evaluation, based mainly on insights drawn from participation in and data collected about the Shona Independent Churches. Although this reflection may seem critical of the evaluations of other researchers, the intention is not to arrive at final, definitive pronouncements. It is more a matter of erecting a *few signposts* indicating a positive direction in which theologians and fellow Christians should move if a just and fair assessment of the phenomenon is to be achieved. I still have to analyse in depth the scores of Independent Church sermons which my research assistants and I have tape-recorded over the years — a daunting task which should actually be undertaken by a whole team of researchers. The outcome of this exercise should, however, be illuminating.

I am also fully aware of the limitations of attempting to "measure" the Christian nature of the Independent Churches in terms of the Reformed *notae ecclesiae*. A more conclusive assessment would need to make use of further criteria such as the role of the church in society, incarnational theology, perceptions of salvation and so on.

So far I have been led, in erecting these preliminary signposts, by my own gut-level response to the religious life of friends rather than by a thorough-going theological analysis of the mass of data at my disposal. In the final analysis an integration of both these approaches will be required. With the passing of the years I have actually evaded the challenge of a full-scale theological assessment of Independentism. Who, after all, wants to have the final word about the deepest, most unfathomable religious sentiments of close associates and friends? In this existence hope and change always appear to relativize judgment! We can but grope and feel our way intuitively, which of course does not relieve us of the duty of seeking truth and discerning the spirits, but which alerts us to our inevitable involvement in the historical process of movement and of becoming — the pilgrim nature of our earthly existence.

Hence any more probing theological analysis which I may yet undertake can never be anything but provisional. Perhaps at the end of the day I shall have to confess that I had neither the humility nor the appropriate tools for this task. My confession, however, will also include the positive comment that despite the seemingly "heretical" notions held by many Independents, they have — through their lives, both their earthy celebrations and their unquestionable awareness of God — made me profoundly aware of what I consider to be the caring attitude of Christ.

CHAPTER 1

ORIENTATION

1.1 *INDEPENDENT CHURCHES IN A MISSIOLOGICAL PERSPECTIVE*

Ever since the publication of Bengt Sundkler's pioneering study, *Bantu Prophets in South Africa,* in 1948, the Independent Churches have become a subject for serious, sustained research by missiologists. There are even grounds for asserting that reflection on and evaluation of the Independent Churches in Africa is one of the greatest tasks confronting missiology today.

Firstly, there is the rapid growth both in the number of these churches and in their membership since the beginning of the century, followed by a massive Christian oriented movement which simply cannot be ignored. It amounts to a sort of "spiritual" or "prophetic" revolution in Africa and involves an estimated 7 000 groups[1] with millions of followers.[2] In South Africa the terrific attraction of this kind of movement is highlighted by the great Easter assemblies at Lekhanyane's Zion City near Pietersburg. Statistics indicate that membership of the Methodist Church — the largest missionary agency in South Africa — has remained static at 12 percent of the total Black population for the period 1940 to 1960, whereas during the same period membership of the Independent Churches rose from 9,6 to 20 percent of the total Black population. If one moreover considers that over 30 percent of South Africa's Black population today either belongs to or falls within the direct sphere of influence of churches of this kind, the magnitude of the phenomenon needs no further comment.

1   Barrett, 1968, pp. 78-79. In 1968 Barrett estimated the number of Independent Churches in Africa at between five and six thousand. At the growth rate indicated by him the present total should be seven thousand or more.
2   Ndiokwere, 1981, p. 281. He estimates the number of adherents of these movements at some 20 million.

Since missiology is concerned with the historical process of church growth it needs to pay attention to the historical origin, the expansion and factors that contributed to the origin of the Independent Churches. There is an unmistakable correlation between mission policy, missionary work and the establishment of "young (mission) churches" on the one hand, and the rapid growth of the Independent Churches on the other.

A second reason for studying this movement is the missiological importance of such problems as the following: the focus on the incarnation in the Christian message within a particular culture, as manifested in for instance intelligible preaching and adapted Bible translation; religious environment; the on-going process of indigenization or contextualization of the churches with the accompanying danger of syncretism (e.g. in their organizational structure, leadership, ritual and doctrine); and particularly the process of interpretive communication between the Christian message and non-Christian religions.

The Independent Churches offer a unique opportunity for observing how the Black man once removed from the immediate influence of Western oriented missionaries, deals with his own traditional religion. Here one can see how Christian salvation is proclaimed and experienced in terms of the existential situation and world-view of the Black man, how the gospel is adapted to or presented in confrontation with existing indigenous customs and values. This is a dynamic process with extreme variations between the antipodes of *syncretist distortion,* in which the essential features of the gospel become blurred, and *legitimate indigenization or contextualization,* in which Christian communication is adapted and rendered intelligible without forfeiting crucial scriptural truths. No matter how one judges the nature of this process in a particular church, the fact remains that the "historical churches" can form a vivid picture of the value, mistakes and limitations of their own missionary policy in the past. The sometimes fragmentary scriptural interpretation, emotional expression, holistic approach, pragmatic or materialistic accents and other features of the Indpendent Churches all show the foreignness to the African context of the sober, rationalistic, often dualistically spiritualized approach of Western Christianity. Such contrasts provide valuable insights for those concerned with deciding the course of mission strategy in African in the future.

Thirdly, interchurch relations make a theological evaluation of the Independent Churches imperative. No matter how delicate and complex a task it may be, it is essential for the "historical churches"', determination of policy concerning the rejection of or possible ecumenical co-operation with the Independent Churches. In such an evaluation one is immediately confronted with the question of prejudice and subjectivity. One could state categorically that the following by now traditional approaches simply do not apply any more:

(1) the attitude of antagonism which merely warns against "false prophets" or sectarian separatist parasitizing on Western missionary work;
(2) an amused approach which views the Independent Churches as unimportant curios, and
(3) the totally unconcerned attitude that conveniently ignores the whole troublesome issue.

In a theological evaluation there must be constant awareness of both positive and negative factors. If the evaluation is to be balanced and scientific, there must be sufficient empirical data such as those provided by monographic in-depth studies. Theological literature on the subject contains abundant evidence of categorical statements and summary judgments based on impressionistic data, without proper consideration of the merits of inferences or generalizations about the trends in these groups which are being condemned. The result is that some movements are flatly rejected as unchristian or post-Christian without proper consideration of the tremendous variations of the phenomenon as a whole. This applies particularly to those groups which some missiologists are fond of designating "messianic".

Part of the difficulty of such an evaluation is the fact that literary data on a particular group are often inadequate for really searching theological inquiry. Even a fieldworker with missiological training may have difficulty obtaining a reasonably representative image from the host of often contradictory empirical data about a particular group. This is why theological judgments in this sphere must be cautious and provisional. Missiology must moreover initiate the collection of theologically interpretable data by means of empirical research projects.

1.2 *LITERATURE*

A great many publications about the Independent Churches have
appeared over the past few decades. The following bibliographies
provide a comprehensive survey:

Mitchell, R.C. & Turner, H.W. *A comprehensive bibliography
    of modern African religious movements,* 2nd edition. North-
    western University Press, 1968.
Turner, H.W. Bibliography of modern African religious move-
    ments, Supplement I. *Journal of Religion in Africa,* 7:3,
    1968.
Turner, H.W. Bibliography of modern African religious move-
    ments, Supplement II. *Journal of Religon in Africa,* 3:3,
    1970.

H.W. Turner periodically updates these bibliographies with
"supplements" which already list some 2 000 titles. Barrett gives
an analysis of how the literature has grown.[3] The rise of protest,
renewal and revivalist movements (e.g. the Harris movements in
the Ivory Coast, 1913; the Nomya Luo mission in Kenya, 1914;
the Chilembwe rebellion in Nyasaland, 1915; the prophetic movements in the Congo, 1921; and the Aladura revival in Western
Nigeria, 1925) unleashed a flood of descriptive publications.
Contemporary observers did not realize that they were dealing
with a phenomenon of continental dimensions. By and large
they were critical of and alarmed by the new movements which
they interpreted as a local misconception of the Christian message. At the historic gathering of the International Missionary
Council at Tambaram in 1938 this concern was voiced in a request that special research be undertaken into the so-called
"Separatist Churches" in Africa.

The turning-point came in 1948 with the publication of Bengt
Sundkler's *Bantu Prophets in South Africa.* His perceptive distinctions and meticulous scientific research, focusing mainly on
the Zulu churches, not only put South African Independent
Churches on the map, but also established a new field of scientific

3   Barrett 1968, p. 37f

inquiry. Barrett shows how Sundkler's work led to a trebling of the literature, and how the accent in the later studies shifted from the descriptive to the more analytical and scientific.[4]

By way of orientation, and with no claims to completeness, I have listed in the Appendix the better known and most significant publications in this field.

As regards an overall perspective Barrett's *Schism and Renewal* is probably the most comprehensive study to date. Its aim is to analyse this phenomenon in Africa in its totality and to arrive at an explanatory theory for the principal reasons for its origin. The very enormity of the subject causes Barrett sometimes to lapse into superficiality and untenable generalizations. Nevertheless he produces valuable new perspectives which help to clarify the connection between mission strategies and church schisms.

With the *regional studies* listed in the Appendix, I have included a few discerning remarks for the benefit of those who are not familiar with the literature on Independency. Incomplete as it is, the bibliography covers a wide field and includes most of the classic studies on the subject. A sound knowledge of the phenomenon concerned assumes at least reasonable familiarity with the works by Barrett, Daneel, Sundkler and Turner.

1.3 TERMINOLOGY

The term "Independent Churches" is a provisional, general designation for a diversified, varied phenomenon that cannot readily be accommodated by any one term. Within the broader socio-political framework these religious groups represent a phenomenon coinciding with the expansion of the Western sphere of power and civilization in the Third World over the past few centuries. In the resultant process of acculturation the Third World peoples were radically influenced by the Europeans. This influence was all-pervasive and, apart from religion, also affected the economic, political, social and cultured spheres of life. In view of this the Independent Churches cannot be isolated from the broad context of conflict and development in the Third World,

4   Ibid., pp. 40-41

but must be studied as *part of a large-scale, sweeping process of acculturation*. Remember too that this kind of movement serves not only an acculturative and religious function, but is a major *sociological phenomenon* manifest wherever social structures are unhinged and traditional societal patterns superseded. Sociologically, therefore, such movements are *reorientiation centres* where people embrace norms and find security in the midst of to them unmanageable change. This is the justification for the descriptive title of this book: *Quest for belonging*. In spite of theological objections, then, there is some sociological justification for the rapid proliferation of church movements.

The terminology used depends largely on the premises of the researcher and his field. *Political scientists* speak of resistance movements and revolutionary cults; *psychologists* of deprivation cults, referring to a reaction against the removal of certain privileges; *sociologists* refer to religious associations, popular movements or separatist sects; *anthropologists* call them adaptive or acculturative movements, or even nativistic or revivalist groups and *missiologists* employ descriptive terms such as sectarian, syncretist, eschatological, chiliastic, messianic, visionary or prophetic movements.

The problem with using the above *theological* qualifications is that they are loaded terms, implying value-judgements. In most instances they refer to only a few prominent trends of certain groups and can therefore not be applied generally. Such concepts as syncretist, separatist or sectarian are relevant to some movements, yet have a prejorative flavour. In addition the theological terminology is limited in that it does not reflect the close interrelationship with socio-political and cultural factors.

In looking for a blanket term one must guard both against pejorative terms and against absolutizing some tendency that constitutes only part of the overall picture. Thus the term "prophetic church" is too narrow since many churches have no recognized prophetic office. "Native churches" could have been useful except for the derogatory connotations of the term "native" in modern Africa. Calling them "independent" or "indigenous" churches could be confusing since these terms are commonly used to indicate the "young" churches that grew from the involvement of Western mission churches and then, without breaking with the latter, developed into "independent", "indigenous" churches.

The designation "Independent Churches" offers the most acceptable, generalized title without any obvious or implied value-judgment. "Independent" is an apposite adjective, since in their organization and worship these groups are in fact independent of the Western mission churches that had initially imported the Christian message. Besides, members of these movements like to see themselves as independent. Turner explicitly defines an African Independent Church as

> "a church which has been founded in Africa, by Africans, and primarily for Africans".[5]

This definition captures three essential features, namely that the Independent Churches are of African origin, were founded by Africans and, despite the fact that some of them are not exclusivist and admit White members, are largely adapted to the needs, life-view and life-style of Black people. The use of the term "church" is, firstly, apposite and technically correct since the leaders all see their movements as churches of Christ and wish to be recognized as such. Secondly, using this term as a general definition implies a tentative rather than an absolute theological evaluation. Even in a tentative theological evaluation one could argue that the majority of these groups, either wholly or in part, manifest the *notae ecclesiae* which are considered normative for a church in, for instance, the Reformed tradition. Throughout the preaching of the gospel and a concern with scriptural truths are focal; the sacraments of baptism and holy communion are administered, and discipline is common to all these churches, even though the moral standards are often much adapted to tribal law and traditional codes of conduct. When it comes to a more specific theological evaluation one would in all fairness have to inquire into the usages of individual groups. In our final chapter it will become evident that a theological evaluation in this field would have to be an extremely delicate and complex undertaking.

The designation "Independent Churches" presupposes a *demarcation of the field* which excludes, inter alia, *protest* move-

5   Turner, 1967(c), p. 17

ments within the "historical" or "established" churches. Examples of such protest movements are the revivalist movement in East Africa, the Order of Ethiopia which is affiliated with the Anglican church (Church of the Province of South Africa) and even what is known as Black theology. Inasmuch as these movements still operate within the framework of the "historical" churches they fall outside a discussion of the Independent Churches.

Our three-point definition above can be amplified by the following sociologically oriented definition: an Independent Church is a new movement arising from the interaction between a tribal community and its religion on one hand, and a heterogeneous foreign culture intruding with its (Christian) religion on the other. In several respects the new movement deviates significantly from the classical religious traditions of both the cultures involved. Elements of both traditions are renewed, modified and embodied in a new religious sytem.[6]

One could ask how the churches that are *not* Independent Churches should be defined. The term "mission churches", referring to the products of Western missionary activity, is awkward in that it implies that these churches are dependent on missionary agencies. Turner's suggestion[7] that we speak of "older churches" has some merit since the Independent Churches are mostly of fairly recent origin. But this raises a fresh problem: that of the distinction between "older churches" and "young churches", which grew from the intervention of the "older churches" in the mission field, whereas what is wanted is actually a blanket term for both. Probably "historical churches" would effectively pinpoint the distinction, not merely because it refers to historically earlier groups, but also because churches of this kind are more directly linked with the Christian community of past ages. By contrast, the Independent Churches have no such historical continuity with the early Christian church, although some of them naturally claim and experience a strong emotional and ideological bond with the first Christian community.

When we speak of Independent Churches we must always

6   Bosch, 1973, p. 7
7   Turner, op. cit., pp. 18-21

remember that we are dealing with a dynamically changing rather than a static phenomenon. Thus some groups develop on sectarian lines whereas others, influenced by renewal movements within their own ranks, grow into churches of a more specifically Christian nature. Others, owing to a process of degeneration, can no longer be called Christian. The *Guta raJehovah* (City of God) movement of *Mai Chaza* in eastern Zimbabwe, for instance, has deliberately replaced the Bible with a revelational book of its own and produced a highly heretical reinterpretation of the Holy Trinity, so that it has forfeited its claim to being a church of Christ.

When it comes to interchurch relations there is a marked increase in the interaction between the historical and the Independent Churches today. Among the historical churches there is a growing realization that the Independent Churches are creatively producing new, indigenized usages which are effective in the traditional tribal contexts and which are in many respects more acceptable theologically than was at first thought. Thus there is growing interest in the Independent Churches' approach to the traditional religion.

For their part the Independent Churches too are beginning to break down their isolation by means of various organizations such as the African Independent Churches' Association (AICA) and the Reformed Independent Churches' Association (RICA) in South Africa;[8] then there is the African Independent Churches' Conference (AICC) *(Fambidzano yamaKereke avatema),* founded in 1972 by a number of Shona Independent Churches. This latter body became a member of the Rhodesia Christian Conference and the Rhodesia Christian Council (national council of the World Council of Churches) at quite an early stage. The church of Simon Kimbangu in Zaire has been a member of the World Council of Churches for some time.

Various attempts have been made to provide proper theological training for candidates from these movements. Edward Lekhan-

---

8 Sundkler (1961, p. 50) describes early attempts at amalgamation by the Independent Churches in South Africa and West (1975, p. 142f) describes the successes and failures of a body such as the AICA.

yane, former leader of the Zion Christian Church, completed a course at the Dutch Reformed Theological School near Pietersburg, and several students belonging to Independent Churches (including some Shona Zionists) were highly successful at the Lutheran theological college at Mapumulo.

The efforts of theological institutes established specifically for this purpose are highly significant too. At one stage the AICA started a theological college with the aid of the Christian Institute, but unfortunately it floundered as a result of poor financial administration. For the past ten years the theological training centre of the aforementioned *Fambidzano* (AICC) has been presenting a highly successful extension training programme in Zimbabwe. Hundreds of Shona candidates from twenty to thirty Independent Churches have completed this two-year course. Today this programme, originally initiated by me, is run by a team of some fifteen Shona lecturers, mainly Zionists (trained at Mapumulo, Epworth in Salisbury, Unisa and by *Fambidzano* itself) under the able and dedicated leadership of Peter Makamba. Peter's father, Bishop Makamba, was one of the Zionist "pioneers" in Rhodesia during the twenties and is today regarded as the "father" of *Fambidzano,* in which capacity he opens all major gatherings with prayer.

In Zaire Dr Marie-Louise Martin has been principal of the Kimbanguist theological school for some years.

One result of the historical churches' growing involvement with the Independent Churches and the greater emphasis on scientific study of these movements has been the establishment in 1973 of a Study Centre for new Religious Movements under the leadership of Prof. Harold W. Turner. At present this research centre has its headquarters at Selly Oaks and co-ordinates studies of new religious movements in various parts of the world.

1.4 TYPOLOGY

The general designation "Independent Churches" is sufficient to differentiate a particular type of church movement from other churches, but further differentiation is necessary in view of the great variety of groups with divergent trends. Naturally any classification of groups according to stereotyped characteristics is a Western academic enterprise, undertaken purely for the sake of clarity. It can at best provide a relative categorization since some groups fit none of the given categories and others, owing to a process of change, switch from one category to another.

H.W. Turner's typology, partly based on Sundkler's work, is manageable and lucid and we shall be using it as a guideline throughout.[9] Turner's basic distinction is between groups that are non-Christian or manifest very slight Christian tendencies, and those which are more obviously Christian. These two main categories are subdivided into further categories.

1.4.1 PRE-CHRISTIAN OR EARLY CHRISTIAN MOVEMENTS

1.4.1.1 Neo-pagan movements

These movements represent a large-scale reversion to the traditional religion. The abrogation of ancient sanctions and social patterns as a result of Western culture and the influence of Western religion was keenly felt and an attempt was made to achieve a new stability by consciously refashioning and renewing the ancient cult. In anthropological terminology this category has been variously designated, according to specific features, as

— *revivalist,* in cases of deliberate reversion to ancient ways, for instance the People of God and the Cult of the Ancestral Spirits in Kenya and the association of Ancient Religious Societies of African Descendants in Nigeria. The latter is trying to revive the traditional religion through a combination of tradition, training of priests and the creation of sanctuaries;
— *nativistic:* the purging of foreign influences because of powerful racial awareness, nationalism or tribal reintegration;
— *vitalistic:* selected elements of the extraneous religion are

---

9 Turner, 1967(c)

used in a predominantly traditionalist context. Examples of *nativistic-vitalistic* movements are the National Church of Nigeria, the Church of Orunmila and the Adulawo Movement in Nigeria, the Church of the Ancestors in Malawi and the Herero Church in South West Africa; in South Africa the *iNkonzo yeSizwe* and the *Bantu Ngqika-Ntsikana Church* could also be classed in this category;

— *syncretist:* pagan and new religious elements are fused in a synthesis which remains essentially traditional and therefore un-Christian — an example would be the Deima cult of the Ivory Coast.

When one considers the Shona Independent Churches of Zimbabwe the problems of a classification according to this typology emerge forcefully. *Mai Chaza's Guta reJehovah* (City of God) movement could be typified as neo-pagan, but does not fit readily into any of the subcategories. It is *revivalist* in the sense that the ancient creation myths are revived in a new guise, with both *Mai Chaza* and *Mwari* as the original creators of the earth (and the Zimbabwe ruins in particular); it is *nativistic* in its initial resistance to schooling by Black nationalist and tribal forces (the Manyika tribe in the eastern regions); it is *vitalistic* in that an aspect of Christian faith is found in the traditionally oriented healing practices; and it is *syncretist* in its moral codes which are neither traditional nor strictly Christian. When one considers the African Congregational Church — a nonprophetic church whose Shona name, *Chibarirwe* (place of our birth, i.e. of our ancestors), immediately underscores traditional custom — the neo-pagan trend is at once obvious. Thus many church council members actively join in the ancestor cult. Yet there is such a marked Christian orientation throughout this church, for instance in its observance of monogamy and its Christ-centred preaching, that it cannot simply be slotted into this category.

1.4.1.2 *Hebraic movements*

These movements differ from neo-paganism in that they have radically departed from paganism and have made faith in one

God as defined in the Old Testament a key tenet. However, they have not yet reached a predominantly Christian position.[10]

In this category Turner makes a distinction between Israelite and Judaistic movements. The former place the accent on the replacement of paganism with a message of joy and deliverance effected by a loving God. There are striking parallels with the Old Testament people of God, so that Israelite movements are able to proceed from the promises of the Old Testament towards a Judaistic or Christian faith. One example is the West African movement which arose as a result of the travels of the prophet William Wade Harris.

When such movements fail to experience the realization of the Old Testament promises and to develop along Christian lines they stagnate, resulting in a critical attitude similar to that of Judaism at the time of Christ. An example of such a "Judaistic" movement is the Turban cult of Kenya, which preaches repentance at the behest of a wrathful Spirit of God and prepares for the persecution of God's people.

These groups are further characterized by a strongly legalistic approach based on codes of moral conduct, ritualism, exclusivism accompanied by antagonism to the White race, and occasionally a messianic hope fixed on the coming of a Black Messiah. Turner cites the God's Kingdom Society as an example. This movement mentions Christ as mediator, but in actual fact it adheres to the Old Testament rather than the New, as is evident from the replacement of communion with the Feast of Tabernacles. The emphasis is on righteousness as a condition for entering God's kingdom.

Also in this category is the Church of Christ of James Limba in Port Elizabeth.

In a strict sense none of the neo-pagan or Hebraic movements could be typified as Christian, so that they fall beyond the scope of our study. We should, however, note them by way of contrast with groups that are more or less Christian. Besides, there are some groups that are classified Christian which are moving in the direction of neo-paganism or Hebraism, or at least show such tendencies.

10 Ibid., p. 8f

1.4.2 CHRISTIAN MOVEMENTS

1.4.2.1 Ethiopian-type churches

Independent Churches designated "Ethiopian" are in the first instance non-prophetic and lay no claim to any special manifestations of the Holy Spirit. By contrast with prophetic churches they do not practise "Jordan" baptism. Their church services are less conspicuously emotional, they seldom exorcise evil spirits nor do they have elaborate witch-hunting rites. They have fewer rules about the use of liquor or medicine and the eating of pork, and their forms of worship are more in line with those of historical (particularly Protestant) churches than those of prophetic movements.

The Ethiopian-type churches originated largely as a reaction against White and White-dominated mission churches.[11] Political development and the knowledge that a colonial power had been successfully resisted in East Africa for the first time bred an awareness that God concerns himself with Africa in a special way. Such texts as Psalm 68: 31, which says that Ethiopia hastens to stretch out her hands to God, are interpreted as a sign that the oppressed Black people have a specially appointed place in God's plan of salvation. This text is linked to the conversion of the Ethiopian chamberlain and it is claimed that Africa responded to Christ's message of salvation long before the European peoples did. This led to the rise of a sort of "Ethiopian" ideology with a marked psychological sense of self-esteem and responsibility for spreading God's kingdom in Africa.

The "Ethiopian" ideology took root mainly in South and East Africa. It had its heyday between about 1890 and 1920, when most of these churches originated. Some of the non-prophetic churches that originated later but are still classified in this category show a decline of the specifically "Ethiopian" ideology.

As for the Shona Independent Churches, the racist reactionary factor features to a greater or lesser extent in *all* these groups and can therefore not serve as a key criterion for distinguishing

---

11 Sundkler, 1961, p. 53. These churches, according to Sundkler, broke away from White mission churches mainly on racist grounds.

between Ethiopian-type and prophetic churches. There are even indications that the First Ethiopian Church is much less militantly anti-White than some Zionist or Apostle churches. Hence the features distinguishing "Ethiopian" from Spirit-type churches in the Shona context are religious and organizational rather than socio-political.[12]

1.4.2.2 Spirit-type churches

Opinions differ greatly as to the most apposite designation for this category of churches. The most outstanding common feature among them is their special emphasis on the work of the Holy Spirit, manifested in speaking in tongues, prophetic activity of diverse kinds and faith healing. In Zimbabwe these groups set themselves apart from others by adopting the popular name of *maKereke dzoMweya* (churches of the Spirit), hence my personal preference for the term "Spirit-type" or "prophetic" churches. Sundkler prefers to call them Zionist churches because so many of these prophetic groups are Zionist — the word "Zion" often features in their names and they have indigenized concepts of a kingdom of God in which the holy city of Zion — either in a symbolic or a concrete sense — occupies a focal position.

My objection to this term is that some prophetic movements specifically do not want to be considered Zionist, so that the designation is not general enough. Thus the Apostle Church of Johane Maranke, commonly known as the *vaPostori* (Apostles), claims to represent a more authentic version of Christianity than the Zionist churches because in Africa they, through the inspiration of the Holy Spirit, are living according to the example of the first Apostles of Jesus Christ.[13] If this had been an insignificant little group one could still perhaps have maintained the qualification "Zionist", but since it is the largest Independent Church in Zimbabwe, with thousands of members in Zambia, Zaire and Malawi as well, it cannot be classified with a number of divergent "Zion churches" against whom it often reacts vehemently.

12 Daneel, 1971(a), p. 350
13 Ibid., p. 315f

In Nigeria the term *Aludura* (prayerful) churches is used, while in the Ivory Coast they are known as Harris churches because of the evangelization accomplished by the prophet, Harris. Others speak of Spiritual churches. Turner prefers to call them "prophet-healing churches", to reflect the two major emphases of these groups, namely revelations of God's Spirit through prophets and a message of salvation in which faith healing occupies a key position.

On the whole the Spirit-type churches are of more recent origin than the Ethiopian type. In South Africa and Zimbabwe their heyday came only after 1920, while the Aladura churches in Nigeria originated mainly between 1910 and 1950.

Turner believes that the diversity of accents on the work of the Holy Spirit justifies a subdivision into *soteriological* and *revelational churches*. The soteriological churches place the main emphasis on prophetically guided faith healing. Redemption is interpreted mainly as deliverance from disease caused by demonic forces — especially witches, wizards and evil spirits. Because of the persistent emphasis on healing one could also refer to them as "therapeutic churches". By contrast the "revelational churches" place the accent on revelations given to prophets through the inspiration of the Holy Spirit. In this way the Spirit regulates church activities and the lives of individual members.

Although this classification might well apply to the prophetic churches of Nigeria, it does not tally with the realities of the Shona Spirit-type churches. In the majority of Zionist and Apostle churches in Zimbabwe both these poles of prophetic activity are represented. There are shifts of emphasis, but these are mainly among different congregations of the same church, depending on the tastes and talents of the prophets concerned. Thus in Bishop Mutendi's Zion Christian Church the accent at church headquarters, in the so-called hospital, is on therapeutic prophetism, whereas at assemblies it is on prophetic revelation because here the guidance of the Spirit in the church's planning is of focal importance. When one moves from one ZCC congregation to another one finds here a therapeutically oriented prophet with facilities for visiting "patients", and there a revelational prophets whose forte is revelations and interpretations during church services. There are also prophets who are considered expert in both fields. Hence among Shona prophetic movements one can-

partial shift in emphasis within individual groups based on con-
not apply an exclusive subdivison to each group, but merely a
gregational variation in accordance with the presence of prophetic charisma and the circumstances in which religious activities develop.

1.4.2.3 *Messianic churches*

Some researchers classify the so-called "messianic churches" in
the same category as the Spirit-type churches. There is some
justification for this in that both are largely prophetic movements, the difference being that in messianic churches the leader
is elevated to messianic status. In these movements the attention
of members is often captured by the eminence of the leader —
his mystical powers, miracles and mediation between God and
his followers — to such an extent that he usurps Christ's position,
either wholly or in part. In extreme cases where the Christology
is manifestly usurped by the Black Messiah, who is to some extent deified, we are in effect confronted with Black Messianism
which can be typified only as non-Christian or post-Christian.

The problem is how to evaluate the empirical phenomenon.
Sundkler initially used mediation at the gates of heaven as a
criterion for a basic distinction of Messianism.[14] The crucial question is here: who stands at the gates of heaven, Jesus Christ or the
Black Messiah? If the answer is the Black Messiah, then Christ's
mediatorship is either violated or superseded and the designation
"Black Messianism" is applicable. However, my own research
among the Shona Independent Churches showed that many
Zionist prophetic leaders were attributed with the functions of
"custodian of the heavenly gates", yet this special task was never
interpreted in an exclusivist sense as replacing Christ as Mediator.
It was rather that these leaders performed an *introductory* function so as to fulfil their earthly responsibilities to the end, and
not that they guaranteed their followers access to heaven, circum-
venting Christ's mediation and the judgment of God. Similar
views are found even in prophetic groups characterized by a

14 Sundkler, 1961, p. 323

41

strong emphasis on Christology. In such cases one can at most speak of Spirit-type churches with messianic tendencies.[15] It would seem that the concept "messianic" is used far too casually and categorically in the literature. As a result certain movements are theologically condemned as degenerate, whereas in fact they represent a legitimate christianizing process of indigenization or contextualization.[16] One must therefore exercise extreme caution when applying the term "messianic" to the Independent Churches. We shall return to this later.

What we have said here demonstrates that a typology of the Independent Churches is no more than a tentative aid to enable us to introduce some measure of order into this vast field. Within the broad distinctions there must be scope for fluidity, variation and often subtle processes of change.

15 Daneel, 1982(a)
16 See my criticism of Beyerhaus, Oosthuizen, and Martin in my inaugural address: "Swart Messianisme" — Verwording of kontekstualisasie". UNISA, 1982(a)

CHAPTER 2

INDEPENDENT CHURCHES: AN HISTORICAL PERSPECTIVE

2.1 ORIGIN AND EXPANSION OF THE INDEPENDENT CHURCHES

It is not mere chance that our attention is confined to the Independent Churches south of the Sahara, but because these movements do not abound anywhere on earth to the extent that they do in Africa. A comparison between African countries moreover indicates that no other country on the continent has as many of these churches as the Republic of South Africa.

This fact should not be assessed negatively. The proliferation of churches in Africa in fact indicates that Africa and Oceania are the only two non-Western cultural areas where the Christian message had a large-scale positive reception. Indeed, these are the only areas where Christianity has progressed rapidly since the christianizing of the Mediterranean and European peoples during the first millennium after Christ. Thus the absence of similar Independent Churches in such countries as Japan, China, India and Pakistan indicates that the gospel failed to find any great response there.

The schismatic movement in Africa got under way only towards the end of the last century (apart from a few earlier movements to be mentioned in due course) and gained proper momentum in the twentieth century. David Barrett produced the most comprehensive interpretation of statistical data for the whole of Africa. In his *Schism and renewal in Africa* he calculates the position of the Independent Churches in 34 African countries for the year 1967.[1] It appears that in that year there were 5 031 separate movements in Africa with an estimated 6 868 880 adherents. The average size per group across the whole of Africa is calculated at 1 380.

1 Barrett, 1968, pp. 78-79

There are innumerable differences between these groups.

— In *size* they range from minute groups comprising one or two families to the enormous movements of Lekhanyane (ZCC in South Africa), Johane Maranke (African Apostolic Church of Maranke in Zimbabwe) and the Kimbangu church in Zaire. The churches of Lekhanyane and Kimbangu most likely have several million members each.

— As for *origin*, there are groups that broke away from the historical churches, those who grew as a result of further schisms within the ranks of the breakaways, and movements that arose around a prophetic figure, drawing their members from various churches and from the non-Christian environment.

— With regard to *stability*, some of the smaller groups disappear quite soon owing to lack of organization and motivation, while others are established groups with church headquarters and soundly organized congregations that consolidate and expand.

— When it comes to *doctrine* and *forms of worship,* there are groups which largely follow the historical churches from which they originally broke away and others who try to give an original reinterpretation of the gospel message in an African context and to adapt church usages culturally and in terms of religion.

— As regards *vitality* there are introverted, static and consequently dwindling groups, as opposed to mission oriented churches which expand across tribal and even national boundaries.[2]

Barrett's table shows that in 1967 there were 3 000 separate groups in South Africa with a total of 3 100 000 adherents. In respect of other countries where there are many of these movements, he lists the following statistics: Zaire, 500 groups, 1 000 000 adherents; Nigeria, 500 groups, 600 000 adherents; Ke-

2   Hastings, 1971, p. 193. See also Daneel, 1980

nya, 160 groups, 600 000 adherents; Ghana, 200 groups, 200 000 adherents; Zimbabwe, 100 groups, 500 000 adherents. These statistics are by now outdated. The number of Independent Churches in South Africa alone probably exceeds 4 000. However, it is extremely difficult to obtain accurate statistical data in this field.

As for the ratio to the total number of Christians, Barrett calculated that in 1970 the Independent Churches made up just below 10 percent of the Christian population of Africa.[3] However, John Mbiti puts this percentage at 20 percent,[4] and G.C. Oosthuizen at 25 percent[5] of the Christian population of Africa.

The growth of this movement shows marked fluctuations. Every year several small groups disappear, but a number of new ones emerge. By 1967 Barrett estimated that for every ten to twelve groups that fizzle out each year, some 100 new churches are born and canvass some 100 000 new members annually. If one adds to this the gains in membership of the existing churches, then the total movement is growing at a rate of three to four hundred thousand members per year.

An important question is whether the growth rate of the Independent Churches is slowing down or not. It would seem that up to 1970 these churches grew phenomenally, in terms of both new groups and overall membership. But there are signs that their heyday is passing. Census statistics in South Africa indicate that whereas in 1960 the Independent Churches represented 21 percent of all Christians, this percentage had dropped to 18,3 by 1970. But are these figures accurate? Is it merely a temporary fluctuation? And does the growing popularity of Lekhanyane's ZCC in recent years not indicate a renewed spurt of growth? Turner and Hastings are of the opinion that elsewhere in Africa a decline in growth rate must be expected. Whatever the prognosis, the fact remains that the Independent Churches represent one of the cardinal developments of Christianity in twentieth-century Africa.

3 Barrett, 1970, pp. 39-54
4 Mbiti, 1969, p. 232
5 Oosthuizen, 1968(b), p. 197

2.2 THE BIRTH OF A MOVEMENT: DONNA BEATRICE

We have pointed out that most of the surviving Independent Churches were established in this century, and a few towards the end of the nineteenth century.

However, the actual roots of this entire movement extend much further back into the past. Therefore it is not just fascinating but actually important to devote some attention to the history of the first Independent Church movement in Africa south of the Sahara. Interestingly enough, the moving spirit behind this movement was a woman, Kimpa Vita, renamed Beatrice at her baptism. By the year 1700 she was twenty years old, living in the then Portuguese kingdom of the Congo, near the town of Sao Salvador (in what is today known as Angola). Donna Beatrice, as she came to be known, claimed that the spirit of St Anthony had taken possession of her (cf. the traditional pagan soothsayer and magician whose spirit was possessed by that of an ancestor). Beatrice abandoned all her worldly goods and began to proclaim the coming judgment of God. Her preaching was a powerful protest against the Catholic church, particularly its formalism and externalism. She aimed at destroying all crosses, crucifixes and images of Christ because, she said, they had simply become new fetishes replacing the old.

Of particular importance, however, was her message that Christ came into the world as an African in Sao Salvador and that he had Black apostles. Here for the first time we encounter the idea of a Black Christ; in other words, the first inklings of Black Theology. Her proclamation gave expression to a deep yearning: the yearning for a Christ who would identify with the despised African. How could the White Christ of the Portuguese images, the Christ of the exploiters — how could he ever help the suffering African, pining for liberty?

There was yet another element in her preaching. She proclaimed a utopia, a paradise on earth and the restoration of the ancient Kongo empire. According to the traditional concepts of Africa, wealth and success are naturally signs of the blessing of God (or of the ancestors).

Beatrice rapidly became a national heroine, a focus of reintegration for all scattered and dissatisfied groups. She was venerated as a saint. She then announced practical measures: the chiefs must all assemble in Sao Salvador in order to restore the ancient Kongo empire under a new king. That was in 1706. The (Portuguese) authorities imprisoned her and she was condemned to be burnt at the stake as a heretic. Like Joan of Arc she died with the name of Jesus on her lips, and her adherents were forcibly subdued.[6]

2.3 DEVELOPMENT OF THE MOVEMENT IN SOUTHERN AFRICA

We have dwelt in some detail on the history of Donna Beatrice, not simply because she was the first Christian prophetess in Africa but particularly because in her, and in her preaching, we may observe certain themes which were to recur time and again in many different forms in Africa. We observe, for example, that the prophet usually appears in times of crisis, and is usually commissioned by means of dreams or visions to a particular task. Whether, in the case of Donna Beatrice we are dealing with an authentic Christian movement is difficult to determine today, on account of the dearth of contemporary records. Later, however, remarkable parallels with Donna Beatrice appeared in South Africa, such as Mantsopa Makheta (born in Lesotho in 1793) and particularly the Xhosa prophetess, Nongqause, whose visions in 1856 and 1857 led to the famous national suicide episode of the Xhosa. However, one could certainly not call Nongqause a Christian prophetess; the only "Christian" element in her message was that the deceased ancestors would, on a particular day, all rise from the dead.

Later in the nineteenth century, from about 1870 onwards, we find a gathering momentum in the emergence of modern Independent Churches in many African countries. Here we are faced with prophets who — with certain exceptions — are unmistakably Christian, who summon the people to conversion, repentance and amendment of life, prophets through whom Christ performs his

6   Martin, 1971, pp. 30-35

work of healing and sanctification, prophets who recapitulate the history of salvation, but who also run a risk of mingling Christian and pagan elements.

In the progress of the Independent Churches we may also detect definite shifts of emphasis. Some of the early personalities, like Donna Beatrice, Hendrik Witbooi (who was a kind of political Messiah among the Herero of South West Africa and died in a skirmish with the Germans in 1905), Enoch Mgijima[7] (leader of the "Israelites" who rebelled against the South African government near Queenstown in 1921; in the ensuing armed conflict 183 of his followers died) and other similar figures, were in many respects strongly nativistic and millennialistic, with a distinct anti-White orientation. Although such prophet figures still occur occasionally today, there is an unmistakable shift away from these elements to a more ecclesiastic and Christian approach.

Besides, the explicitly nativistic and anti-White movements were mainly confined to the Congo and Southern Africa. From the outset, the independent groups in West Africa were more peaceful, less millennialistic and messianic, also more interested in reformation and the application of Christian principles in the terminology of Africa.

We shall now trace the historical development of the "Ethiopian" and Spirit-type churches.

The first major schism in South Africa took place in 1884, when Nehemiah Tile, a Black minister of the Methodist church, broke away to form the Tembu National Church, with Paramount Chief Ngangelizwe of the Tembu tribe in the Transkei as its nominal head (just as the British queen is the nominal head of the Church of England). The schism was apparently preceded by unrest among the church's Black members about White control in the Methodist church and a desire to assimilate more traditional and national elements into the church.

Similar schisms occurred elsewhere. In Sekukuniland (Transvaal) a German missionary J.A. Winter, raised strong objections to the unwillingness of his White colleagues to permit Black leadership in the Lutheran church. Under his leadership, the Lutheran Bapedi Church was then founded. Winter's logic was,

7   Sundkler, 1961, pp. 72-73

however, the cause of his downfall; hardly was the Black church founded when it dismissed its founder as a White interloper. That was in 1889. In the same year, an Anglican evangelist in Pretoria, Khanyane Napo, defected from the Anglicans to found his own organization, the Africa Church.[8]

2.3.1 *Ethiopian-type churches*

It was in 1892 that the name "Ethiopian" appeared for the first time. In that year a Methodist minister on the Witwatersrand, Mangena Mokone, protested against what he called racial segregation in the church and, together with a group of supporters, founded the Ethiopian Church. Unlike the schisms of Tile and Winter, Mokone's did not involve only one tribal group, because he had a vision of a church with a wide horizon embracing all the Black tribes. He succeeded in gathering round him a talented group of co-workers, including Khanyane Napo, S.J. Brander, Jonas Goduke (Tile's successor) and James M. Dwane.

Under the influence of Mokone and his adherents the term "Ethiopian" began to feature more frequently in the designations of newly established churches. Mokone himself attached great significance to Psalm 68: 31: "Let Ethiopia hasten to stretch out her hands to God." As mentioned earlier, this text was associated with the baptism of the Ethiopian court official (Ac 8) so as to substantiate ideologically a direct link with the early church and bypass the influence of European churches. Mokone interpreted these texts as a promise concerning the evangelization of Africa and as justification for an independent Black church leadership. Other scriptural passages eventually gained prominence in the "Ethiopian" movement to validate its separate existence — the rescue of the infant Jesus from Herod through his parents' flight to Africa (Egypt), and the fact that Simon of Cyrene, a native of Africa, helped to carry Jesus' cross.

The Abyssinian victory over the Whites at Adowa in 1896 caused a stir among "Ethiopians" in South Africa. From the beginning the Zulu followers of the American Negro Baptists

8 Ibid., pp. 38-39

(who began missionary work in Natal in 1899) called themselves the *ama-Kushi,* i.e. the Cushites (Ethiopians). The Italo-Abyssinian war in 1935 also served to stimulate an Ethiopian mythology in South Africa, and fervent prayers for an Abyssinian victory were offered at nocturnal prayer meetings.

Let us now revert briefly to Mokone and his supporters. The most able of these was undoubtedly James Dwane. Through his good offices, Mokone's Ethiopian Church came into contact with the African Methodist Episcopal Church (AMEC), a Negro church which had been established as far back 1815 in Philadelphia, USA, by the Negro minister, Richard Allen, in protest against the colour bar in the Methodist church. Dwane visited this group in America and on his return persuaded the majority of Ethiopian leaders to follow him in joining the AMEC, with Dwane himself as the leader (assistant bishop) in South Africa. Eventually, however, Dwane became dissatisfied with the state of affairs and in 1900 he and a large number of followers joined the Anglican church as the Order of Ethiopia.

The majority of "Ethiopians" did not follow Dwane but remained in the AMEC. Some groups, however, defected at a later stage, for example Brander with his Ethiopian Catholic Church in Zion (1904).

Other major "Ethiopian" churches include P.J. Mzimba's African Presbyterian Church (1898), a group which broke away from the Scottish (Presbyterian) mission. There were also secessions from the Congregationalists, such as the African Congregational Church, under the powerful leadership of Gardiner B. Mvuyana, as well as the Shaka Zulu Church, founded in 1924. Besides Tile's Tembu National Church, there was another important breakaway from the Methodist church, namely that of the Bantu Methodist Church (also known as the Donkey Church) in 1932.

With reference to the spread of "Ethiopianism" in the erstwhile Rhodesia, it is interesting to note that as long ago as 1903 the Anglican bishop of Rhodesia in a letter to the then High Commissioner warned that the members of this movement had sociopolitical aspirations and would therefore foment racial friction. As a result foreign and South African leaders of the AMEC, despite frequent requests for admission, were banned from the colony. However, the admission of Fingu labourers to the Bulawayo district and Sotho settlers to the Fort Victoria area meant that "Ethiopian" notions began to spread among the Ndebele and Shona before 1910. Up to 1920 the Rev. Magatho, a Sotho minister of the AMEC who established a church and a school near Bulawayo in 1906, played a prominent part in politics, specially in the Ndebele's attempts to secure sufficient land for establishing a "national home".[9] Magatho was in contact with the Sotho settlers in the Victoria province, but there is little evidence that this early form of "Ethiopianism" had any note-worthy influence on the politico-religious life of the Shona tribes.

The earliest "Ethiopian" church among the south-eastern Shona, the First Ethiopian Church (FEC),[10] was founded by Mu-pambi Chidembo, a muNdau from the Bikita district who had worked as a migrant labourer in the Transvaal from 1890 to 1910 where he came into contact with the South African "Ethio-pians". In 1910 he returned to Bikita district, now a bishop, and proceeded to establish FEC congregations among the Duma, one of the Shona tribes. He also proselytized in the Gutu, Ndanga and Chipinga districts, but his influence remained restricted until the forties when his nephew, Nheya Gavure, instilled new life into this church. By this time there was hardly any contact with the South African "Ethiopians" and when asked about the back-ground of their movement, Chidembo's followers could only say that "Chidembo had brought the *Topia* church with him from Johannesburg".

After Gavure was promoted to leader of the *Topia* church in 1952 it flourished in the south-eastern districts, mainly Bikita and Zaka. By this time the original "Ethiopian" ideology with its marked racist and anti-White sentiments had become obscured. At any rate this ideology did not dominate the church's pro-clamation during the sixties and seventies. Bishop Gavure's per-sonal integrity and spiritual ardour did much to keep congrega-tional work biblically oriented, so that it presented a manifestly Christian image. He was also a leading figure in the burgeoning

9 Ranger, 1964, p. 57, in Daneel 1971(a), pp. 350-351
10 Daneel, 1971(a), p. 369f.

ecumenical efforts among Shona Independent Churches after 1972 and for many years was president of *Fambidzano* (the council of Independent Shona Churches).

After the FEC one of the most influential Ethiopian-type churches among the Shona was the African Congregational Church. Sengwayo, a muRozvi from the Chipinga district, resigned as an evangelist of the American Board Mission as a result of friction with the White missionaries at Mt Selinda. He had encountered the successors of Mvuyana, Samuel Dube and Ma-Khoba in South Africa during the thirties and had felt a close affinity with them because of the similarity in their background — reaction against the conduct of the American Board Mission, which had resulted in schism and the establishment of the Zulu Congregational Church. They promoted him to clerical office *(mufundisi)* and he returned to Rhodesia to establish and expand the African Congregational Church in the Chipinga district. In 1942 he obtained government recognition for his church. All the key figures who helped him to establish the ACC among the VaNdau in Chipinga (the Reverends Dzukuso, Pahla, Sibambo and Makoni) were former members of the American Board Mission.

In 1950 there was a breakthrough in church growth when influential leaders such as Moses Ruwana, Zvobgo and Chirasha-nye with their followers from the DR Mission church, began joining the ACC. Within a few years thousands of new members from the Victoria, Gutu and Bikita districts (many of them from the DR Mission Church) joined this "Ethiopian" movement. Moses Ruwana was the key figure during this flourishing period in the life of the ACC.

Under Ruwana's influence this church's reliance on traditional customs came to the fore. Its popular name, *Chibarirwe* (derived from *kubereka,* give birth to, that which was born for us, place of our ancestors), expressed its reaction against the historical churches and its recognition of traditional usage. During this period the vernacular name gained general recognition. However, this deliberate Africanization led to fresh reaction and reform, culminating in schism and the establishment of the African Reformed Church *(Shonganiso* Mission) in 1953. The leaders were the Revd Zvobgo — father of the present Minister of Justice in the Mugabe government — and Sibambo. The new church drew

52

closer to the doctrine of the Reformed Mission Church by making monogamy, abstinence from liquor and a prohibition on divination *(kushopera),* and hence by implication on ancestor worship — qualifications for membership. In the years that followed Zvobgo successfully launched his own school and various activities similar to those of the DR missions. Zvobgo himself stated: "The organization of our African Reformed Church is not directed at breaking down the work of the DR missionaries, but to further our own activities in the spirit of remembrance that our church originated from the *'vaDutchi'* our spiritual fathers."[11]

A typical feature of the expansion of Ethiopian-type churches among the Shona was the impulses from South Africa which gave rise to schism and the origin of new churches. However, by contrast with the "Ethiopian" movement in South Africa, the *Topia* and *Chibarirwe* churches achieved full autonomy at an early stage. Despite unmistakable elements of Shona reaction against the historical churches, the latter — and the DR Churches in particular — left their mark on the Ethiopian-type churches because of their early influence on the key figures prior to schism and their continuing influence on youth through their control of the educational system. Anti-White sentiments were most marked among the *Chibarirwe,* also evident in their attempt to adapt the church to traditional customs.

When one compares the position in Zimbabwe with that in South Africa, there is one striking difference: when the growth rate among Ethiopian-type churches in South Africa was beginning to decline noticeably by the thirties, they were just beginning to flourish among the Shona. Thus in Zimbabwe the rise of prophetic and non-prophetic movements largely coincided, whereas in South Africa they developed in two separate phases (Ethiopian-type, 1890-1920; Spirit-type, 1920-1970).

2.3.2 *Spirit-type churches*

The prophetic movement in South Africa only advanced substantially (in terms of numbers) after the initial heyday of the

11 Ibid., p. 368

"Ethiopian" groups. However, once this popular form of religion got off the ground it soon grew into a far more numerous and influential movement than that of the "Ethiopians". The prevalence of such terms as Zion, Jerusalem, Apostolic, Full Gospel, Pentecostal and the like in the designations of South African Independent Churches in itself indicates that most of them are strongly pentecostally inclined, or at least give pre-eminence to the work of the Holy Spirit.

The driving force behind this entire movement was an apocalyptic church in America, the Christian Catholic Apostolic Church in Zion, established by John Alexander Dowie in 1896. This church placed its main emphasis on divine healing, adult baptism by immersion, and the conviction that the second coming was imminent. In Zion City, near Chicago, a new theocratic kingdom was established.

In 1904, Daniel Bryant, one of Dowie's "overseers", visited South Africa and baptised the first group of converts. One of the early converts was a White, P.L. le Roux, a man of devout and childlike faith who exercised an unobtrusive but profound influence on the entire movement. Through the agency of le Roux and others, the Zionist movement gradually acquired a marked pentecostal slant. Le Roux himself was "baptized in the Holy Spirit" in 1908.[12]

In that year le Roux and several prominent Black leaders founded the Zion Apostolic Church. This was followed by a series of schisms, one of which led to the establishment of the Zion Apostolic Church of South Africa under Bishop Mhlangu, in 1917. This church was to have great significance for Shona migrant labourers in South Africa. This was the church with which the pioneers of Zionism in Rhodesia — Makamba, Mtisi and Masuka — first became involved. On his return to Rhodesia Masuka acted as chief representative of Mhlangu's church for many years, while Mtisi established his own Zion City near Umtali and Makamba launched an independent branch of the Zion Apostolic Church in the Bikita district. The Zionist move-

12 Sundkler (1976, p. 16f) gives a detailed account of the work of the Revd le Roux and the first group of Black leaders of the Zionist movement in South Africa.

ment gave rise to innumerable splinter groups such as the Zion Protestant Church, the Zion Sabbath Church, the Zion Apostolic Church of Jesus Christ[13] and the like.

In South Africa the energetic and influential "Edward of Basutoland" broke away from Mhlangu's ZAC of SA in 1920 and founded the Zion Apostolic Faith Mission. In 1923 two Shona migrant labourers, Samuel Mutendi and Andreas Shoko, were baptized in this ZAFM. On his return to Rhodesia in 1931 Shoko became leader of the Shona branch of this movement, while in 1925 Mutendi, along with Lekhanyane, broke away from the ZAFM and established the Zion Christian Church. Like Lekhanyane in the Transvaal, Mutendi expanded the ZCC in the erstwhile Rhodesia into a widespread and well-organized movement from his headquarters which he called Zion City. In the early years there was no substantial difference between the ZCC and other Zionist groups among the Shona. In all of them faith healing, inspiration by the Spirit and "Jordan baptism" were focal points. One distinction was that the ZCC wore uniforms and the star of Zion, whereas the official dress of other Zionists was invariably long, multicoloured robes tied with sacred cords *(ndaza)*. This led to distinctive terms in the Shona vernacular, the ZCC on the one hand and the *vaZioni veNdaza* (Zionists of the sacred cords) on the other.

Organizationally the Shona Zionist churches, which grew rapidly during the thirties, soon became independent of the South African movement. Ideologically the bonds were maintained and were strengthened by sporadic mutual visits. To some Zionist leaders the ties with South African Zionist churches had mainly prestige value in the Shona context. Occasionally minor schisms were justified by citing the support of some South African Zionist leader.

Of all these Zionist churches Bishop Mutendi's ZCC attracted most attention at a national level. Mutendi gained publicity as a sort of resistance hero who effectively dodged the oppressive measures of the administration. A descendant of the royal house of the Rozvi, he invoked the bygone glory of this dynasty and as a result many more Shona chiefs were baptized in his church than

13 Daneel, 1971(a), p. 300

in any of the other Independent Churches in Rhodesia. In Mutendi's "holy city" chiefs and ordinary ZCC members could attend the great feasts and experience a taste of a "kingdom" of their own, free of White domination and subject only to a venerated authority. Because of Mutendi's fame as a miracle-worker, benefactor and resistance figure his leadership eventually developed overtones of what one could call "Messianism". However, in a church full of contrasts the sentiments that found expression were not only those of tradition and tribal politics, but also progressive modern trends. Mutendi and his sons applied and promoted modern agricultural methods and ran a school of their own in collaboration with the central government.

Apart from the Zionists, the Spirit-type churches that developed into nation-wide movements from the early thirties onwards were mainly the African Apostolic Church of Johane Maranke and Mai Chaza's *Guta raJehovah* (City of God), both originating in the Umtali area. We shall concentrate on the AACJM, among the Shona commonly known as the *vaPostori* (Apostles). Whereas many of the Zionist leaders had a DR (mission church) background, Johane Maranke and the nucleus of his movement's leadership came from the American Methodist Mission. Johane had his visions and calling written up in a book entitled *The new revelation of the Apostles (Umboo utsva hwavaPostori),* in which he is identified with biblical leaders, especially Joseph and Moses.[14] He also refers to other church leaders' experiences, for instance those of John Masowe, a Shona prophet whom Sundkler describes as a Black Messiah, and Alice Lenshina of the Lumpa Church in Zambia. Such experiences imply a "death" and a visit to heaven, where the visionary receives a special commission directly from God. In this way his vocation is of unassailable authenticity. On 17 July 1932 Johane experienced an outpouring of the Holy Spirit in the vicinity of Mount Nyengwe. He heard a voice commanding him: "You are John the Baptist, an apostle. Go forth and do my work. Go to every country, preach and convert the people. Command them not to commit adultery, steal or become angry. Baptize people and observe the sabbath! "

14 Ibid., p. 316f

Although terrified by the experience, Johane at once obeyed and in the course of the next few days baptized many of his relations in the new Apostle Church. Until his death the course of his life was directed by this commission and he undertook regular campaigns, some of which took him into the heart of the Congo, baptizing thousands of people.

Johane's basic strategy was to proclaim a fervently apocalyptic message, heal people by laying on of hands and then initiate them into his church by means of a "Jordan" baptism. On his campaigns his cousin, Simon Mushati, acted as prophet to interpret the guidance of God's Spirit for the Apostles' programme. Those who were baptized were encouraged to go and preach in their own villages and expand the Apostle Church. As a result congregations mushroomed all over in both rural and urban areas. At an early stage a hierarchical leadership was devised and consistently applied in all congregations. It comprised baptists, prophets, evangelists and judges as the key offices, each subdivided into five orders. Whereas initially Johane had confined himself exclusively to preaching and baptizing, the expanding church eventually demanded more of his time for organizational work and the conducting of *Pendi* (Pentecostal feasts). A church district was not really complete without its own *Pendi* centre where several congregations could assemble for the visits of Johane and Simon Mushati. In addition to preaching, baptism, teaching and organization, the key event at such assemblies was the administration of the sacrament of bread and wine.

Johane's father, Momberume, and his two brothers Conorio and Anrod, usually stayed at home, constituting a sort of consolidatory advisory council at headquarters. The emphasis in the Apostle Church was not so much on the construction of a holy city where people could visit the "emissary of God". Johane was far too restless a wanderer and evangelist for that. But at home Momberume and a number of "judges" *(vatongi)* dealt with all disciplinary matters, while Conorio acted as faith healer and Anrod as advisor on matters of church organization.

The *New revelation* provides little factual information about church growth because of the focus on Johane's personal experiences. Nonetheless one gets some idea from certain "texts" about activities in the course of Johane's journeys through rural villages. Thus in chapter 14: 2 Johane says: "I went to all the villages to preach, speak in tongues and drive out *shavi* spirits. I healed people, performed miracles and even walked on fire." In chapter 15 there is a description of a large church gathering in 1932, on which occasion Johane fell into the "Jordan" and announced that God's kingdom was at hand. Those who had come from beer-drinking sessions were freed of evil spirits.

Consistent features in these descriptions are the rejection of the "things of this world", for instance in confrontation with traditional customs (burning of all medicines, fetishes and rejection of ancestor worship), a high ideal of sanctity associated with Old Testament laws, and an apocalyptic message to move people to repentance.

Within eight years Johane's church had grown phenomenally. Over a hundred *Pendi* centres had sprung up throughout the country and were ministered to every year. Country-wide journeys were undertaken on foot, by bicycle or ox cart, until eventually the church could afford Landrovers. By 1957 Johane's older sons had to be appointed to help minister to the many church centres every year.

Johane operated southwards into the Transvaal and the Free State, but his targets outside Zimbabwe were chiefly Zambia, Malawi, Mozambique and Zaire. Thus he had a tremendous following among the Kasai. When in the 1960s Abero celebrated communion in the vicinity of Elizabethville and Chingulu over 10 000 Apostles participated. Similar numbers joined in communion feasts in the vicinity of Port Herald and Blantyre. Thus Johane was one of the foremost African prophetic leaders, a man with a missionary vision who for thirty years travelled, preached and baptized indefatigably. Numerically his church did not achieve the size of those of Kimbangu and Lenkhanyane, but it is still one of the most widely dispersed movements in Africa and the largest Independent Church in Zimbabwe.

As so often happens in the Independent Churches when a founder-leader dies, Johane's death in 1963 triggered off a power struggle. Prophet Simon Mushati and certain other leaders protested against the way in which Anrod, Johane's brother, and his eldest sons Abero and Makebo took over the leadership of the church. This conflict culminated in schism, as a result of which

Simon and a few thousand adherents are still continuing with their own African Apostolic Church today.[15]

Among the many Spirit-type churches which originated around the beginning of this century, and whose growth rate accelerated during the twenties and thirties, the most prominent are the following: the *amaNazareta* of Isaiah Shembe and the Zion Christian Church of Engenas Lekhanyane in South Africa; Mutendi's Zion Christian Church and Johane Maranke's African Apostolic Church in Zimbabwe; Alice Lenshina's Lumpa Church in Zambia; Simon Kimbangu's Church of Jesus Christ in Zaire; and the Cherubim and Seraphim Church and the Church of the Lord (Aladura), both in Nigeria.

Women play a strikingly important part in many Spirit-type churches. In more than one instance, a woman is at the head. As examples we may mention: Ma (i.e. Mother) Nku of the St John's Apostolic Faith Church on the Witwatersrand; Mai (i.e. Mother) Chaza's City of God near Umtali in Zimabwe; Christiana Abiodun's Cherubim and Seraphim Society in Nigeria; Alice Lenshina's Lumpa Church in Zambia; and Gaudencia Aoko's Maria Legio Church in Kenya. Some of these women received their special vocation at a remarkably young age. We have already referred to the fact that Donna Beatrice was hardly 20 years old when St Anthony took possession of her. Alice Lenshina was 29 years of age when she received her call, and Gaudencia Aoko was only 20.

Even where women are not actually at the head of a movement, they often occupy prominent positions in the organization. Thus, Simon Kimbangu's wife, Mwilu Marie, was for many years (while her husband was in prison and even after his death) an unobtrusive yet active inspiration for the entire Kimbanguist movement.

Today the Spirit-type movement is very much stronger than the "Ethiopian". By far the majority of members of the Independent Churches belong to this group. However, it is not possible to obtain statistics of this ratio, partly because a large number of Independent Churches are both "Ethiopian" and prophetic while others could hardly be classified as either one or the other.

15 Ibid., pp. 331-338

2.4 THE KIMBANGU CHURCH IN ZAIRE

Before we leave the subject entirely, it may be worthwhile to relate briefly the history of one of the Independent Churches, namely the Kimbangu Church.[16] We select this church, not simply because it was for a long time the largest Independent Church in Africa, but also because its history opens up many significant theological perspectives which will help greatly in our attempt to understand the movement in other parts of Africa as well.

Simon Kimbangu was a teacher and evangelist at the Baptist mission in the village of N'Kamba in what was then the Belgian Congo. During the 1918 flu epidemic he heard a voice calling him one night to a special kind of service. However, he did not heed the voice until three years later when, on 16 April 1921, he performed a miraculous healing. Other healing miracles followed: the lame, the blind, the deaf and cripples were healed, each time with the explicit declaration that this had happened in the name of Jesus. It was as if a new Pentecost had dawned on N'Kamba and this was in fact how the people experienced it: Simon was the chosen instrument of the Holy Spirit; the Holy Spirit was poured out, not only in Jerusalem but also here in Africa, in N'Kamba, the "new Jerusalem".

Kimbangu preached as well as healed, and his theme was quite simple: "Throw away the fetishes (magical objects and amulets) and trust in God alone! " According to reports, one could see discarded fetishes all along the roadsides leading from N'Kamba. Did Kimbangu, through his preaching, simply substitute more powerful fetishes? He himself did not see it this way. His preaching also emphasised moral chastity and monogamy (cf. by contrast the polygamy of Lekhanyane and Shembe) and he forbade his followers to attend pagan dances. His preaching revealed no anti-White tendencies; in fact he explicitly preached obedience to the authorities and love of one's enemies.

Thousands of people flocked to N'Kamba to hear this prophet. In the mission churches, too, there was a tremendous revival. One missionary reported: "Our church buildings are filled to

16 In this regard see particularly Martin, 1971

overflowing, while those of the Catholics are emptying. From every side we hear requests for teachers and educational material; in three months we have sold 500 hymn books." Another missionary wrote: "This is the most remarkable movement this country has ever seen." However, the Baptist missionaries in more than one respect remained sceptical and wary of this movement. The nub of the matter, as far as the Black Christians were concerned, was quite simple: "You do not believe it because he is Black." The missionary's labours had, in fact, borne a fruit which the missionary himself did not expect . . .

Kimbangu's public ministry was to be short-lived. The pilgrimages undertaken by hundreds of people to N'Kamba aroused the suspicion of the Belgian authorities: here was insurrection brewing. Several officials were sent to investigate the matter. The report of one of these colonial officials, Leon Morel, is important in that it contains remarkable missiological insight, interspersed with misconceptions and fallacious arguments. Morel writes: "Kimbangu wants to establish a religion related to the mentality of the African, a religion which will incorporate characteristic features of Protestantism, with, however, fetishist practices added . . . The religions of Europe are full of abstractions which have no affinity with the mentality of the African, who longs rather for concrete facts and protection. Kimbangu's doctrine speaks to him because it is supported by assimilable facts . . . It is necessary, therefore, to fight Kimbangu, for his tendency is towards pan-Africanism."

What made matters worse was that from the outset there were political elements which wanted to use Kimbangu's popularity for their own ends. They were called "Ngunzists" or "false prophets" and although Kimbangu himself, and his eventual successors, repeatedly repudiated them, it was not easy for the Belgian authorities to distinguish between the true Kimbanguists and the false. The fact that his followers — drawn, mostly, from the Baptist mission — sang hymns like "Onward Christian soldiers" and "Stand up, stand up for Jesus" (hymns which were quite alien to the Catholic civil servants) did not help to calm the fears of the Belgians.

The Catholic missionaries, for their part, increasingly urged swift and firm action. On 6 June 1921, barely two months after the beginning of the movement, Kimbangu brought his public ministry to a close and went underground. While the movement continued to grow, and while many adherents were imprisoned, the police sought in vain for the leader. On 12 August a state of emergency was declared. A month later, on 12 September, Kimbangu voluntarily gave himself up to the authorities, explicitly invoking the example of Jesus in Gethsemane. On 3 October he was sentenced to 120 lashes and the death penalty, and that in front of a military court before whom no witnesses or defence counsel appeared. From Protestant missionaries and political groups came pleas for clemency strongly opposed by Catholic missionaries. The pleas for mercy were heeded and Kimbangu was sentenced to life imprisonment. He was not to serve this sentence in his home environment, but in Elizabethville (now Lumbumbashi) in Katanga, thousands of kilometres from his home. He was never released and died in prison on 12 October 1951.

The remarkable thing is that the movement did not end with Kimbangu's imprisonment. Despite the fact that his public ministry had lasted a scant two months, the movement he initiated grew from strength to strength. Two of his three young sons were taken from their mother when he was imprisoned and placed in Catholic boarding schools. However, this was where they received the very training which they were to need later as leaders of the movement. In the fifties, Joseph, the youngest, now the head of the church, was private secretary to the last Belgian governor-general, while Charles, the eldest, served in several cabinets from 1960 onwards.

To put an end to the movement, the Belgian authorities began applying strict measures after 1921. Many Kimbanguists were imprisoned, deported to thirty different areas of the Congo, and subjected to all sorts of restrictions. It is calculated that a total of 37 000 heads of families were banned during the period 1921-1957; the total number of individuals was over 100 000. These deportations, instead of destroying the movement, helped to spread it across the entire country. At the same time, however, pseudo-Kimbanguism or Ngunzism was also spread abroad, which did not improve matters for either the Kimbanguists or the Belgians. Some of these Ngunzist elements wanted to elevate Kimbangu, to "the God of the Blacks", a new Messiah. He would, they said, drive the Whites into the sea. At this point the Bible was forgotten. A glorious (mythological) past was projected onto the future, but there was no longer a genuine eschatology. The cross of Christ was obscured. Among many so-called Kimbanguists magical elements were prominent. In fact, they were more like pagan diviners than members of a Christian church. Ngunzist peripheral groups which grew up with the passage of time include the Congolese Salvation Army (an offshoot of the famous Salvation Army); Simon Mpadi's *Eglise des Noirs* (Church of the Blacks), also known as the Khaki Church; Andre Matswa's Amical Balali movement in Congo-Brazzaville; and Emmanuel Bamba's church *Le Salut de Jesus-Christ par le temoin Simon Kimbangu,* a movement which broke away from the Kimbangu movement.

The measures taken by the government could not separate the chaff from the wheat, with the result that all were treated alike. Many hymns written and sung at that time testify to suffering under persecution, as witness the following:

> . . . Jesus is a prisoner
> Jesus was whipped.
> They whip us too,
> We, the Blacks, are prisoners,
> The White man is free . . .
> . . . We suffer inexpressibly
> But through thy power
> No one can deter us . . .

None of these hymns call for revenge. In fact, they frequently mention that the Whites, like the Blacks, are followers of Jesus.

At this stage the Kimbanguists were not yet organized as a separate denomination, but remained members of their several churches (including the Roman Catholic Church). It was only in 1956 that the Kimbanguists began de facto to detach themselves from these churches and officially organize their own religious worship. The movement had now become a church; it took the name *Eglise de Jesus-Christ sur la terre par le prophete Simon Kimbangu* (EJCSK), the Church of Jesus Christ on earth through the prophet Simon Kimbangu.

However, persecution and intimidation did not abate, for the movement was still regarded as illegal. The turning-point eventually came in 1957. A deputation of leading Kimbanguists went with a petition, signed by 600 people, to the Belgian governor-general Petillon. The petition stated: 'We suffer too greatly. Wherever we gather for prayer, we are arrested by your soldiers. So as not to burden the police with extra work we shall all gather, unarmed, in the King Baudouin stadium; there you may imprison us all or shoot us all." The alternative, not explicitly stated, was nevertheless implied: " . . . or guarantee our religious liberty! " Petillon in fact, had no choice, and promised to exert himself in the cause of religious liberty. However, it was not until December 1959 (six months before the Congo was granted independence) that the Kimbangu Church was granted official recognition. A few months earlier Simon Kimbangu's widow, Mwilu Marie had died. For almost forty years she had unobtrusively inspired the entire movement.

Since the independence of the Congo, the Kimbangu Church has grown phenomenally. Special attention has been given to education. By 1968 there were already about 100 000 children in Kimbangu church schools. They have also founded their own clinics, brickyards, agricultural settlements, tailor shops and so on. The village of N'Kamba, where Kimbangu began his activities, occupies a focal place and has since been renamed N'Kamba-Jerusalem. After all, this was where salvation history was repeated, here the new Pentecost dawned, here God revealed himself to the dishonoured, suffering Black race. Simon Kimbangu was re-interred in the town in 1960, and a mausoleum was erected in his honour.

Apart from the parallels with Jerusalem and Pentecost, other scriptural parallels have been cited. The period 1921-1960 is often compared to the Israelites' forty years sojourn in the wilderness; Simon Kimbangu's voluntary surrender to the authorities in 1921 with that of Jesus in Gethsemane. He is also linked with Moses because he freed them from the slavery of superstition, witchcraft and sickness and — eventually — from the yoke of colonial rule. The colonial government has been compared with King Herod who wanted to kill the infant Jesus. Another saying is: "The world did not love father Simon, just as it did not love Christ." Thus the life of Kimbangu is time and again seen as concretization of the biblical message. Just as Jesus healed the sick, raised the dead, proclaiming salvation, so did Simon Kimbangu. As he suffered innocently, so did Simon. The qualitative differences were, however, steadfastly emphasized: the death of Jesus was an atonement, while the suffering endured by Simon was not. Simon was no more than an apostle, an ambassador, but through the concrete events of his life Jesus was, as it were, portrayed before the eyes of the Congolese (cf. Gl 3: 1). Just as Paul bore in his body the marks of Jesus (cf. Gl 6: 17), so also did Simon. Through Simon Kimbangu, many people saw Christ.

That there are latent dangers in this viewpoint and others like it is not to be denied. Undoubtedly, in the minds of many simple Kimbanguists, Simon took the place of Christ. It is, however, significant that the church's leadership discouraged such tendencies.

Simon Kimbangu's second son, Solomon Dialungana, the least educated of the three brothers, produced a catechism in 1957 which did, in fact, contain dangerous statements. In it, Simon Kimbangu is identified with "the other comforter" whom Jesus promised, his bodily return is proclaimed, and it is stated, with reference to John 1: 1 "he was with God in the beginning". These and similar utterances partly express the naivete of people not yet accustomed to couching a catechism in verbal terms and to whom our Western practice of theology is wholly foreign. It is significant, on the other hand, that a more recent edition of this catechism does not mention Simon Kimbangu.

Perhaps Simon Kimbangu's "theological" significance for the church is best expressed in an impressive carving in N'Kamba, a photograph of which appears on the cover of Dr Martin's book. It portrays Simon Kimbangu as Simon of Cyrene, who carried Jesus' cross. He is not a new Christ, yet he is more than John the Baptist whose finger points to Jesus. He is Simon of Cyrene (from Africa) who walks with Jesus along his path of suffering and helps to bear his cross.

Today the three sons of Simon lead the Kimbangu Church. Charles Kisolokele is the eldest, then comes Solomon K. Dialungana, while Joseph Diangienda, the youngest, occupies the supreme office. According to the reports of observers, all three are true, humble Christians. Joseph Diangienda in particular commands respect on all sides. In 1966 he wrote an important statement on "Church and politics" which can, in a sense, be regarded as the manifesto of the Kimbanguists. It is explicitly anti-

Marxist and also anti-racist. It is strongly opposed to violence, though this does not mean that the Kimbanguists refuse (as do Jehovah's Witnesses) to perform their military service, but only that when persecuted for their faith they will not resort to armed violence.

The Kimbangu Church's government is hierarchic. It is therefore quite different from that of the Baptists from whom they originally sprang. A church order was drawn up in 1960, which lays down that Kimbanguists may not take part in any political conflict, and that they are opposed to any form of discrimination on grounds of race or colour. In addition to the Ten Commandments, their followers are required to obey the following commands: obedience to the authorities; mutual love and love for enemies (Mt 5: 43-45); abstinence from alcohol, tobacco, dancing and immorality; there is to be no fetish cult; they are to pay their taxes; they are to abandon all thoughts of vengeance; they are to refrain from eating pork and the flesh of monkeys. Monogamy is rigidly upheld. Services are held on Sunday, and the sermons frequently refer to Simon Kimbangu. Feast days are held from time to time and on these occasions special collections are taken. The atmosphere is festive and joyous, and as a result church members do not seek their merriment elsewhere. If Joseph Diangienda is present, the sick and others who need help come to him after the service, when, quite unostentatiously, he speaks with them and lays hands upon them, praying for healing or in blessing. Neither people nor ministers wear special clothes.

The members of this church are extremely generous. In 1966 they were able to build a church in Kinshasa seating 3 000 worshippers. Widows, orphans and neglected children are cared for in settlements and elsewhere. Although they practise prayer for healing with laying on of hands, they do not reject or condemn medical help: they already have their own clinics with qualified nurses in attendance.

During the years of persecution they could not, of course, celebrate *communion*. Even after the church was recognized, they did not immediately institute the sacrament, but considered it prayerfully for many years. Eventually the first communion was celebrated during the jubilee festivities on 6 April 1971, fifty years after Simon had begun his public ministry. Three hundred and fifty thousand believers gathered on this occasion. The eucharistic elements were bread baked from a mixture of potatoes, maize and bananas, and wine made of honey and water.

In our further discussion of the Independent Churches, it will be a good thing to bear in mind the remarkable history of the Kimbanguists. Without in any way holding up this church as an ideal model of an Independent Church, it will be a useful standard for comparison with other movements.

We have already referred to some disturbing trends in the Kimbangu Church. There are others too, such as the water of N'Kamba, which is used for healing purposes. Believers take it with them in large vessels as far as Congo-Brazzaville, Rwanda and Kitwe in Zambia. This water is applied to afflicted parts of the body, and it is also drunk. Here undoubtedly magical tendencies are lurking. The same is true of the soil of N'Kamba, small quantities of which are taken away by visitors as a "pledge" (cf. 2 Kings 5: 17). There is also the danger of pharisaism and legalism, particularly in the attitude of some that "we Kimbanguists" are not like "worldly people". Sin is too easily viewed as a transgression of *commandments* rather than the breach of a personal relationship.

However, the Kimbangu Church possesses within itself the corrective for these mistaken tendencies. The *Bible* is the consistent focal point of religious and community life, and not as a fetish, but as a source of life. This does not mean that the Kimbanguists are safe from all heresy, but they are at least armed for the struggle against un-Christian elements.

CHAPTER 3

FACTORS INFLUENCING THE ORIGIN AND GROWTH OF THE INDEPENDENT CHURCHES

An analysis of the factors influencing the origin and growth of the Independent Churches is extremly important for missiology. It shows what mistakes were committed by historical missioning churches in the past and provides valuable insights into the type of reactions that could be expected to a particular policy or circumstance. Such an analysis moreover promotes understanding of the African's interpretation of Scripture and the "theological" emphasis he places in terms of his existential situation.

In this chapter we shall first consider various theories concerning the causes for the origin of the Independent Churches as presented in the literature and then isolate a number of factors for more particular attention. It is always extremely difficult to distinguish major causes from the host of background factors that influenced (and continue to influence) church formation, either directly or indirectly. Whereas it is a fairly simple matter to determine which general political, sociological and economic factors are conducive to the formation of new churches, it is by no means easy to arrive at a representative or tenable theory when it comes to the individual groups or their members. Thus in the same group it may well be that the founder-leader broke away from a historical church in protest against a particular church policy. Over the years people join this new church for a variety of other reasons ranging from the political and sociological to the religious — factors in which the original cause of the reaction hardly features any more. Unless one has a historical perspective on the variety of successive factors one could easily arrive at a mistaken theory based on the initial phase of the group's origin. Thus one could erroneously typify it as a reactionary phenomenon, whereas in actual fact it could have developed into a missionary movement whose existence and growth are not (or at least not exclusively) attributable to reaction against the historical (mission) churches.

3.1 THEORIES ABOUT CAUSAL FACTORS IN THE LITERATURE

Some researchers have tried to reduce the complexity of causes to a few basic background factors. Thus Sundkler, Balandier and Andersson stress the *socio-political* situation in which such movements originate. They see the fundamental causes as social injustice resulting from a policy of segregation, alienation from tribal territories and racial tension generally. Sundkler maintains that "separatism" is largely a result of a colour bar maintained even in the church of Christ.[1] The desire of the "disinherited" to own land gives rise to a particular type of leadership, namely a Moses figure who will lead his followers to the "promised land" (some plot of land or farm) where a church colony is then established.[2]

Andersson postulates a causal connection between the origin of "messianic" movements in the Congo and the desire for political co-determination,[3] and Balandier points out that this phenomenon originated in a colonial situation where the colonizers oppressed the colonized.[4] Lucy Mair, on the other hand, explains the Independent Churches simply in terms of a correlation between the emergence of cults and the lack of political representation.[5] Thus the Independent Churches are defined as *political protest movements* against a background of colonial paternalism and the rise of Black nationalism.

Kuper and Knoob point out that *ethnic factors* play a crucial part in the formation of Independent Churches. Kuper maintains that the continuing secession of churches reflects an accepted custom in the traditional tribal structure (in Swaziland). The custom of a kinship group to secede and become independent on the death of the head of the family is projected directly onto the structure of the church.[6] Knoob feels that the main cause of

---

1   Sundkler, 1961, p. 37
2   Ibid., pp. 33, 331
3   Andersson, 1958
4   Balandier, 1953, pp. 41-65
5   Mair, 1963, p. 181
6   Kuper, 1946, pp. 117-189

"separatism" is the lack of social security, especially when people leave the sheltered existence at the mission station. This author believes that when studying "separatism" one should proceed according to an *ethno-historical* approach which in the first instance allows for the realities of African society. Africans still cling to the small kinship group as the ideal for social living.

> *Das Idealbild der Grossfamilie wird auf die Kirchengemeinde uebertragen, wie frueher auf Klan und Stamm.*[7]

Sundkler also suggests that a comparative study will reveal a morphological similarity between the "pattern" of tribal culture and the types of Christian prophetic movements to which it gives birth.[8]

Harold Turner classified the causal factors into four categories:

(1) acculturative or circumstantial factors;
(2) contributory factors (psychological pressure, cultural and social disintegration, conflict between two systems, political domination, exploitation, etc.);
(3) precipitating factors (personal crises, epidemics, new taxes, war, healing miracles, appearance of a charismatic personality, etc.); and
(4) enabling factors. Here Turner refers to the fact that among the world's major religions Christianity displays a remarkable ability to allow new religious movements to arise within its own framework. Elements such as the Christian gospel's special appeal for the poor and the oppressed, the possibility of a group and its leaders identifying with the people of Israel, biblical eschatological promises of a better future — these are all factors which enables such churches to come into being.

Turner emphasizes a different facet from the aforementioned authors. With reference to the Independent Churches in West

7 Knoob, 1961, pp. 116, 122
8 Sundkler, 1961, p. 300

Africa he demonstrates convincingly that the main causes for their formation were *not* socio-political, economic or ethnic factors. He stresses the *basically religious nature* of these movements.[9] In the midst of crumbling traditional structures these churches represent a creative religious movement which provides security, fellowship and spiritual guidance in the context of the newly established groups. He describes the Church of the Lord as a "vital development" at a point when the African past is confronted with the challenge of the new world of the Bible. The origin and growth of this church relate directly to the work of the Holy Spirit.[10]

G.C. Oosthuizen classified the various causes into twelve groups: [11]

1. Political causes (racial discrimination, colonialism, etc.)
2. Economic causes (restrictions, job reservation, etc.)
3. Sociological causes (colour bar, striving for social justice, etc.)
4. Historical causes (missionary paternalism, colonial history, etc.)
5. Denominational causes (multiplication of missionary societies; unhealthy competition; discrepant disciplinary measures; disputes)
6. Religious causes (inability of Whites to convey the gospel within the context of another religious culture; exclusive concentration on the salvation of souls, etc.)
7. Ethnic causes (function of the extended family; the need for small, intimate groups; the desire for a visible mediator; the struggle against disease; the role of visions and dreams; the legalistic character of traditional community life; the desire for ritual; the role of emotion; disillusionment with Christianity; missionaries' ignorance of the indigenous language; tribal connections, etc.)

9 Turner, 1967(a), p. xiv
10 Turner, 1967(b), pp. 371-372
11 Oosthuizen, 1968(b), pp. 209-221

8. Ecclesiastical causes (neglect of pastoral care; misunderstandings about discipline; ineffective catechising; neglect of the diaconate; misuse of church finances; reluctance to encourage indigenous leadership; lack of opportunity for the laity to serve, etc.)
9. Non-religious causes (the role of symbolic colours, dress, processions, ceremonies; the missionary's insensitivity in personal relationships; ambition, jealousy and suspicion; etc.).
10. Poor communication
11. The Bible as a cause (polarity between the written word and the Spirit-inspiration of the prophet; literal interpretation of Scripture; the Bible as a fetish; the role of women in the Bible; etc.)
12. Theological causes (misconceptions, particularly about the concept of God, the Messiah, the Holy Spirit, the church, the concept of sin, the sacraments, attitude to Scripture, eschatology and the resurrection).

Oosthuizen believes that it is a fallacy to regard the Independent Churches as nationalistic movements with political aims, although he acknowledges that "Ethiopianism" is a reaction against the superior attitude of Westerners. He writes:

> Although the deepest motive of many independent movements has been *religious* one of their essential points is the transferring to the spiritual and ecclesiastical plane of the *opposition to white authority,* which could be made effective only by reconstructing the African communities under African leadership (my italics).[12]

In a very readable essay in his book *Mission and ministry*,[13] Adrian Hastings suggests ten main causes for the rise of these movements:

1. A missionary attitude and missionary theology which, one way or another, justifies schism

12 Oosthuizen, 1968(a), p. 7
13 Hastings, 1971, pp. 208-209

2. The multiplication of Protestant missions in one area
3. A lack (in some churches) of ritual and an opportunity to concretize the sacral
4. The need for small local congregations, where a feeling of security and fellowship can develop
5. A tribal structure which stresses decentralization
6. Certain needs which the historical churches ignored
7. Limited promotion of indigenous ministers
8. A colour bar in the community reflected in the church
9. Rapid social change, leading to instability and a sense of insecurity
10. Lack of opportunity for Black leadership in the political, civic and industrial spheres.

These ten factors, says Hastings, work cumulatively. As more of them occur in a particular country, so the possibility of independent church formation increases. He finds all ten factors operative in South Africa, a large number of them in Kenya and Zambia, but hardly any in Tanzania and Rwanda.

David Barrett's analysis of the causes of "independency" in his comprehensive study, *Schism and renewal in Africa,* is highly significant. Having studied the phenomenon among the Luo in Kenya, he then consulted the most relevant literature to determine which factors are considered important. Thereupon he selected a representative sample of 336 tribal units in Africa, to whom he put eighteen key questions for purposes of statistical comparison. The questions concern background factors conducive to the formation of Independent Churches. The more of these factors are present in a tribal unit, the more favourable the "tribal *Zeitgeist*" is for schism. With the aid of experts from other disciplines the eighteen questions were processed at seven levels of analysis so as to arrive at a general theory.[14]

The first analytical level was aimed at "national correlates of independency". It was found that schisms were more common among peoples where a large number of (Protestant) missionaries were labouring; where the concentration of Whites pro rata to the Black population was high; where the standard of living (of

14 Barrett, 1968, pp. 5-7

the White elite) was high; where the percentage of literates was high; and so on. The second and third levels of analysis concerned "tribal correlates of independency". These movements occur most frequently among polygamous tribes where ancestor worship features prominently, where missionaries have been active for a long time and the Bible has been translated into the indigenous language.

The last four levels of analysis all concern the theme, "reaction to mission". In his discussion of the eighteen key questions in this section Barret tries to substantiate his basic hypothesis, namely that

> independency is a societal reaction to mission arising out of a tribal *Zeitgeist* or climate of opinion in which Christian missions were believed to be illegitimately mounting an attack against African traditional society and in particular its basic unit, the family.[15]

The missionaries' attack on polygamy is a conditioning factor whose effects are mainly at an unconscious level. Drastic condemnation of the ancestor cult implies an onslaught on the very foundations of the African tribal and family structure. Such attacks by missionaries were experienced as a direct threat to a fundamental aspect of Black society and could not but provoke strong reaction. Thus Barrett concludes that the Independent Churches represent a reaction to mission rather than to colonialism (although he does not rule out colonialism as a causal factor). He also demonstrates that a community's claims to spiritual independence increase the moment the Bible is published in the indigenous language. Initially the missionary has absolute control over Scripture and his interpretation is binding. Unrestricted access to the Bible provides the African with an independent source of reference, and moreover one which is in all probability more closely related to his own society than to the White man's. The discrepancy between missionary practice and biblical norms did not pass unnoticed.

Statistical analysis of data from 724 tribes led Barrett to con-

15 Ibid., p. 116

clude that in tribes where only parts of the Bible had been translated there was a 56 percent probability of separatism; tribes with access to the New Testament had a 67 percent probability, and those with the whole Bible in their own language an 81 percent probability of schism.[16]

Finally Barrett describes the fundamental cause of the Independent Church movement as a whole in this theory, to wit:

> *A failure in sensitivity, the failure of missions at one small point to demonstrate consistently the fullness of the biblical concept of love as sensitive understanding towards others as equals, the failure to study or understand African society, religion and psychology in any depth, together with a dawning African perception from the vernacular Scriptures of the catastrophic nature of this failure and of the urgent necessity to remedy it in order that Christianity may survive on African soil* (Barrett's italics).[17]

Barrett then elaborates on the threefold failure of mission under three themes: *philadelphia,* Africanism and biblicism Firstly there is a lack of brotherly love (the biblical concept of *philadelphia)* and a paternalistic attitude towards converts; secondly, the lack of sympathetic contact results in an imperfect understanding of the overall tradition complex (Africanism), so that the good and the bad in traditional customs cannot be distinguished; and thirdly, most missionaries failed to spot the parallels between African society and the biblical faith. Instead of using or christianizing traditional customs they condemned or proscribed them for Christians.[18]

3.2   NINE CRUCIAL FACTORS

Among the host of factors mentioned by researchers as causes for the origin of the Independent Churches David Bosch isolated

16 Ibid., p. 131
17 Ibid., p. 156
18 Ibid., p. 157

nine of the most significant ones for discussion.[19] Thus he provides a useful classificatory outline which one could profitably study. Apart from a few insertions in the form of comments and modifications by way of summary, we reproduce the whole of Bosch's discussion:

(1) *Poor communication:* Bosch refers to Barrett's basic theory on the failure of mission to understand the society, religion and psychology of the African, also its failure to actualize the biblical concept of love — see above.[20] Concurring with this, Bosch cites poor communication as a cardinal cause of church schism. He argues thus:

In a single sentence Barrett in fact raises quite a few issues, all of which we may reduce to one phrase: lack of communication, or, as Barrett himself describes it in the heading of the chapter from which the above quotation is taken, "a failure in love". Until well into the twentieth century Western missionaries still did not generally accept that Christianity in Africa would have to be different from Christianity in Europe. When it did begin to differ there were often deliberate attempts to put the lid on such distinctive developments and to channel African church life back into the stereotyped patterns of the West. In the final analysis this lack of understanding of the African is indeed, as Barrett rightly observes, "a failure in love". There was a form of love for the African, but it was paternalistic — the love of a superior being who knows what is good for an inferior one.

We may mention one or two general examples. Many missions totally ignored the role which ritual, ceremonial and symbols can fulfil. The emphasis was placed wholly on the intellectual aspect; emotion must be suppressed as something belonging to a lower order. There was also little understanding for the very real belief in witchcraft and evil spirits. Missionaries often poked fun at this and — typically — labelled it "childish". Thus polygamy which, within the context of African tribal life actually makes sense in many respects, was simply equated with unchastity. Beer-drinking was bluntly dismissd as "abuse of liquor" without any

19 Bosch, 1973, p. 33f
20 Barrett, op cit., p. 156

76

realization of its role in ritual or the fact that it symbolized fellowship and brotherhood.

As a result of these and similar symptoms of lack of communication, the gospel — the good news — began to sound a negative note for many of its African hearers. Eugene Nida put it this way:

> . . . unfortunately some of the unique elements of the gospel are not the things we really talk about. We rather teach people that Christianity involves a new set of taboos: You mustn't drink; you mustn't smoke; you mustn't have more than one wife, etc. And so people often have a very strange idea of what this thing Christianity really is all about.[21]

In this way, he says, "the good news about salvation becomes the bad news about monogamy".

All these indications of lack of communication or lack of love — which ultimately boil down to the same thing — gradually created a favourable climate for schism. When other factors were added the whole "atmosphere" became ripe for secession.

In an unpublished doctoral thesis submitted to the University of Pretoria, H.L. Pretorius describes this inability to communicate the gospel properly to the Black man in his cultural context as "cosmological underestimation". He shows that this inability to communicate is manifested particularly in four areas, namely those of the ancestor cult, magic, illness and sexuality. The errors and "cosmological underestimation" on these points were a large-scale cause for the establishment of Independent Churches. Christ was proclaimed to the Black man as the answer to questions which a White man would ask, the fulfilment of needs felt by the European — the Saviour of the world in terms of a European world-view. The missionaries simply could not see the validity of a completely different cosmological system of thought.[22]

(2) White missionaries often proclaimed a *superficial, impoverished gospel*. This point is, in a sense, linked with the first, but

21 Nida, 1971, p. 97
22 Pretorius, 1972

stresses another aspect of the problem. The preaching of the Word and the catechesis were often extremely superficial and did not even touch on many facets of the life or struggle of the African. The basic cause of this was the impoverished gospel which the missionaries brought to Africa. The majority of them were products of the Pietistic revival in Europe and America, and/or of Puritanism. Hence to them salvation meant saving souls. Their Puritan background led many of them to define sin exclusively in terms of sex, licentiousness, pleasure, carnal indulgence, etc. The result was, basically, a "gospel" of do's and don'ts. The list of forbidden things was particularly long, the list of things that were permitted very short; it consisted mainly of church going, Bible reading, prayer and hymn singing. There were few attempts to show people that one's daily work is also a form of worship. In fact, about the whole area of a man's physical needs, daily struggle for existence and human requirements the missionary was strangely silent. He could proclaim a gospel of the *soul's* salvation, but not of the salvation of the entire *man*. This inability was most clearly expressed in the sphere of *illness;* here the church simply had no message, and it was precisely this vacuum that was later filled by the Zionists with their message of deliverance.

Many churches did provide medical services, but this was only a partial solution to the problem, and in some respects aggravated it. First it was obvious that the medical personnel, in spite of what they confessed verbally, went about their hospital work with no religious assumptions; that is, they did not rely on divine intervention but on their medical expertise. Second, most churches made it part of their explicit mission policy to build hospitals with the specific aim of "winning souls". Medical care was thus no more than an aid to real work of mission; the proclamation of the Word which would lead to the salvation of the soul. The healing of the body, the salvation of the entire man, fell outside the missionary purpose. The same was true, to a certain extent, of mission schools. For many years the only purpose in erecting mission schools was that they could help people to read the Bible. Often they simply did not realize that a general, comprehensive education would help to "save" the African as a whole human being.

This exposition is — we readily acknowledge — somewhat extreme and one-sided. In most instances the reality was not quite as bad as all that. Deep in the subconscious of the African, however — and this is what really concerns us — this is how it was experienced: Christian religion is for Sundays only and has little bearing on Monday's events. From Monday to Saturday life is ruled by taboos. It is this state of affairs which (at least in part) explains the legalistic tendency of African churches.

This becomes all the more poignant when we remember that in traditional African life, religion is inseparable from the rest of daily life and behaviour. Religion, cultural life, social life, national life, the economy are all interwoven. They are at most colours of the same spectrum. By contrast Christianity — so, at least, it appeared — was something different. Religion could be practised in isolation from other aspects of life.

This state of affairs prepared the way for the rise of the Independent Churches. There was a silent, as yet inarticulate yearning for a religion which would embrace all of life and would fill the whole day. The Independent Churches, once they came into being, did have social, political and economic implications. It could not be otherwise. As such they also prepared the way for political independence in various countries. In a previous chapter we have referred to the part played by the Kimbangu Church in this respect.

(3) *The phenomenon of rapid social change, industrialization, urbanization, and the secularism that accompanies these changes:* It would seem that the mere fact of contact and social change is not enough to generate the large-scale birth of new groups. The *extent* of the contact and the change, their persistence, their sudden *intensification,* and the degree of *interference* by the outgroup — all these affect our problem. Besides, it appears that some peoples are exceptionally sensitive to extraneous influence, while others, can "tolerate" much more before they feel impelled to react in one way or another.

It is clear, however, that large-scale urbanization and industrialization must have a radical effect even on groups with a high degree of resistance, the more so if the members of that group are illiterate or semi-literate. The situation is naturally aggravated by such contributory factors as migratory labour and herding people together in large, impersonal housing units. In such circumstances, where people are far away from their homes (the "natural" surroundings in which they practised their traditional religion), they begin to seek new anchors. For reasons given above and others to be considered later, the historic churches were often not in a position to offer the kind of "home" for which such people yearned. This is where the Independent Churches stepped into the breach. F.B. Welbourne and B.A. Ogot aptly named their study of two Independent Churches in West Kenya (the "Church of Christ in Africa" and the "African Israel Church Nineveh") *A place to feel at home.*[23] In the midst of the upheaval, insecurity and exposure of city life these churches offer an anchor, security, a haven in which to shelter from the storm. Their creation of comforting support systems for alienated individuals is the manifestation of the ongoing *quest for belonging.*

The process of industrialization also led to secularism. One of the first effects of secularism on Christian life is that it begins to be lived at two levels: the religious level (chiefly the individual spiritual life) and the secular level of "normal" everyday life. Thus we return to the point made in section 2. In addition, secularization is an escalating process: the religious level of life decreases and the other increases. In more and more areas, God becomes dispensable. Black Christians sense this subtle threat subconsciously: they sense that Western Christians have no answers to this problem. They sense, that White Christians, on account of their dualistic world-view, have segregated the sacred from the profane. There is only one solution, and that is to reunite the two in a new synthesis. This the Independent Churches, particularly those of the Spirit-type, offer to do.

(4) *The relationship between Black and White:* This cause has been mentioned several times in the literature since the publication of Sundkler's book, and before that. It is not true, however, that this factor was operative only in South Africa. Throughout Africa colonialism was an essential factor in this process, and wherever there was colonialism there was, by definition, a difference in status between Black and White. To take but one ex-

---

23 Welbourn & Ogot, 1966

ample, residential segregation was a fact in all the cities and large towns of Africa before independence. In some instances, this persisted after independence also. We can therefore confidently say that to a greater or lesser extent the whole spectrum of Black-White relations played a part in the formation of Independent Churches in practically all African countries.

South Africa occupies a special position in this respect. Comparatively speaking, the number of Whites in South Africa was infinitely larger than elsewhere. The bulk of the country's area (87 percent) eventually came into the hands of Whites, and Bantu in these "White" areas were regarded as aliens and temporary workers. Factors such as job reservation, and the scant opportunity for advancement (political, economic and even ecclesiastic) for the Bantu made the situation even more critical. Here the churches must be singled out: even though there were no legal restrictions, there were virtually no attempts to place Black ministers in responsible positions. Thus the entire situation paved the way for schism. The development of leadership in the Independent Churches served as a safety valve, a "surrogate" for the development of leadership in other spheres of society.

(5) *H.W. Turner's precipitating factors:* By this we mean that in a particular situation the "climate" has already been prepared — inter alia by the aforementioned factors — whereupon certain things happen which, in this pregnant atmosphere, give birth to independent movements. Such precipitating factors may be a personal crisis such as the sudden demise of the two children of the young Gaudencia Aoko of Kenya. This as it were roused her from a dream, and led to the founding of the Maria Legio Church, a group which broke away from the Roman Catholic church (originally with 93 000 adherents). A similar case was the crisis surrounding the original ministry of Simon Kimbangu in the Congo in 1921. A miracle of healing, or the ministry of a charismatic personality, can be such a precipitating factor. In Ghana the prophet Harris began his ministry just when, following the outbreak of the First World War, there were serious disruptions in commerce and economic problems. This contributed greatly to his success. In Melanesia contact with the affluence of American soldiers during the Second World War led to the establishment of a number of religious movements. The incomprehensible

discipline of a White missionary or chance meeting with a Negro church leader from America may also be precipitating factors. It is, in fact, impossible to draw up a complete list of the events of incidents that could act as precipitating factors. It is important to note, however, that they are not as a rule, factors, for they presume a climate ripened by other factors to the opportune moment for actual schism.

(6) *Disillusionment as a factor:* By this we mean that the tribal population, after initially turning to Christianity and dramatically turning away from tribal religion, can reach a point where they experience various forms of intense disillusionment, and this can lead to the establishment of new church groups. Disillusionment may be because the glorious eschatological end-time, the second coming of Christ, and the "resurrection of all things", so ardently proclaimed by the missionaries, do not materialize — the New Testament problem of the *Naherwartung.* Disillusionment may also ensue when the Bible is eventually translated into the vernacular, and it then appears that this book does not, after all, reveal all the secrets of the Westerner's power and success. There may be disillusionment because Western medicines cannot cure "spiritual" ills, or when it is discovered that the Western church working among a particular tribe is only one of a multitude of these churches, and a very young one of that. When, in addition, it is ascertained that church names like Anglican, Lutheran, Wesleyan, Dutch Reformed, etc., do not even appear in the Bible, the disillusionment may be complete, and it becomes logical to try to bypass the multiplicity of Western churches and return to the Bible itself. It was for such reasons that Bishop Limba of Port Elizabeth called his church *Ibandla likaKrestu* (Congregation of Christ) for, according to Matthew 16:18, these were the words which Christ himself used to describe his community. Bishop Mutendi of the Zion Christian Church in Zimbabwe drew a fascinating diagram which graphically portrays the whole history of Christianity.[24] According to this diagram the Christian church of the first four centuries was the Zion Church. Thereafter, for one or other reason, it became the Roman Catholic

24 Daneel, 1971(a), pp. 492-493

Church, but in 1923 Mutendi's Zion Christian Church was established as a direct likeness of the original church. From this mainstream (Zion Church — Roman Catholic Church — Zion Christian Church) all the other denominations broke away.

In the light of such data the influence of disillusionment as a factor cannot be underestimated. It can also express itself in other ways, for example the general disillusionment of second-generation Christians who did not share in the dramatic events experienced by those of the first generation. Schism offers them — unconsciously — a chance of psychological compensation for what they have missed.

(7) *Western denominationalism:* We shall return to this later, when we discuss the difference between the Protestant churches and the Roman Catholic Church as far as the formation of Independent Churches is concerned. Meanwhile we shall simply point out that the multiplicity of Protestant missions — sometimes even initiated by different missionary societies of the same European church — undoubtedly had a detrimental effect on Christianity in Africa. In this respect South Africa is a vivid example, for nowhere else on the entire continent have so many missionary groups concentrated on a single territory. As a matter of fact, there are few missionary bodies in the Western world which do not have a mission in South Africa.

In various countries, African as well as Asian, Protestant missions have successfully concluded a comity agreement, in terms of which a particular missionary territory was divided up between different missionary agencies in a way that largely excluded overlapping. In South Africa, in spite of several attempts, no such agreement was ever achieved. This inevitably led to considerable confusion.

What made matters even worse was that the various missionary groups in one territory competed and slandered one another. In addition, the qualifications for membership differed, as did disciplinary regulations. A member who was dissatisfied with the discipline meted out by his church could therefore easily transfer to another church in the same locality where his "transgression" would be regarded in a less serious light — or he might simply not divulge the real reason for his switch of allegiance.

South Africa is, of course, not the only country in Africa to have experienced large-scale overlapping and multiplication of missionary bodies. It happened in other countries as well, though not to the same extent. R.L. Wishlade reports, for example, that in one district in Malawi — Mlanje — no fewer than eleven separate White missions were active when he was engaged in research there.[25]

Such fragmentation not only led to actual schism; at a deeper level it planted the idea in the African mind that schism was nothing extraordinary. In other words, in the subconcious mind of the African Christian it became a justification for schism.

(8) *The translation of the Bible into the tribal vernacular:* David Barrett referred to this factor.[26] That the Bible should be a factor in the formation of Independent Churches is at first sight so startling that this point needs some clarification. We should realize that translated portions of Scripture are often the very first printed literature to appear in any African language. A great deal of trouble is taken to teach people to read simply to enable them to read the Bible. In fact, this was, for many years, the main purpose of mission schools: to enable people to read the Bible in their own tongue. Often the ability to read was a condition for the baptism of adult converts. This psychological "pressure" led the African to attach tremendous importance to the printed word.

The appearance of the first portions of Scripture in the vernacular heralded another significant change: now, for the first time, it was possible to distinguish between the missionary and Scripture. The Scripture passages translated into the vernacular became an independent standard of reference, and intelligent Christians soon began to realize that certain things in Scripture sounded different from what the missionary had told them, that the missionary was silent about certain scriptural values whereas others he exaggerated. There was, for example, the discovery that the Bible does not speak only of the soul and its redemption, but also of social justice, in a way that the missionaries tended to conceal; that there was in Scripture a spontaneity, a vitality

25 Wishlade, 1965, p. 143
26 Barrett, 1968, pp. 127-134

84

and a dynamic which was apparently largely lacking in the rigid structures of the missionary agencies.

Particularly striking was the agreement between the African word-view and that of the Old Testament. Almost immediately, the Western missionary's condemnation of polygamy was questioned, since the Old Testament expresses no concern about it, and people like Abraham ("the father of all the faithful") and Moses and David ("the man after God's own heart") were all polygamists. Along with this went the impression that the Old Testament evidently allowed more latitude for fertility and sexuality than did the missions.

Perhaps of even greater importance than the role of polygamy and fertility in the Old Testament, was that it apparently supported some form of *ancestor cult*. In the Independent Churches, the fifth commandment has the same prominence as the fourth commandment has among Seventh Day Adventists. The fact that Paul calls "honour your father and your mother" "the first commandment with a promise" appears to substantiate this view, particularly when we recall that the specific promise "that your days may be long" links up closely with traditional African spirituality. Some of the other features of Scripture, such as the long genealogies and expressions like "he was gathered to his fathers" strengthened the suspicion that the missionaries distorted the message at this point.

It should not surprise us that African Christians should have jumped to conclusions of this kind. It is still true today that by far the greater majority of literate Africans can read only their own language, and that the Bible (or portions of it) is, in many cases, the only literature available to them (apart from a hymn book). Hence there is very little that can be used for purposes of comparison, and the Bible in the vernacular serves as an "oracle" in all spheres of life. Another consequence is an extremely fundamentalist and literal interpretation of Scripture.

The translation of the Bible into the vernacular is also a factor in a new process of growing self-awareness: this hitherto unrecognized people is nevertheless important enough to have the Word of God in its own language! The sudden importance and significance of the mother tongue — and by implication of one's own culture and traditions — thus becomes a factor in a new process of national awakening.

Although Barrett claims correctly that Bible translation into indigenous languages was a factor favouring the emergence of Independent Churches, this must be seen in relation to other aspects. Thus it is true — as we have already shown — that one of the causes of the movement is the radical and sustained exposure of the culture of a particular African people to Western culture and religion. Without exception, translations of Scripture appear only after prolonged contact with a particular people and are to be regarded as product of prolonged cross-cultural influence. Independent Churches are perhaps formed not so much as a result of a people receiving the Bible in their own language, but rather of such prolonged cultural exposure.

Here is an additional factor: as a rule, Scripture in the vernacular first appears, among more numerous peoples, that is, those with a large potential readership. Hence if we compare the formation of Independent Churches in a tribe consisting of two million people (who have their own Bible) with the same phenomenon in a tribe which has 50 000 people (as yet without its own Bible) it is logical to expect that the first tribe, by virtue of its greater numbers, will have a greater potential for schism than the second, and that in such a case it will matter little whether the Bible is translated or not. In his scale of religious tension, Barrett did in fact include the size of the tribe as a contributory factor (in his second question) but he did not correlate it with the availability of the Bible.

(9) *The traditional structures* of a particular people may be of such a nature that they encourage or discourage the formation of Independent Churches. A very interesting example of discouragement is the Baganda people of Uganda. The Baganda have a centuries-old structure of central authority and through different hierarchical channels every Muganda is related to and subjected to those above him. Missionary work among the Baganda has been conducted mainly by the Anglican and Roman Catholic churches. The Anglicans went so far as to link their ecclesiastical hierarchy at almost every point with the traditional hierarchical structure of the kingdom of Baganda. One effect of this centralized structure of authority of the traditional state of Buganda was that in the ecclesiastical sphere too there were very few schisms.

At the other end of the scale to the Baganda we may mention the Luo people of Kenya. Traditionally the Luo have never had a central authority structure. In the words of Barrett, they are "an eminently peaceable and domesticated people ... with no tradition of hierarchical or other oppressive rule"; they are "one of the richest, most intelligent, literate and progressive of the Lake peoples".[27] In addition, the Luo have a long history of relatively good relations with Whites, nor were there any White settlers on Luo territory. In 1957, only fifty years after the first Luo was baptised, there was in the Anglican Church (by far the strongest Protestant church among the Luo) a large number of well-trained indigenous ministers and a well-organized congregational structure. Long before Kenya became independent, both the Anglican and Roman Catholic dioceses had Black bishops. Economically, the Luo were better off than most other tribes in Kenya.

For all that, the number of Independent Churches among the Luo, particularly during the past twenty years, has reached amazing proportions. It is striking that this tendency increased by leaps and bounds after Kenya achieved independence (in 1963). By 1967, about 20 percent of the entire Luo population (230 000 out of a total of 1 250 000) belonged to Independent Churches.

In the light of all these facts, one cannot help thinking that a basic cause of schism is the traditional structure of the Luo community. Unlike the Baganda, the Luo tend to organize themselves politically and economically into small, independent groups. They also have a remarkable susceptibility to charismatic (as opposed to hereditary and institutionalized) leadership.

B.A. Pauw observed the same trend among the Tswana people. He writes: " ... tribal unity was not inviolable, and the splitting of tribes is not an uncommon feature in the history of the Tswana." Among the Tswana the normal cultic group is the extended family which in the normal course of events is gradually subdivided into new cultic units. The idea of the church as an overarching cultic unit is thus foreign to the Tswana. "Under these circumstances, unless the unity of the Church is very strongly accentuated, malcontents easily secede, and ... this is an im-

27 Ibid., p. 14

portant factor in the progressive fragmentation within separation."[28]

In his book on the formation of Independent Churches in southern Malawi, R.L. Wishlade also mentions the remarkable resistance of the Baganda to schisms (to which we have already referred) and contrasts this with the situation in southern Malawi. In this region, the tribes' traditional structures show striking similarities to that of the Luo and the Tswana: "Here conflicts in the indigenous kinship and residential system, political system, and in the sects lead easily to secession ... The political units of both the Taung Reserve and Southern Nyasaland were ... traditionally both liable to fission, and the values supporting such action have persisted."[29]

3.3 PROTESTANTISM, CATHOLICISM AND THE FORMATION OF INDEPENDENT CHURCHES

We now come to another major issue, which is not so much a cause of the formation of churches as something pertaining directly to the whole matter of causes and factors. This is the incidence of separation among (or in relation to) Protestant as opposed to Roman Catholic churches.[30]

Several investigators have argued that secessions hardly ever occur in the Roman Catholic Church, but this is not entirely in accordance with the facts. True, secessions take place mainly with Protestant churches, but particularly since the nineteen-sixties there have been an increasing number of secessions from the Roman Catholic Church as well. In 1955 the Catholic Church of the Sacred Heart was founded among the Bemba of Zambia. In Zaire there are six Independent Churches which broke away from the Roman Catholic Church. A particularly interesting case in point is the *Legio Maria*, the Legion of Mary Church which came into being in 1963 among the Luo people of Kenya; the

28 Pauw, 1960, p. 237
29 Wishlade, op. cit., p. 143
30 Turner, 1969, pp. 255-264

leader of this movement, Gaudencia Aoko, seceded from the Roman Catholic Church and rapidly gained 90 000 adherents, most of them ex-Catholics.

It should also be borne in mind that new schismatic movements among the Protestant churches, frequently recruit large numbers of adherents from the Roman Catholic Church. Thus the prophet Harris built up a large following in 1913 in the Ivory Coast in an area where there was at that time no Protestant mission, though there was a Roman Catholic mission. Alice Lenshina's Lumpa Church in Zambia also proved to have considerable attraction for Roman Catholics. Such examples could be multiplied.

For all that, it is undoubtedly true that the Roman Catholic Church in Africa is more resistent to schism. This is not merely interesting but also instructive in that one can trace the most important factors causing this difference by comparing these two churches.

(1) The Roman Catholic Church, with its strict and centralized hierarchical system, has never aspired to Venn's and Anderson's ideals of "self-governing, self-extending and self-sustaining" churches or congregations. For a long time, this mission ideal exercised a decisive influence on the thought of the entire Protestant missionary endeavour. As far as the Roman Catholic Church was concerned, the local congregation was nothing more than a cog in the wheel of the hierarchical structure of the universal church. Thus we have a basic ecclesiological difference which must undoubtedly influence the eventual incidence of schisms.

(2) We have already referred to the role played by translations of the Bible in stimulating schism. Protestant missionaries realized the need for translations of the Bible much earlier than the Roman Catholics, and did much to produce such translations. For this reason alone — according to Barrett's scale of religious tension — the possibility of schism is that much greater in the Protestant churches. What is even more important than the availability of a Bible in the vernacular as opposed to its non-availability in the Roman Catholic Church is *the difference in the attitude of these two churches towards the Bible*. The nature of Protestant preaching is such that the Bible was placed above the

church as a source of authority; it is the objective, supra-personal and supra-ecclesiastical criterion by which every individual has to be measured. To the Roman Catholic missionary, on the other hand, the Bible was par excellence the book of the (Roman Catholic) church which could be adequately interpreted only by the clergy of that church. The words of Adrian Hastings (himself a Roman Catholic) are significant: "African Protestants have often been offered the Bible without any adequate balancing ecclesiology." Among Catholic Christians it was otherwise: "Their knowledge of it has been carefully mediated via the clergy. What they have had of Scripture, they have had flanked by a strong doctrine of the Church. They have never possessed the Bible as an ostensibly independent source of authority, something whereby they could easily judge missionaries."[31] To Protestant Africans, the Bible was a higher authority than the missionary. They could therefore turn their backs on the missionary and follow the "Bible" fairly easily if it seemed that the missionary's conduct and teaching conflicted with the Bible.

(3)   We have just mentioned a matter associated with the attitude towards the Bible which needs to be specified more clearly in its own right, namely the authority of the Roman Catholic priest as opposed to that of the Protestant missionary. This whole matter is illustrated by Axel-Ivar Berglund in an article entitled "Church and culture change in a Zulu tribal community" in which he discusses the roles of the Lutheran, Roman Catholic and Congregationalist churches in the Mapumulo district of Zululand. He writes:

"While Congregationalists tend to be very free towards their authorities within the Church and often choose their own way without consulting the minister of the congregation, the Roman Catholics represent exactly the opposite approach. They tend to be far more dependent on their parish priests and submissive to their advice and decisions. The Lutherans stand somewhere in between the two. At an ecumenical gathering recently a Roman Catholic made a special effort to make known that it was with the knowledge and

31 Hastings, 1971, p. 204

consent of his parish priest that he was present and even passed a word of greeting from the latter. A Congregationalist who happened to sit next to me commented on the man's strong underlining of the fact that he was there with consent and greetings — he, the Congregationalist, had never thought it necessary to consult his Church authorities on the question of attending the meeting or not! As far as he was concerned, it was his private affair if he attended, and it had nothing to do with his minister at all! "

Berglund relates this state of affairs to the "dubious honour ascribed to the Lutherans and Congregationalists of the Mapumulo District who have formed several breakaway Independent Churches, while the Roman Catholics have, as far as I know, not a single one".[32]

Here we have a basic difference between the two ecclesiastical traditions. Voisin, a Belgian (Roman Catholic) civil servant in the then Belgian Congo, who investigated the Kimbanguistic movement in 1925, even spoke of the new movement as a direct religious outcome of the individualism taught by the Baptist mission.[33]

(4) Protestant missionaries also encouraged, much sooner and more energetically, the development of an indigenous ministry. The earliest ministers were usually people with meagre theological training who were ordained with little ceremony. By contrast, the Roman Catholic Church from the beginning insisted on extraordinarily high qualifications for the priestly office, with the result that very few candidates were ordained as priests, but the ones who were, were steeped in Roman Catholic ecclesiastical tradition. The ordination of a priest was moreover an impressive business, one of the seven Roman Catholic sacraments, further enhanced by various rites, vestments and so on.

By contrast, no special ritual attended the ordination of a Protestant minister. All these factors encouraged the idea among Protestants that anyone could appoint himself a minister —

[32] Berglund, 1971, pp. 56-57
[33] Martin, 1971, p. 120

another factor conducive to schism. To this we may add the absence of a sanctioned interpretation of the apostolic succession in most Protestant churches.

(5) We also need to note that ritual in general — not only that involved in the ordination of a priest — occupies a central place in the life of the Roman Catholic Church. In the Protestant churches it was, to a large extent, lacking. It would seem that the ritual of Roman Catholicism made a great impression on the African and that it offered him a satisfaction which he could not find in the Protestant churches. In many instances where independent groups separated from Protestant churches they adopted Catholic forms of ritual. Sundkler rightly observes: "Protestant missions brought the Zulus into contact with a form of Christianity which was centred round a book. The Independent Church changed the stress and evolved a form of religion centred round a set of rites."[34] He cites various examples to support his view, viz. the Ethiopian Catholic Church of Africa and the Ethiopian Catholic Church in Zion. The use of Roman Catholic titles — bishop, archbishop, cardinal, and even pope — points in the same direction.

(6) The difference in approach to traditional African religion and customs is particularly important. The divergent theological traditions — the natural theology of Rome and the Protestant emphasis on the total corruption *(corruptio totalis)* of human nature — bred completely different approaches as regards adaptation to or rejection of indigenous customs. Both churches envisaged the establishment of indigenous churches as an outcome of missionary work, but in the Protestant tradition this in no way meant the assimilation of indigenous customs as if these had somehow escaped sin and possessed an intrinsic virtue or merit. The accent was rather on a radical break with paganism and hence with traditional values. These values and customs could only be assimilated by the church if they were totally transformed and renewed in Christ. Such a theological atmosphere left little leeway for adaptation or accommodation. Bavinck writes:

34 Sundkler, 1961, p. 181

"The Christian life does not adapt itself to the heathen forms of life, but takes it into possession, and by doing so, renews it."[35]

By contrast the natural theology of Catholicism allows far greater flexibility with regard to indigenous customs. Those which were considered intrinsically good were simply incorporated into the church. This is why Catholic missiologists speak of building bridges between Christianity and the indigenous cultures, a synthesis of Christian and pagan truths and a reverent collection of "connecting links" which must be incorporated into the new structure of revelation and reconciliation.[36] This is pre-eminently a position which favours accommodation and assimilation. Accommodation allows for the adaptation of the missionary and his message to the customs of the non-Christian, while assimilation permits the integration of such customs into Christianity. One therefore finds that, by contrast with the rigid "principle of discontinuity" which characterizes the contact between Protestant Christianity and pagandom, many popes have regarded their church as the protector of the natural cultures of the pagans. In the encyclical *Summi Pontificatus* Pope Pius XII states:

> Anything whatever that has found acceptance in a people's way of life, provided only that it be not inextricably bound up with superstition and error, is at all times weighed sympathetically and, if possible, retained intact and unmarred.[37]

If one looks at the realities of missionary work, more specifically among the southern Shona where the DR Mission Church and the Roman Catholic Church provide the ecclesiological backdrop of the formation of Shona Independent Churches, one observes that during the pioneering phase at any rate the different theological backgrounds were not a significant factor. Early

---

35 Daneel, 1971(a), p. 245
36 Buhlmann, 1950, p. 62; Daneel 1971(a), p. 246
37 **Summi Pontificatus** in Burke, 1957, p. 57; Daneel, 1971(a) pp. **246-247**

missionaries such as the Revd A.A. Louw (DRC) and Fr Prestage (RC) both espoused a radical break with indigenous customs. Louw's main emphasis was on personal conversion and the Shona language as the one "point of contact" between Christianity and Shona culture. After an attempt at studying traditional Shona ideas and religion Fr Prestage concluded that the overriding fear of the ancestors and the concomitant power of spirit mediums made it impossible for the church to use these traditional foundation.[38] But as the indigenous Shona congregations grew and a policy with regard to traditional customs had to be formulated, the differences in approach emerged more clearly. I shall cite a few examples because this is a direct cause for the defection of church members and, as far as the Shona are concerned, *the main reason why the DR Mission Church lost more of its members than did the Catholics*.

When it came to traditional marriage customs, the DR Mission Church had great reservations about the *roora* (bride-price) and in terms of canon law categorically rejected the traditional elopements, levirate customs, substitutory measures in cases of barrenness and the like. These were all regarded as forms of immorality *(upombwe)*. In its endeavour to maintain a high standard of morality it rigorously applied canon law in this regard. An analysis of disciplinary measures applied in one mission congregation (Alheit in the Gutu district) over a period of nine years showed that 76 percent of the 519 disciplinary cases involved immorality *(upombwe)*, and many of these were elopements *(kutizisa)*. Of the 519 disciplinary cases only 37 percent of the parties involved retained their membership of the church. If one considers moreover that since 1950 the DR Mission Church placed some 500 to 800 members under church discipline every year, and that only some 40 to 60 percent of these people remained members of the church, then the loss of members through reaction against the church's view of traditional marriage customs is considerable. Those members who were perturbed by the disciplinary measures invariably joined an Independent Church.

By contrast the Roman Catholic disciplinary system was consistently more flexible. Not only was its attitude towards tradi-

38 Daneel, 1971(a) p. 247, with refernce to Gann, 1965, p. 206

tional marriage customs less intransigent, but in its application of discipline — for instance withholding communion — its penalties were imposed for far shorter periods than those of the DR Mission Church. Oskar Niederberger reports only marginal losses of RC members as a result of disciplinary measures.[39] Fr Haag, head of one of the Catholic missions among the southern Shona, said that church members were not disciplined for engaging in the common practice of elopement *(kutizisa).* The parties were merely encouraged to have the marriage solemnized in church as well. Haag maintained that immorality cases are not necessarily investigated:

> If the matter becames public through a village court or through rumours, the priest intervenes, but if the guilty party shows a penitent spirit and confesses, it is all right.

Haag's comment reflects yet again the somewhat optimistic, flexible approach of the RCC. By contrast with the DR Mission Church, whose members are supervised by *vatariri* (overseers) and whose church council is virtually a court "trying" the cases of offenders, the RCC uses the confessional, where members' lapses are handled in privacy and therefore provoke a less direct reaction.

When it comes to traditional religious customs,[40] the DR Mission Church rejects the ancient cult of the Supreme Being, all rites connected with the ancestors, divination and visits to traditional "doctors" *(n'anga).* The *Katekisma* condemns all ancestor rites as breaches of the first commandment. One gets the impression that in its reflection on the ancestor cult the church placed the emphasis so much on the aspect of worship, idolatry and satanic rejection of God that no thought was given to any assimilative transformation or the conscious substitution of Christian parallels for certain rites. Individual missionaries, to be sure, took an interest in and sought deeper insight into the traditional world-view, but *the overall trend was one of elimination and to some extent repudiation of the ancient spirit world instead of conscious confrontation and/or dialogue with existing Shona*

39 Personal interview
40 Daneel, 1971(a), pp. 262-277; Daneel, 1973, pp. 57-64

religious views. One seldom hears a searching exposition of the spirit world in sermons; in hospital visiting the traditionally oriented causes of disease that matter so much to the patient are seldom mentioned; and in their pastoral work some Black ministers avoid the contentious subject of continued involvement with the traditional religion. Evidence of the fact that condemnation led to repudiation is provided by the aforementioned 519 disciplinary cases in the Alheit congregation. Only *one* of these cases concerned participation in *n'anga* divination, which could have implied ancestor worship. In other words, discipline is almost never exercised for participation in *kupira midzimu* (ancestor worship ceremonies), despite the church's condemnation of these and the sure knowledge among church leaders that many members periodically take part in these rites. The net result is that both the old and the new faith exist side by side in the lives of church members without any clear-cut exposition. Because the Christian message does not penetrate consistently to all levels of church members' existential experience, which is still largely influenced by the traditional world-view, many members of the DR Mission Church find the new faith unsatisfactory. Thus the Independent Churches, who either overtly accept the ancient customs or condemn them but provide similar, christianized rites as substitutes, become attractive.

After the pioneering phase the RCC increasingly regarded the traditional Shona religion as a sort of *praeparatio evangelica* which had to find its fulfilment within the framework of Christianity. Ancestral veneration *(kupira midzimu)* was not seen as a threat to the worship of the Christian God and was assimilated into the church in a modified form. At quite an early stage the traditional rain-making ceremonies were replaced by church ceremonies which included many symbolic acts that were meaningful to the Shona. In 1966 a modified burial ceremony was adopted by the RCC where the dead are addressed by both priest and congregation.[41] In this rite the emphasis is on communication with the spirits of the family's ancestors and it implicitly acknowledges that the ancestors act as mediators between the deceased and the Christian God. The liturgy makes no distinction between

41 Daneel, 1973, p. 61

pagan ancestors and departed saints. Attempts by Catholic priests, notably Fr Kumbirai, to christianize the principal rite of all ancestor worship, the *kugadzira* (when the deceased is elevated to the rank of ancestor, i.e. *mudzimu*) are characterized by the retention of traditional facets. In particular the recognition of the living as mediators for the dead, and vice versa, is preserved. There is communication between the living and the deceased and the protective function of the ancestors is retained in modified form. Such a process of adaptation raises some major theological issues. When one examines the liturgical forms for addressing the ancestors one may wonder whether the process of christianizing or adapting the ancient customs has been sufficiently thorough. However, the important thing is that by manifest reflection on customs that are of vital importance to Africans and by adapting rites in a way that they may on the whole be interpreted as recognition of the Black man's traditions and identity, the RCC has created an atmosphere which could help to counteract strong reaction and schism. Whatever theological criticism or reservations one may have about the RCC's policy of accommodation among the Shona, the fact is that it has done much to promote cohesion and deter individual defection, by contrast with the situation in the DRC.

(7) A final difference between the Roman Catholic and Protestant approaches was mentioned earlier as a general factor, but must be mentioned again in this context for the sake of completeness: the fact that Protestantism reached Africa in divergent forms, while Catholicism consistently presented a united front. This undoubtedly greatly weakened and relativized the Protestant message. In addition, the Roman Catholic missionary could proclaim with perfect confidence that his church went back in an unbroken line to the New Testament period, while many Protestant groups could at most claim an independent history of a few decades.

3.4 REACTION TO MISSION?

From the approach we have adopted thus far in this chapter, one might easily get the impression that the Independent Churches originated mainly as protest movements in reaction to mission.

The very use of the factors that cause the origin of these churches to establish what mistakes the mission churches have committed seems to presuppose that their origin and growth were a direct reaction to missionary work. Many of the above theories similarly assume that *the formation of Independent Churches as such originated within the mission churches in Africa.* Barrett's book *Schism and renewal* and his basic theory of the Independent Churches as a reaction to mission give an impression of groups of people who had previously belonged to one or several mission churches. Sundkler creates a similar impression with his concept of separatism and his description of the dynamics of fission in the churches. He describes three phases in the origin of new churches: the initial schism, the integration of the new church, and then a fresh crisis followed by the next schism. Even though there are no statistics to corroborate this, it could well be that the Independent Churches in South Africa draw the majority of their adherents from the mission churches. Turner demonstrates that the Church of the Lord in West Africa recruits up to 75 percent of its members from the historical churches.

Hence, although one cannot deny that reaction is a factor, it remains essential to qualify this more precisely so as to arrive at a fair ultimate assessment of the phenomenon. Amongst the Southern Shona there is no question of the *classical schism* as described by Sundkler. None of the *Ndaza* Zionist leaders or Mutendi effected a schism by defecting from one of the mission churches with a faction of its members during a time of crisis. Nor can this be said of Bishop Chidembo of the First Ethiopian Church or Johane Maranke. The latter worked at Umtali for quite a long time before returning to his tribal area to establish his Apostle Church among traditionalists and mission church members alike. Only in the case of Sengwayo one could maintain that there was mounting tension within the American Board Mission, culminating in the breakaway of several prominent office-bearers round about the same time. However, case studies of the key figures indicate that there was no question of a co-ordinated schism organized by Sengwayo. Such leaders as Dzukuso and Pahla had already been dismissed from the mission church on account of polygamous marriages *before* they decided to join the ACC *(Chibarirwe).* These data lead to a significant conclusion, namely that among the Shona the Independent

Churches did *not* originate through a drastic exodus from the mission churches as mass movements within a short time. In most cases the leaders had to conduct prolonged recruiting campaigns before their churches began to expand to a noteworthy extent. *Besides, statistics for the churches that I have studied indicate that the majority (about 60 percent) of Independent Church members were never full members of any of the mission churches.*[42]

An attempt was made, through interviews with a large number of Shona Independent Church members, to asses the extent of reaction as an explicit factor in their defection from one church and joining the other. Since the majority of respondents had never belonged to a mission church the percentage of manifestly critical ones was significantly low. At most one could speak of a fairly strong *indirect reaction* to mission in that in their choice of a religious affiliation these people's preference for certain attractive practices in the Independent Churches could imply rejection of the influence of mission on African life generally. This indirect reaction is probably largely subconscious. The fact that many of the Independent Church members had attended mission schools and even catechism classes without ever seeking full membership of the mission churches also points to an indirect reaction. Such reaction as did emerge from interviews, in the case of "Ethiopians", focused mainly on the rigid application of church rules pertaining to moral conduct, marriage codes and the use of alcohol. Among the Spirit-type churches the standard criticism was that "Jordan" baptism, faith healing and the work of the Holy Spirit are not given enough emphasis in the mission churches. A representative opinion here is that of an eminent *muPostori*, Chakaza, a son-in-law of Johane:

> "The mission churches do not follow the instructions of the Bible. *Therefore the DR and RCC do not have the Holy Spirit.* Some of their members practise traditional religion; they secretly go to the *n'anga* and participate in Holy Communion shortly afterwards. This, we Apostles do not allow. It is sinful. Only the Holy Spirit, working through our prophets, reveals hidden sins such as wizardry, visits to the

42 Daneel, 1974, p. 13f

n'anga, use of medicine and adultery. The sinners *must* repent in public before they are allowed to participate in the Sacraments. *Only through the Spirit can people be helped to stop doing wrong.* Besides, this Spirit of the Apostolic Church is the *real* Holy Spirit referred to in the New Testament.[43]

No matter how much one stresses the reaction factor, or what distinctions one makes (for instance direct and indirect/subconscious criticism), there are insufficient grounds to call the Shona Independent Churches protest movements. Nor are there adequate reasons for reducing the basic cause for the origin of the movement, as Barrett does, to a "failure of missions in love". Barrett's threefold qualification of the failure of mission is broad enough to encompass all the "mistakes" made by missionaries, but often these mistakes were not the result of a lack of love or understanding, but of inspired conviction and a host of other factors. *The significant point to emerge from all this is that to reduce the causal factors for the origin of Independent Churches to reaction to the mistakes made by missions implies a one-sided view which does not sufficiently acknowledge the creativity and originality within these churches.* Their creative response to God's Word is codetermined by far more than just an apparently negative reaction to mission. Their interpretations of the Bible, distinctive forms of worship and modified rites are part of an authentic, indigenous reaction to the gospel, an independent momentum free of European supervision and of the radical spirit which would have characterized a real reaction to mission.

When one examines the Independent Churches in their own right one finds that the reaction to mission is usually confined merely to the initial period of a group, or that it never played a dominant part at all. A study of their continued growth moreover shows that reaction to mission may be incidental, that Independent Church leaders are inspired by God's Word in their evangelism, that their churches expand because of the unique development of a missionary vision[44] and that they are able to act without being biased in any way by demominational differences and

43 Ibid., pp. 27-28
44 Daneel, 1980(a)

prejudices. Their adapted rites with regard to faith healing, rain-making, fertility, magic and the like are not necessarily or exclusively prompted by pragmatic considerations concerning the proselytizing value of such adaptation, but are also products of a conscious, existential involvement with the "good news" of the Christian God, regardless of the prescriptions or views of some Western oriented mission church. This is why my work on the origin and growth of the Shona Independent Churches is not confined to the colonial or missionary situation with its resultant reactionary phenomenon, but includes a study of adapted church rites, the refashioning of ancestor rites, prophetic faith healing and prophetic combating of magic.[45]

The Independent Churches' real attraction for members and growth derive from their original, creative attempts to relate the good news of the gospel in a meaningful and symbolically intelligible way to the innermost needs of Africa. In doing so they are in a process of and have to a large extent already succeeded in creating truly African *havens of belonging*.

45 Daneel, 1974, chapters 2 to 5

CHAPTER 4

CHURCH AND COMMUNITY

In this chapter we shall examine the Independent Churches in the various environments where they occur, namely rural tribal communities and urban areas. We shall try to determine how the church structures fit into the rural village and how they influence and even change existing social structures. Attention will also be paid to such issues as economic stratification, participation in agricultural activities and political involvement.

The accent will be largely on the Independent Churches as a rural phenomenon, for the following reason. The main breeding-ground for these movements is still the communal lands (formerly called 'reserves') where one finds tribal communities and farms run by Blacks. This is where the large church colonies such as those of Shembe, Lekhanyane, Mutendi and others are located, as are the Mount Zions and "Jordan" rivers which play such a cardinal symbolic role in the Spirit-type churches. The Independent Churches have most influence in a rural context. Their proselytizing techniques are largely geared to the life-style of agrarian communities where a substistence economy is closely interwoven with and to a large extent maintained by the traditional religion. By means of real adaptations and by offering alternatives to rain-making rites, the ancestor cult, healing practices and the belief in magic — that is, by offering a new, comprehensible and relevant spiritual infrastucture for rural community life — these churches achieve their greatest impact and most fertile growth in these areas.

In South Africa urban areas, notably the Reef, also constitute a major growth point for the Independent Churches.[1] Probably more Independent Churches originate and grow in the Reef urban conglomerate than in any other urban area in the whole of Africa. Sundkler claims that the Reef as a whole has had a decisive influence on the development of the Independent Church

---

1 Sundkler, 1961, p. 80f

movement in South Africa.[2] But by and large the majority of these churches in Africa are a rural phenomenon and establish urban congregations subsequently, partly as a result of migratory labour. In such cases the urban congregations are primarily designed to provide a spiritual haven for migrant labourers who sojourn temporarily or periodically in the cities. As a result some urban congregations rely on members coming from elsewhere and display little recruiting intiative. Others eventually adapt to urban conditions to such an extent that, in addition to their rural orientation, they can also initiate urban expansion. However, in most prophetic mass movements it is rare for such urban development to outstrip growth in rural areas.

4.1 INDEPENDENT CHURCHES AND THE RURAL COMMUNITY

4.1.1 Church headquarters and village structure

Among the Shona churches there are different types of church headquarters. Firstly there are the large *church colonies* such as Bishop Mutendi's Zion City (formerly in Bikita, now in the Gokwe district) and the Apostle centre in the Umtali district where the entire village structure (the "line" system of the village community consists of a number of family units living in groups of huts arranged along an imaginary "line" across a wide area) has been drastically modified through geographical rearrangement on a centralized basis. Secondly, there are the *medium-sized headquarters* which affect village structure less dramatically, even though the leader's church building (and/or school) obtrudes among the huts of other villagers. This category is marked by the formation of subcommunities within the village and a clustering of buildings. Influential *Ndaza* Zionist leaders, such as Masuka and Makamba, and the "Ethiopian" leaders of the First Ethiopian Church and the African Reformed Church *(Shonganiso* Mission) have headquarters of this kind. Thirdly, there are the *small headquarters* with almost no physical manifestations except

2   Ibid., p. 80

possibly a few symbols or Bible texts on the wall of a hut to distinguish the bishop or church president's abode from his neighbours'. Fourthly, there are the *floating type of church headquarters* such as those of the ACC *(Chibarirwe)* where the home of the leader has little centralizing or consolidating impact. Church conferences are held in the various circuits on a rotational basis and for the duration of these gatherings that place becomes the temporary organizational centre of the church.

Mutendi's Zion City with its concentration of Western-style houses and traditional huts represented a radical departure from the old village structure. The white painted houses, schools, offices and elegant cars contrasted dramatically with the somewhat drab huts of neighbouring villages. The Zionist community was also much larger than the ordinary village. The "man of God" not only needed a substantial team of followers to administer his "holy city" and control agricultural projects, but he also employed the services of various prophetic faith healers to minister to the patients in the colony's "hospital" (in the sixties Mutendi's hospital at Bikita comprised some 200 huts).[3]

By contrast with the heterogeneous religious affiliation pattern of other rural villages, Mutendi's "village" developed a homogeneous religious pattern under one personality who was both headman and religious leader. In reality the village as a whole was transformed into a church headquarters. This inspired villagers with a strong communal motivation, namely to work together to construct their own "Jerusalem". It seldom happens that an entire community can be united and mobilized for such a long period by means of a common *Leitmotiv*. By contrast with the traditional headman, who in his religious capacity has only sporadic contact with the villagers, (for instance when someone brings a pot of beer to 'buy' the traditional day of rest [*chisi*] from the ancestors, or when rain-making rites have to be arranged), Mutendi acted as the religious leader of his followers every day. Through a combination of religious authority, mystical power and tribal jurisdiction Mutendi united his fellow villagers in a common effort.

3   Mutendi died in 1974, which is why we use the past tense when referring specifically to him.

The daily programme in Zion City started early with a prayer service led by the "man of God" personally. Preaching, prayer, dancing and song concluded with a blessing through laying on of hands for school children before they departed to their classrooms. While the prophets went about attending to their patients, the programme for the day's work was decided by Mutendi and some of his officials. Thus the day started on a shared religious basis.

Tasks in the "holy city" were many and various. Building projects required brick-making; roads and buildings needed to be maintained; the grounds had to be kept clean; every day work progressed in the fields; church administrative functions included the admission of new patients and interviews with visiting congregational leaders. "Patients" and temporary residents were fed in return for work in the fields, resulting in a *mutual aid system:* in exchange for prophetic therapy and pastoral care people helped in the fields or on building projects.

Mutendi himself always tried to engage in church activities in an advisory capacity in the course of the morning. After a midday break for rest and prayer he discussed household affairs with his sixteen wives and gave them biblical instruction. Later in the afternoon he dealt with church matters at the open-air meeting place. "Court sessions" were held regularly to discuss finances, planning of projects and campaigns and to decide disciplinary cases. Regular informal discussions with church delegations from all over the country and tribal headmen who came to Moriah for counsel also formed part of the afternoon sessions of the *dare* (court). Often tribal politics — especially border disputes between tribes and succession disputes — was the topic of discussion.

Regular visits from paramount chiefs from as far afield as Buhera, Nuanetsi, Chibi and Shabani gave Mutendi's headquarters a prestige equal to that of the traditional priestly colony at Matonjeni[4] near Bulawayo, but unrivalled by any ordinary rural village. Because of the regular visits of chiefs, Zionist officials and "patients" from all over the country, Zion City had an effective information system and was therefore in close touch

4 Daneel, 1970(a)

with educational, religious and politico-economic developments in the country. In this respect the Zionist headquarters evolved as an open, outward-looking community despite its highly exclusive religious tendencies. By contrast the social structure of ordinary rural villages is much more traditional, conservative and introverted with a far more restricted communication network.

The influence of such a Zionist community on neighbouring villages is various. Despite the exclusiveness of their Zionist dogma, contact between them and non-Zionists in the immediate vicinity is invariably amicable and without overt tension. Traditionalists and other non-Zionists even helped to build Mutendi's school and then sent their children to be taught in Zion City. On the other hand, in some villages inhabited by ex-Zionists and strong supporters of the traditional faith the prevailing attitude is one of envy and outspoken antagonism. Schismatic Zionist leaders disputed Mutendi's leadership, while traditionalists upholding the ancient cult — for instance the *n'anga*, "priests" of the ancestor cult and "messengers" who still rely on the rain-providing Supreme Being at the cultic caves of Matonjeni — reacted strongly against Mutendi's outspoken attacks on certain aspects of the traditional religion.

Naturally the large church colonies have a far more conspicuous and far-reaching impact on the surrounding community than the medium-sized or small headquarters. In the case of the latter, membership of the "mother" church is scattered among various villages and there is no daily display of the group solidarity which was such a striking feature of the activities in Zion City.

4.1.2   *Rural congregations*

Most Independent Church headquarters have a number of remote circuits or districts, the boundaries of which usually coincide with administrative district boundaries. Each circuit has its own leadership hierarchy and congregations worshipping at their various meeting places, either in the open air or in church buildings. A survey was conducted in the Chingombe tribal area in the Gutu district, one of the most densely populated rural areas in Zimbabwe with a heavy concentration of Independent Church

congregations. The aim was to find out how congregations function in the village context. Thus, while the description in this
section is mainly of one specific area, it represents certain trends
that occur fairly generally elsewhere as well.

One of the most remarkable features of the Chingombe congregations is that even the tiniest church is dispersed over an
enormous geographical area. Usually a congregation is composed
of families and friends from several villages. Although congregations are not based purely on grounds of kinship, it is remarkable
that a number of geographically dispersed yet related families
often form the nucleus of a (historical or Independent) congregation, in the same way that a group of related families form the
nucleus of a village (as opposed to non-related villagers) and
determine its tribal identity. It is exceptional for a village community to belong to only one congregation, and where it does
happen, the influence of congregational activities is less radical
than in the case of the large church headquarters outlined above.
Instead of demonstrating group solidarity through isolation, it is
customary for members of both the mission church and Independent Churches to join forces in village activities. On week days
villagers of different denominations work side by side in the fields
in ordinary work-day garb so that it is difficult to tell which
groups they represent. Thus a *Ndaza* Zionist bishop might visit
his village headman in Chingombe who is a pastor in the *Chibarirwe* to organize a team of workers for some farming operation.
The two men appear together, both dressed in khaki, wearing no
insignia of ecclesiastic rank. While they are thus engaged in discussing village projects or advising workers in the fields the
religious prejudices and the Zionist claim that the *Chibarirwe* are
a bunch of heathen are irrelevant and probably forgotten. On one
occasion I watched an entire village community working together
transporting manure to the fields. The work-party was composed
of a *n'anga,* several traditionalists, Roman Catholics, Protestants,
a *Chibarirwe* pastor, a Zionist bishop and several Zionist prophets.
In payment the Zionists were given unfermented sweet beer
(mangisi), the mission church members and traditionalists received strong beer and the younger helpers who had to buy
school books received cash. Thus denominational boundaries are
easily overcome in a communal project as long as the "payment"
is adapted to the prescriptions and needs of the various groups.

The decisive motivation for communal action was the common interest of the entire village in the agrarian sense, rather than denominational interests.

This does not mean that religious differences do not feature at all in everyday village life. Devout Zionist and Apostle clergy often exhort their followers to practise greater chastity and sanctity, as inspired by the Holy Spirit, in their village life. Those who heed these appeals seldom dissociate themselves from agricultural activities, but will protest against the village headman's annual collection of gifts for the rain petition to the Supreme Being *(Mwari)* at Matonjeni, and his collection of sorghum *(rukweza)* for the local rain-making rite *(mukwerere)*. A motivated denominational group may band together and form a work-party to perform piecework *(mugwazo)* such as planting, ploughing and harvesting in neighbouring villages for cash or other remuneration. Usually such activities occur when a congregation is trying to raise money to erect a building or for a major conference. But this *mugwazo* exercise does not replace the traditional village labour system *(nhimbe)* — it merely supplements it. What it boils down to is that in a labour context members of any church can join in a village community (which temporarily supersedes denominational ties), a kinship group or a specific group of church members.

With the rise of the Independent Churches new leadership structures naturally developed in rural villages. People of little importance or with little tribal jurisdiction in the village court have status in their church. Sometimes leadership roles are reversed in the congregation, thus bypassing the traditional principle of seniority. This happens when an alien *(mutorwa)*, unrelated to the tribal leaders of the village and therefore acting in an advisory capacity only in the village court, appoints the village headman as a junior office-bearer in a church of which he is a pastor or bishop. It also happens when a son appoints his own father to a junior position in the hierarchy of his church. However, in such cases of "reversed authority" it is customary to appoint the headman or a senior kinsman as "judge" *(mutongi)* — probably the most appropriate office for one accustomed to settling cases *(kutonga mhosva)* in the tribal context. The incumbent of such a position remains subordinate to the leader of the congregation but is less subject to pressure from above than a junior evangelist, deacon or prophet. In this way tribal status is accommodated in a church context. There are also cases where the church leader and village headman are one and the same person.

One wonders whether the presence of different churches, each with its own code of loyalty, and the subordinate positions sometimes occupied by village headmen in their local churches have any direct effect on village court procedures. Do the village headmen's church factions ever exercise pressure on them to manipulate court verdicts? From court sessions that I have personally attended it would seem to be rare for church members to act as pressure groups in the *dare*. Demonstrations of church solidarity (be it historical or independent) are not common at this level. Church members usually attend court sessions in ordinary dress. Cases before the court on occasion involve internal conflicts within a particular denomination, in which event the members concerned seldom hesitate to put their cards on the table. Because the Independent Churches subscribe to the traditional codes for marriage, *roora* and illicit sexual intercourse, the headman's handling of domestic matters is rarely questioned unless there has been a misconstruction or partisanship.

The only occasions when Zionists and *vaPostori* attend court proceedings in their long robes is when the case involves witchcraft or sorcery. When a prophet is called upon by a headman to conduct a witch hunt he may insist on a "village baptism". This means that every villager must publicly confess in the "Jordan" and be baptized by the appointed prophet so as to establish who is responsible for the disharmony or death in the village. During the baptism the baptizing prophet and his co-religionists will be robed, possibly in an attempt to avoid suspicion, but this does not stop the prophet from subjecting them to the same "trial by baptism" and even occasionally to single out one of them as the sorcerer or witch.

During the court session following such a baptism members of that prophetic church may band together and try to obtain a conciliatory verdict for the witch or sorcerer, irrespective of the religious affiliation of the accused. The prophet himself usually leaves the village community soon after the baptism. Hence one finds the paradoxical state of affairs where an outsider (usually a prophet renowned as a witch hunter) hunts down witches or sorcerers in a village, and members of that prophet's church subsequently plead for conciliatory measures instead of the traditional penalties (banishment or death) by explicitly appealing to Christian love. Such appeals are not always successful and prophetic witch hunts may lead to the burning down of huts and physical violence in an attempt to expel the guilty party from the community. Hence prophetic activities can have drastic consequences, whatever the prophet's own motives may be, and the charge that "prophets break up families" *(vaprofita vanoputsa mhuri)* is not altogether unfounded. The important thing is, however, that in these circumstances members of the prophetic churches present a united front in the village court and insist, often with considerable success, on the application of a non-traditional code which offers the guilty party space and hope instead of elimination. In this way Christian norms are sometimes introduced into traditional jurisdiction, even if it is not always a proper break-through in the Christian sense.

In the sphere of labour and the sessions of village courts, then, church membership and divergent denominational loyalties do not as a rule drastically affect communal village activities. Instead of replacing old customs with new ones, these churches — and especially the Spirit-type, which one would actually expect to have a polarizing effect on account of their strict codes of conduct — adapt remarkably well to rural village life.

It is in the specifically religious sphere when people gather for worship that the differences emerge vividly. Here, dressed in robes or uniforms at services or meetings, church members distinguish themselves as groups *separate* from the rest of the village community. These are the occasions when the Apostles and Zionists incite one another to sanctification by the Spirit through isolation from the heathen *(vahedheni)* — who in extreme cases include all non-Zionists or non-Apostles. As we said earlier, in practical affairs this proclaimed exclusiveness makes way for remarkable flexibility.

4.2 INDEPENDENT CHURCHES AND SCHOOLS

4.2.1 Mission controlled schools

During the first phase of the growth of Independent Churches among the Shona (1922-1935) the *Ndaza Zionists* were openly opposed to mission schools. This was based on religious prejudice, one-sided scriptural interpretation and reaction to missionary control of schools. The Revd Orner, a missionary of the American Board Mission at Mount Selinda in the Chipinga district, refers to Zionist resistance to the school system. In 1932 he wrote to the Director of Native Development:

> The chief message with these 'Zionist' people is that education is not a good thing and nobody ought to go to school . . . They also preach that those who have joined the church of the white missionaries have the mark of the beast on their foreheads, as mentioned in Revelations . . . As a result of this movement we had to close the Musane school and as you already know the attendance at Mutema has dropped to that of about 25.[5]

The DR Mission Church experienced similar problems during the thirties. In 1932 the Assistant Commissioner at Buhera referred to the loss of scholars in DR mission schools as a result of Zionist opposition.[6] The authorities investigated the Zionist activities, but since there was little evidence of subversion only a few Zionist preachers were charged and prosecuted.

The universal African aspiration to educational advancement meant that Zionists and other Independent Church leaders changed their attitudes and began to encourage their youth to procure advanced training. Instead of opposing mission schools the Independent Churches began to participate in the missions' school building programmes and sent their children to mission

---

5 Report by the Revd Orner, 1932, in **National Archives of Zimbabwe**, S 138/140; Daneel, 1971(a), p. 415
6 Assistant Native Commissioner's letter to the Commissioner, The Range, 26/1932, in **National Archives of Zimbabwe**, S 138/140.

controlled schools. Thus in rural areas a sort of *interdependence* developed. While the Independent Churches relied on the missions, for the education of their children, the mission church members began to employ — overtly or covertly — the faith-healing and revelational-counselling services of the prophets. Such a pattern of interdependence naturally stimulates religious mobility. Mission church members may join a prophetic church temporarily or permanently for a course of faith healing, whereas scholars from the Independent Churches may join a mission church either temporarily or permanently while they receive their schooling.

At the time of my study of the Chingombe tribal area there were 110 villages and a religious distribution of roughly 42 percent mission church, 41 percent Independent Church and 17 percent traditionalist adults. This population was catered for by six lower primary and two higher primary schools. Apart from one Roman Catholic school these were all run by the DR Mission Church. The religious pattern that emerged was the following. Lower primary school children remain under the direct influence of their parents and take part in the religious activities of the household. At this level children from Independent Church homes consider themselves members of their parents' church and thus avoid attending services at the mission schools. Later on participation in mission church activities becomes important with a view to further study. Such pragmatically motivated "religious change" usually occurs after the child has reached standard three and the issue of continuing to higher primary school arises. He will now voluntarily receive religious instruction in addition to class teaching and refer to himself as a DR member. To the Chingombe community DR membership and advanced education have therefore become synonymous, even though in practice religious membership was not always the decisive factor in a child's progress to higher primary education.

The religious situation changes drastically for a scholar from an Independent Church background who qualifies for higher primary school and then has to go to a boarding school. In this context, such as at Alheit mission where the majority of higher primary pupils belong to the mission church and the Independent Churches are regarded as consisting of illiterates, there is considerable pressure on pupils belonging to these churches to conform with the prevailing norms. In these circumstances the children may attend mission church catechism classes and consciously avoid Independent Church services. Some may even refuse to talk about their churches at home.

But the close connection between higher primary pupils and the mission church does not necessarily culminate in steadfast membership. A study of 215 school-leavers in 1966, a year after these children had left schools, underscored the religious mobility of the rural situation. Virtually all the lower primary school-leavers were active in their parents' churches. Only 50 percent of the school-leavers from Independent Church homes had remained stable members of the mission church. The rest had all "reverted" to their original churches. Hence in these cases attendance of catechism classes and even formal confirmation had been no more than a "temporary affiliation".

In view of the fact that in 1966 the DR Mission Church retained the membership of only 13 out of 86 Independent Church school-leavers, the recruitment of Independent Church youth through control of schools clearly affected only a minority of cases. In most cases the so-called DR scholars returned to their Independent Churches. What sometimes appeared to be a numerical preponderance of DR members pro rata to other denominations was actually a purely temporary phenomenon based on control of schools.

But despite this mobility of membership one must not underestimate the fundamental importance which the continuous influence of mission churches had on the Independent Churches through their control of the educational system. The presence of large numbers of Independent Church children in mission schools combatted isolation and promoted interaction. While mission church representatives continued to teach religion in lower and higher primary schools *they influenced the basic Christian concept-formation in the Independent Churches*. As a result the theological concepts in the mission and Independent Churches were often fairly homogeneous despite the emphasis on differences which were often more a matter of identity projection than essential disagreement. Even though Independent Church leaders may be loath to admit it, their theological insights and those of their adherents are often based largely on mission church instruction rather than on their own. As mission control over

113

educational systems declines with growing political independence in Africa, the religious interaction and influencing mentioned above will also diminish.

4.2.2 *Independent church schools*

The initial opposition to schools among Independent Churches in due course changed to respect and then to an ambition to run their own schools. During the sixties the matter of opening their own schools was often raised at Independent Church conferences, especially among the *Ndaza* Zionists and *Chibarirwe*. Only the *vaPostori* believed that involvement in the educational system was not really the task of "true followers of Christ".

There were two main reasons why the Independent Churches insist on running their own schools. First, they maintain that the mission authorities favour their own scholars when it comes to higher primary education. A ZCC office-bearer in Chingombe said:

> My children only get as far as standard three. They all apply for further schooling in DR schools, but they are not accepted. The children of influential DR members are given places in the higher classes in preference to our children because we are Zionists. Church affiliation counts for more than high marks.

In the second place, Independent Church members feel that they risk losing the membership of scholars who continue their studies at mission schools.

Bishop Mutendi and the Revd Zvobgo (ARC *Shonganiso* Mission) in particular managed to secure official recognition for their own schools. Mutendi started building huts for "school instruction" quite early on and came into conflict with the authorities because of this.[7] However, this was at a time when the rapidly growing Zionist movement was considered a political threat. Mutendi was arrested for "illegally opening schools".

7   Daneel, 1971(a), p. 422

Thirty years later a large school was erected by Mutendi's Zionist community at his headquarters in Bikita. Even so Zionist control was not complete, for Mutendi had to employ DR teachers and a school manager from this mission church. Nonetheless, psychologically the fact that they had their own school was a major advance to the Zionists and they were content as long as they could take charge of their children's religious instruction themselves. To them the school was a prestige project and a symbol of their competence.

In Mutendi's case the school building project was executed mainly by his own Zionists, but Zvobgo's *Shonganiso* Mission school in the Mtilikwe reserve (south of Fort Victoria) was built by a rural community belonging to various denominations. Zvobgo's ARC took the initiative in raising the funds and providing the labour for the building projects, but many adults belonging to other churches helped voluntarily, partly because there was no dominant ARC colony. This school with facilities in the sixties for over 300 lower and higher primary pupils arose without any financial aid from the government; a proof of Black perseverance and aspiration.

The presence of Zvobgo's school had no noteworthy impact on the religious affiliations of adults. In this respect the ARC church headquarters and school were a total contrast to those of the ZCC. Chawa's village, which more or less surrounds Zvobgo's school, consisted of 13 adult traditionalists, 14 Zionists, 11 DR Mission Church members, 8 Apostles, 2 members of the *Chibarirwe* and only 4 of the ARC. Even the school children did not display a homogeneous religious pattern. Of the 338 pupils from sub A to standard six (in 1967) only 21 percent were baptized members of Zvobgo's ARC. A total of some 30 to 40 percent of them came from ARC (*Shonganiso* Mission) homes. The rest were the children of traditionalists, or members of the DRC, Zionist groups or *vaPostori*. The majority of pupils had not yet joined a church at the time of the survey.

Once again we see how relative the effect of school control is on religious affiliation. Like the DR Mission Church, Zvobgo managed to use school control to proselytize for his church but, again like the DRC, he was unable to achieve a high correlation between school enrolment and church membership. Nonetheless his efforts had a considerable impact on the community around him. By creating a common goal for these people he managed to unite a religiously heterogenous group to realize an ideal of which all of them could be proud. For many years Zvobgo personally acted as church leader and superintendent of his school. Adults in the vicinity, whether they belonged to his church or not, all boasted to outsiders of "our school that we built". Out of a sense of pride and identification with Zvobgo's achievement they would also readily refer to the ARC as "our church".

One of the Revd Zvobgo's greatest contributions to the rural community was his concern for biblical instruction. Every day he assembled all teachers and pupils on the school grounds to discuss scriptural passages. These sessions took the form of constant communicative interaction between him and the pupils. By means of this emphasis on Bible study and the way he related scriptural truths to the Black man's situation he had a religious impact which extended far beyond the bounds of his own church.

4.3 RURAL ECONOMY

4.3.1 Landownership

There are various reasons why one cannot characterize the Shona Independent Churches as land protest movements. First of all, when interviewed very few members of these churches directly related any discontent about the availability of farmland to membership of an Independent Church. They were critical of legislation in this connection, but so were traditionalists and members of the historical churches. In other words, the Independent Churches were no more involved in the African striving for more land than was any other religious group. Instead of organizing resistance to government controlled development schemes the leaders of the Independent Churches supported these. *Chibarirwe* leaders such as Sengwayo, Pahla and Dzukuso (all owning farms in the so-called African Purchase Areas) and Zionist master farmers "qualified" in the application of Western agricultural methods, encourage their followers both in their sermons and in everyday association to make use of government services so as to farm more effectively and put the avaliable land to better use.

Secondly, the Independent Churches had no more people who were either landless or owned less than the standard allocation than any other religious group. A correlation between landowner-ship and church affiliation in Chingombe showed that those who had little or no land belonged mainly to the mission churches. Hence as far as landownership was concerned the Independent Churches were among the privileged rather than the deprived.[8] This does not imply that the Independent Church members were perfectly satisfied with prevailing conditions, but one would have expected a different correlation if they had identified particularly with disadvantaged local landowners.

Thirdly, there were no signs among the Independent Churches of any conscious attempt at offering economic support to the landless. There was a mutual assistance scheme between church colonies and neighbouring congregations, whereby a group of church members could, say in time of drought, obtain maize from Zion City. But it was not customary for peasants unable to earn a living for lack of land to approach the church colonies for help.

Our rejection of the title "land protest movements" does not imply that these churches were unconcerned about the problems which the government's land distribution policy incurred for Africans. Even though the Independent Churches did not offi-cially represent the protest of discontented landowners, *they pro-vided a forum where frustrations on this score could be voiced without outside interference*. In the face of the social disintegra-tion caused by the reduced powers of land distribution of the ward headman, the often arbitrary delimitation of tribal areas by the administration and the prolonged absences of migrant labourers — in other words, the destruction of the *dunhu* (ward, subdivided tribal territory) which to the Shona meant home — the Independent Churches attempted to replace the crumbling old order with a new Black solidarity.

4.3.2 *Migratory labour*

There is an apparent contradiction in the fact that almost all the precursors of the Independent Churches among the Shona first

---

8   Daneel, 1975, p. 174f

joined these movements while they were migrant labourers in South Africa, but in subsequent years they recruited new members mainly in rural areas rather than in cities where migrant labourers were concentrated. From this one could conclude that the less mobile peasants are more susceptible to the proselytizing activities of the Independent Church missionaries. However, an analysis showed a very real correlation between increasing migratory labour and the growth of Independent Churches. Among the traditionalists and mission church members there was a higher percentage of people who had never been migrant labourers outside their tribal area. As opposed to 66 percent of traditionalist and 58 percent mission church adult males, 75 percent of adult males from Independent Churches had been employed outside Chingombe at some stage or another.

The greater mobility of the Independent Church members is also evident from statistics about periods of employment beyond the national borders (mainly in South Africa): 7 percent traditionalists, 10 percent mission church members and 24 percent Independent Church members. From this one may conclude that *greater mobility and hence greater exposure to outside influences are conducive to susceptibility to the Independent Churches.* Such susceptibility does not result in immediate membership. In most cases migrant labourers did not join these churches until after their return home. It could be that the need for stability, a new identity and "a place to feel at home" was felt more keenly once the migrant labourer was trying to settle back into his tribal area, only to discover that he had in some respects become alienated from it.

4.3.3 *Economic stratification*

Using educational and economic criteria, Sr Mary Aquina postulated the hypothesis that among the rural Karanga (the most numerous of the Shona tribes) Christians from the mission churches represent the upper class, the Ethiopian-type churches the middle class and traditionalists, Zionists and Apostles the lower class.[9] Among the lower class, according to her, the tradi-

9 Aquina, 1969, pp. 114-116

tionalists are the most impoverished, while the Zionists are more affluent than the Apostles. Agriculturally the Zionists distinguish themselves as master farmers, while the *vaPostori* compensate for their social and economic limitations through intense political activity.[10]

Aquina's stratification might well lead one to conclude that the Independent Churches appeal mainly to the economically and socially lowest class of rural society, but I doubt whether this classification can be substantiated. Educationally, it is true, the most advanced people belong to the mission churches, the "middle class" to the Ethiopian-type churches and the least educated to the Spirit-type. But the diversity between the two extreme poles of the relatively "rich" and "poor" is so great that Aquina's classification does not hold water. Economic differences between Zionists and Apostles, both in Chingombe and in the south-eastern districts such as Gutu, Bikita and Umtali, are not as great as Aquina would have it. Like the Zionists, the Apostles number a great many master farmers among their ranks. In Chingombe the *vaPostori* were no worse off than the Zionists as regards landownership and in Umtali, where the Apostle headquarters are situated, they are among the economically most prosperous.

On the basis of occupational differences members of the mission churches tend to preponderate in the "upper class" in Chingombe. Salaried clergy, teachers, clerks and businessmen in the rural centres form the elite of the local community. This is the group that builds Western style houses and drive cars, which are increasingly becoming symbols of status and wealth as opposed to the traditional standard of owning livestock. Independent Church members are more numerous in the "middle class" of skilled and semi-skilled labourers, who include members of government services such as the police, road and rail transport, and tradesmen such as builders, tailors and carpenters.

However, it is a very different picture when one correlates church membership with the various facets of a subsistence economy. In view of the traditional values still espoused by the peasants, it is interesting that members of the Independent Churches are in many ways among the most successful stock farmers. In

10 Ibid., p. 115

terms of herds the Independent Churches are just as strongly represented as the mission church households in the upper bracket (over 12 heads of livestock) and by far the strongest in the middle bracket (6-11 heads). Only 11 percent of Independent Church households owned no livestock at all, as opposed to 28 per cent of traditionalists and 30 per cent of mission church households. In Chingombe the largest livestock owners were consistently members of the *Chibarirwe*. The Independent Church members combined to form the largest percentage of progressive peasants.

To arrive at a comprehensive classification of the subsistence economy in Chingombe in 1966, I allocated a monetary value to each household in the 20 villages that were drawn as a sample, reflecting their livestock ownership and profits from crops. The results were as follows:

	Traditionalist households	Mission church households	Independent church households
Upper class ($280-600)	12%	20%	24%
Middle class ($120-280)	21%	22%	38%
Lower class (below $120)	66%	56%	37%

These statistics indicate that the Independent Churches form the most successful category in the subsistence economy in the Chingombe tribal area. In terms of agricultural activities they represent the strongest "middle class" element and are better represented than the mission churches in the "upper class" as well. *A significant conclusion is that the Independent Churches do not appeal only to the economically under-privileged.* In other words, any simplistic theory that there is a direct correlation between the rapid growth of the Independent Churches and the lot of the impoverished sector of rural society is plainly untenable. The indications are that where these churches have an impact on the ranks of the "poor" and recruit them as members, they immediately encourage them to improve their economic positions. Particularly in the case of Mutendi and *Ndaza* Zionist bishops in farming areas, the example of the leader often inspires his followers to apply modern agricultural techniques and to work together generally to advance the living standard of the movement as a whole. Remember, however, that economic advancement is rarely the exclusive motive for joining an Independent Church.

4.4 POLITICAL INVOLVEMENT

4.4.1 Tribal politics

Between 1920 and 1930 the vanguard of the Independent Churches in the central and south-eastern Shona districts encountered fierce opposition from the tribal authorities. Chiefs, ward headmen and village headmen even made common cause with the government to curb the "impostors".[11] Tribal authorities reacted much more drastically against leaders of the Spirit-type churches than against those of the Ethiopian-type churches. There are two main reasons for this. First, the Zionists engaged in extensive proselytizing campaigns long before the "Ethiopians" did. This was a time when tribal communities were still effectively resisting the mission churches. The chiefs and ward headmen still had important functions in terms of the traditional religion, ones which related directly to tribal politics. Because the Zionists had such a remarkable appeal for tribesmen they felt threatened and reacted strongly. Secondly, some of the customs and doctrines of the prophetic churches conflicted more directly with the traditional custom and tribal mentality than did those of the "Ethiopians". The Zionists' outspoken attacks on ancestor worship, *shavi* spirit possession and the use of medicines prescribed by the *n'anga* were experienced as a disruption of the established order. The prophets were in fact, at least in part, superseding the *n'anga*. They attracted women and children to their colourful ceremonies and appealed to a spiritual power which, they claimed, brooked no compromise with the ancestral spirits.

By contrast the "Ethiopians" were less spectacularly organized. They were smaller groups and their message had less radical im-

11 Daneel, 1971(a), p. 431f

121

plications for the ancestor cult. Besides, they encouraged rather than opposed beer drinking, the use of medicine and visits to the *n'anga,* so that it seemed that they had more respect for the religious heritage of their forebears. In addition the tribal authorities found them more malleable, more predictable, and — because of their greater flexibility towards the traditional religious functions of the headmen — more loyal than the Zionists. Thus Chidembo, founder of the First Ethiopian Church in Bikita, was on excellent terms with local headmen from the start, and Sengwayo, leader of the African Congregational Church, had been paramount chief for years himself and therefore knew from experience how to avoid trouble with tribal authorities during his presidency of the ACC.

By 1940 matters had changed considerably. Some Spirit-type churches had received official government recognition. As it became evident that the Zionists were less disruptive of social structures than had originally been anticipated the tribal authorities themselves began to join these movements. Mutendi, initially regarded with great suspicion, started gaining popularity. As his reputation as a "rain maker" grew the chiefs increasingly came to rely on him. In 1965 he counted fifteen paramount chiefs among the members of his church — a greater number of high-ranking traditional leaders than belonged to any other Independent Church. Mutendi's royal descent from the Rozvi was a major factor in this connection, and the construction of a Zion City with a wide sphere of influence throughout the country made a great impression on tribal leaders who had not forgotten the glory of the once mighty Rozvi dynasty. This church with its impressive headquarters reminded the chiefs and headmen of the organized pan-tribal unity which the Rozvi kings had achieved with their co-ordination of vassal states. Although Mutendi seldom publicly referred to his Rozvi lineage, it was remarkable that at the annual church feasts the chiefs publicly honoured him as if he were royalty.

This constant contact between the chiefs and the "man of God" in Zion City enabled Mutendi to play a prominent part not merely in religion but also in tribal politics. In addition to their regular visits to Zionist headquarters these chiefs appointed ZCC advisors in their tribal courts. These advisors were constantly moving between Zion City and the often remote tribal areas and thus constituted an effective information network. In a sense it represented a modern parallel to the old Supreme Being cult with its information network based on the regular visits of messengers *(vanyai)* from tribal areas to the cultic centre at Matonjeni.[12] In the same way that these messengers constituted a bond between the central religious authority and the tribal areas across the entire country, thus ensuring a perennial politico-religious influence from this central point, so the Zionist advisors enabled Mutendi to exercise a similar influence over a wide area.

In interviews the chiefs themselves made mention of this. Chief Ndanga was profoundly grateful for the support of Mutendi's prophets who enabled him to foresee problems in his tribal territory and take effective countermeasures. Some chiefs believed that Mutendi enabled them to uphold their positions. Chief Gutu (Munyonga), who acted successfully during an interregnum of four years (1963-1967), unreservedly attributed his success to ZCC support. In Munyonga's case the administration was in no hurry to replace an able acting chief whilst there was a power struggle in the district about the rightful successor to the deceased chief. During this period it was commonly accepted that the prayers and advice of Mutendi's prophets actually maintained Munyonga in his position as acting chief. Convinced that the ZCC had a sort of mystical influence on tribal politics in Gutu, chief Mazuru of the same district followed Munyonga's example and was baptized in the Zionist church. The new chief, Chitsa, in due course requested Mutendi to come and "bless his ward" during his ceremonial investiture as headman. Mutendi was moreover explicitly asked to teach the Gutu chiefs how to rule their people in accordance with the Bible. In the case of Chitsa the investiture ceremony was preceded by a "Jordan" baptism at which both Chitsa and chief Munyaradzi of the neighbouring ward were baptized. Mutendi's response to the request of the chiefs and headmen who attended was to instruct them from Isaiah 32: 1 (a king will reign in righteousness) and Romans 11: 26 (the Deliverer will come from Zion).

Prior to the independence of Zimbabwe the chiefs and headmen were often caught in a tricky situation of divided loyalties,

---

12 Daneel, 1970(a), p. 40f

torn between their tribes and the administration. A chief's success dependend largely on his ability to reconcile the often conflicting expectations of these two parties. Constant border disputes and intimidation by extremist Black politicians merely added to the tension, thus enhancing the chief's need for a spiritual anchor and a form of protection. In these circumstances the far-famed protection offered by Mutendi's mystical powers quite understandably had a great attraction. Chief Chitsa's son was convinced that his father joined the ZCC mainly to avert a threatened assassination attempt by tribesmen in a border dispute. Chief Mazuru too relied heavily on Mutendi's prophets to resolve his dilemma when he was under considerable pressure after burning down the huts of a rebellious tribesman. During a time when a charge had been lodged and a lawsuit was pending, regular consultations with a Zionist prophetess offered Mazuru a sympathetic atmosphere in which he could air his frustrations and fears. Such services rendered to chiefs by Zionist prophets have meant that the Independent Churches came to represent a sort of "halfway house"[13] between the traditional religious authorities such as the *n'anga* and spirit medium *(svikiro)* and extremist Black nationalist parties. This "halfway house" enabled the tribal authorities to join in their people's subtle resistance against the infiltration of foreign influences without drastically endangering their position with the administration on which they were dependent.

One of the most dramatic instances of the direct involvement of an Independent Church in tribal politics occurred in 1965 when a border dispute between the Rozvi and the Duma in the Bikita district came to a head. Mutendi supported the Rozvi chief Jiri, in his attempt to retain power in a territory claimed by the Duma chief, Mukangangwi. Bishop Mutendi's Zion City was situated in the contested territory, so that if the case had been decided in favour of the Duma chief Mutendi's own claims to headmanship — which were legitimate under a Rozvi paramount chief! — would automatically have been invalidated. When the District Commissioner's eventual boundary favouring the Duma tribe was announced a protest came directly from Zion City.

13 Ibid., p. 68

Conversant as he was with the tactics of subtle resistance, Mutendi did not wage the battle directly with the District Commissioner, but instead planned and organized Chief Jiri's defence. Tribal delegations' transport to local government offices was provided by Zion City and the outcome was publicized in the religious community so that it could be discussed and prayed about. This interaction provided a chief with moral and religious support in an extremely difficult situation. When the Provincial Commissioner visited the district offices of the government on 16 March 1965 Mutendi personally accompained chief Jiri to see him. During the absence of the "man of God" on this important mission the community in Zion City interceded fervently in prayer and listened to prophecies. In this way it expressed its solidarity with the Rozvi tribesmen in the contested territory.

When it turned out that the District Commissioner's decision was to be upheld the Rozvi in their frustration organized a protest march into Duma territory, where there were Rozvi graves. One of the leaders was Mutendi's son Engenasi who, together with forty other Rozvi tribesmen, was arrested and tried.[14] At this point Mutendi launched an open protest and with the Rozvi delegation instituted Supreme Court proceedings against the Bikita District Commissioner, the Provincial Commissioner and the Minister for the Interior.

Tension in Zion City reached a climax while the Rozvi appeal was being heard in the Supreme Court. Police patrolled the immediate vicinity and the Zionists were in fear of total restriction of their movements. During this phase preaching was directed mainly at consolidating Mutendi's leadership and the ranks of the church. Chief Ndanga, himself a Zionist preacher, addressed the great Easter assembly as follows during the height of the crisis:

Why should we now betray this man [Mutendi]? The very fact that some people in our district are deserting him at this time is a sign that he has been sent by God... Let them rise with strong hearts and stand by him... Let this man build

14 At this stage I was living in Zion City and paid the fines for Enginasi and some others so as to prevent their imprisonment.

up our hearts so that we may be humble. Africa has begun to listen to Mutendi's voice . . . Let this 'chief' sent by God search your hearts. Praise him, for he works through the Spirit of Jesus.

Mutendi's own sermon likewise reflected his involvement in the conflict and the sword hanging over the future of Zion City. After chief Ndanga had finished he spoke thus: "You must persevere in God's ways and not become entangled in heretical activities. Some of you are already overcome by fear as a result of rumours you have heard. Do not fear and do not be angered when people accuse you falsely! Blessed is he who does not dwell among the conceited. The police and the prophets [i.e. the administration and the church] must first listen to God's Word before they set about their work. Then their actions will be successful. In Zechariah 8 God says: 'I have returned to Zion, the city of Jerusalem, therefore it will never be destroyed again.' These words bear us up. This Jerusalem of ours will not be destroyed! Zion is small but strong. Zion will never perish for it belongs to none other than God himself."

But every attempt to have the District Commissioner's decision about the Rozvi-Duma boundary repealed was abortive. Psychologically the Supreme Court case had been worthwhile since the Rozvi under Chief Jiri had at least officially contested at top level a measure that they considered to be unjust. The court case also highlighted the urgency of resettling the Rozvi who had lived in the disputed territory. When it was announced that the government was to open an alternative tribal area for Jiri and his people in Gokwe in the north of the country, Mutendi once more took the initiative, first in reconnoitring the new territory, then in organizing and financing the eventual Rozvi "exodus" to Gokwe. In view of government refusal to provide transport the bishop's assistance was welcomed. To the "man of God" it was a bitter moment when he had to abandon his Zion City, but he preferred to build a new one under a well-disposed Rozvi chief to the insecurity of a city which would always have been the target of an antagonistic Duma chief.

This episode vividly illustrates the tremendous influence on tribal politics of an Independent Church leader. Without Mutendi's intervention the Rozvi tribesmen's protest against an important government measure and the large-scale migration of these people to Gokwe would have taken a much less dramatic course.

The political influence of the majority of Shona Independent Churches is much less conspicuous. Bishop Andreas Shoko, a *Ndaza* Zionist leader in the Chibi district, who also had a number of chiefs and headmen as members of his Zion Apostolic Faith Mission, exploited this fact to a much lesser extent than did Mutendi. But he too advised the chiefs and his influence is indirectly discernible in their positive attitude towards schools and their temperate, healthy race relations.

One would have expected the *Chibarirwe,* who emerged as champions of the "customs of the fathers", to have had a tremendous following among the chiefs. That this did not happen is probably attributable to a lack of dynamic leadership. In a tribal territory like Chingombe, however, this church has considerable influence on local tribal politics because the majority of church-going village headmen belong to this movement. With so many village headmen in its ranks the *Chibarirwe* can sway the election of a ward headman and as a conservative force the church can help to preserve traditional customs and laws in the local courts.

In South Africa, too, close links have been established between the Independent Church leaders and the chiefs. Sundkler shows how the Zionist and messianic leaders in particular reinforce the position of chiefs in Zululand.[15] Some Zionist leaders vie with one another in their deference to the Zulu paramount chief. With the diminution of the chiefs' authority — an almost inevitable development in the modern world — the Independent Church leader emerges to fill this power vacuum. This was pre-eminently true in the case of Shembe. Once this happens, as we have seen in the Mutendi episode, the movement between tribal and church headquarters is reversed. As Sundkler puts it:

> The significant trend is not so much the trek of the prophets to the royal kraal, but rather the pilgrimage of the chiefs to the prophet's temple.[16]

15 Sundkler, 1961, p. 310f
16 Ibid., p. 312

Just as droves of Shona chiefs and headmen descended on Zion City for the great annual feasts of the church, so Zulu chieftains converged on Shembe's Ekuphakameni to join in feasts and talks with the "royal prophet". As in the case of the Shona, the influence the Zulu prophet exercised on the chief was not radical, subversive or revolutionary. In a sense it was an extension of government policy, for prophet and chief were agreed that their goal was to be: *separate* Bantustan and *separate* church! [17]

4.4.2 *National politics*

In the history of the establishment of Independent Churches there have been occasions when some of these groups came into conflict with the authorities. This could create the impression that there must have been some question of subversive political activities. Thus in 1915 the rebellion of John Chilembwe in Nyasaland caused considerable unrest. Not long afterwards, in 1918-1919, the prophets of the Watch Tower proclaimed an imminent day of vengeance in the then Northern Rhodesia, when the Whites would become the slaves of the Blacks. These incidents caused the South African government to be wary. In 1921, when Mgijima, leader of the "Israelite" movement near Queenstown, refused to evacuate his colony from the government property where he had settled without official permission, the authorities decided to clamp down severely. Mgijima's resistance led to the tragic incident at Bulhoek where over a hundred fanatical "Israelites" were killed.[18] There was also the suppression of the prophetic movement of Kimbangu in 1925[19] and the conflict between Alice Lenshina's Lumpa church and the government of newly independent Zambia in the early sixties.

A careful scrutiny of such church-state conflicts reveals that only in rare instances was there any question of deliberate sub-

17 Ibid., p. 312
18 Ibid., p. 72-73
19 Martin, 1975, chapter 7

version by the Independent Churches. The Kimbangu movement was investigated and key figures were cast into prison or deported, but not primarily because these church leaders proclaimed a deliberate policy of resistance and subversion. The radical suppression was rather a result of the prejudices of Catholic priests as expressed in reports to the colonial regime and the popularity of a burgeoning movement which the government experienced as a threat. In the case of Alice Lenshina the conflict was not a result of subversive church policy or proclamation, but rather the reaction of the UNIP political party when she refused it the unconditional support of her church. In other words, the most common cause for conflict and polarization is the Independent Churches' *independence,* not only at the religious but also at the party political level, and their refusal to be manipulated by either political pressure groups or biased public servants.

Among the Shona churches too their reticence with regard to national and party politics was conspicuous. *The preaching of Independent Church leaders reflected manifest sympathy for the Black struggle for political power and Black nationalist sentiments, but this did not lead to wholesale participation in party politics or militant political activities.* On the contrary, in the early sixties the Spirit-type churches frankly rejected all forms of radical opposition to the state as espoused by the then banned nationalist parties, ZANU and ZAPU. Mutendi and other Zionist leaders in particular were critical of subversion and political excesses. Zionist preaching condemned all forms of injustice and violence, whether by White civil servants or extremist Black politicians. In April 1965, at a church service in Zion City, Mutendi appealed to a few thousand of his followers not to join the Black political parties. "If you are true Zionists," he said (our translation), "you must not join movements that move this way and that [i.e. unpredictable political parties]. There are three departments, one of the village headmen, one of headmen and another that I will not mention [ZANU and ZAPU]. If any of our members belong to this third 'department' he or she will have to be suspended for a period. You must avoid the men of politics and follow the ways of God . . . I warn you a second time not to befriend people of that 'department' which is unacceptable to us. Stolen fruit are sweet, but the consequences are invariably grave.

Spreading rumours may be interesting, but the results are rarely constructive. In troubled times like these you must all wear your uniforms so that people will know you as members of this church [which is not involved in party politics]."

Mutendi's preaching was probably conditioned by his know-ledge that the CID was watching his movements. Thus his motives may have been partly pragmatic, in that he felt it was pointless to expose the movement by overt and radical resistance against the established order. Nonetheless his condemnation of the pro-hibited political parties was in keeping with his earlier policy. During the unrest caused by the revolutionary activities of ZANU and ZAPU during the early sixties, not only Mutendi's prophets, but also those of the *Ndaza* Zionists and the *vaPostori* acted as "purifiers of the church". During church services the prophets identified cardbearers of these political parties and then faced them with the choice of either publicly burning their cards or leaving the church. Those who refused to obey were either per-manently or temporarily suspended.

In the Chingombe tribal area there was consensus among tribesmen that none of the Independent Churches was involved in the political activities of ZANU, whose regional headquarters were at the Bhasera business headquarters. The Revd Sithole, who had a considerable following in Gutu, had many *Chibarirwe* members among his adherents, but they participated in ZANU activities as leading members of the headman houses of the Rufu-ra tribe rather than as an organized church group. Still, it is a fact that the Ethiopian-type churches took less drastic action against people who engaged in militant party politics than did the prophetic churches and did not suspend such members. None-theless this greater flexibility among Ethiopian-type church leaders did not result in the exploitation of church gatherings for political purposes. In Chingombe there are several known in-stances where *Chibarirwe* clergy had people removed from their services because they wanted to use the gatherings for political influencing.

During the war that preceded the independence of Zimbabwe the Independent Churches did not overtly join the guerrillas or

130

always support the bush fighters. They were continually under pressure from both government troops and bush fighters. The ZIPRA and ZANLA fighters included two distinct groups: those who explicitly launched the slogan, "Down with Jesus Christ — he is the White man's God! ", and forced Independent Church members to burn their Bibles; and those who sought out Independent Church leaders in rural areas and asked them to offer intercessionary prayers and sing hymns for them. What is less commonly known is that some members of the Independent Churches were martyred for refusing to burn their Bibles. Thus the approach of various Independent Church bishops (with whom I maintained constant contact) was ambivalent. Fundamentally they identified with their people's struggle for independence and power. Some bishops expressed admiration for the way their "young men" (*vakomana,* a popular name for bush fighters) managed to vanish *(nyangarika)* when government troops tried to hunt them down. At the same time they were reserved and cautiously critical about the action which jungle fighters undertook against White churchmen and their own followers.

Finally we must state that it is doubtful whether any of the major Independent Churches became involved in the war to such an extent that one could speak of a total organization or mobilization in the freedom struggle. In individual cases they most certainly assisted the *vakomana* but within the Independent Churches there was much division, as there was in the historical churches, about the approach they should adopt towards the warring parties. In the current situation the Independent Churches are maintaining their independence with regard to party politics and the government. President Banana's insistence on large-scale church unification could put great pressure on the Independent Churches, but it is doubtful whether the politicians' attempts to revive ancestor worship and other traditional customs — a policy diametrically opposed to the prophetic condemnation of the ancestor cult — will result in an outright confrontation between church and state. The government simply cannot afford to antagonize the widespread Independent Churches by insisting on politico-religious reform. It seems more likely that a tacit com-

promise will be arrived at for pragmatic reasons so as to promote
co-operation in the economic and agricultural spheres.

4.5 INDEPENDENT CHURCHES IN URBAN AREAS

As mentioned in the introduction to this chapter, urban congregations of Independent Churches are in a sense *extensions of a
primarily rurally oriented movement*. Among the southern Shona
the general pattern is that most of the major movements have a
few congregations in the urban areas of Bulawayo and Harare,
and in the locations of large towns such as Gweru, Mutare and
Masvingo. A survey in the Mucheke township at Masvingo (population: 20 000) showed that small congregations of virtually all
the Independent Churches from the neighbouring districts of
Gutu, Bikita, Chibi, Zimuto, Ndanga and the like had been established. All of them came about as a result of migrant labourers
who had moved to the urban area as members of their particular
churches. There was mobility in the township community in that
people alternated longer or shorter spells in an urban area with
periodic sojourns in the neighbouring tribal areas. At the same
time there was *mobility of church membership* where people
switched from one Independent Church to another according to
the popularity of preachers and prophets. This switching of
churches was marked by a casual, pragmatic approach, much as
one would change from one club or voluntary association to
another. The dominant trend was for prophetic churches rather
than the Ethiopian type to attract members from other groups.[20]
The greater attraction of the Spirit-type churches in towns and
urban areas probably derives from the fact that the prophets
consciously adapt their "pastoral healing" activities to changed
social conditions and therefore offer solutions to the problems
and upheaval that confront the Black labourer in this environment.

20 West, 1975, p. 202

The *rural orientation* of Independent Church congregations in a town such as Masvingo is caused partly by the regular contact maintained by town-dwellers with their tribal areas. Just as traditionalists often travel to their home villages in the communal lands for important ancestor rites, so town-dwellers attend major church gatherings in the communal lands. Consequently much of the preaching in Masvingo is adapted to events in the communal lands with which the town-dwellers continue to feel an affinity. The rural atmosphere is reinforced by the fact that the services are held out of doors outside the built-up area and because the ritual differs little from that in rural areas.

Along with the rural orientation there are some striking adaptations to town life. Often the sermon deals with life in the urban situation: relations between employers and employees, moral decline and especially the use of alcoholic beverages in beer-halls. Whereas in rural areas the symbolic evils condemned in preaching are sorcery and various forms of traditional spirit possession, the main symbol of evil condemned by urban prophetic groups is the beer-hall. Although moral decline in the townships is caused by several factors, such as the absence of the stabilizing effects of the kinship structure and the weakened authority of the traditional courts, the beer-hall is pre-eminently associated with the forming of extramarital relationships and therefore becomes an object of vehement attacks and condemnation by preachers. When one listens to interviews between prophets and people in need of help at church services, one is struck by the fact that the discussion, more often than in the communal lands, centres on how to find a job, how to maintain a position in business or the striving for material affluence generally. Prominent businessmen sometimes consult both the traditional *n'anga* and the Zionist or Apostle prophets before clinching major transactions. In this way the prophets provide a sort of auxiliary service in the town community which extends far beyond the denominations of the members concerned.

In a large urban area such as Soweto with over a million residents and about 1000 Independent Churches the situation is very different. Here we are dealing with a more established Black urban community, in other words, with city-dwellers whose contacts with rural areas are more sporadic and therefore less dominant. In such a context the churches are more specifically *urban churches* ministering to *urbanites,* so that the process of adaptation is far more profound than in the aforementioned Shona town congregations. The churches in Soweto are not extensions of a predominantly rural phenomenon, but movements that *originate* and *grow* in the city.

Although there are variations in town and urban areas, Martin West's comments on the appeal of the Independent Churches in Soweto and their value in the urban community have sufficient universal validity to warrant our attention.[21] West discusses the problems facing the Black who settles in Soweto. Apart from estrangement from his family and restrictions on social mobility, there is the great disparity between a rural and an urban community. In the city a heterogeneous mass of people are concentrated in a limited area. The kinship structure that forms the basis of the social order in rural communities is lacking and new criteria for a satisfactory social structure are needed. This is where the Independent Churches make an important contribution; where they emerge as 'reorientation centres', and where the nature of their wide ranging activities can best be depicted as a *quest for belonging:*

(1) *Fellowship:* Individuals are encouraged to regard one another as "kinsmen", which breeds a sense of solidarity. In the Independent Churches this is expressed in the common use of the terms "brother" and "sister" between people unrelated by blood. In the Independent Churches members develop a sense of kinship, giving rise to a new kind of "extended family".

(2) *Social intercourse:* The Independent Churches provide scope for forming friendships. In the impersonal metropolis there

21 Ibid., p. 195f

is a great need for the intimate circle of friends where the individual can receive recognition and feel at home. The individual's denomination, which is also his circle of friends, enables him to cope with the problems of urban life in a wide sense.

(3) *Sense of identity:* In a society where the individual is crowded out and feels insecure the development of identity is essential. Thus the Independent Church with its vast hierarchy of leaders in which virtually every adult occupies some sort of official position and carries responsibility accommodates a real need. Instead of isolation and frustration it affords members a new sense of personal worth.

(4) *Protection:* As we have said above, in urban areas Zionist and Apostle prophets are constantly giving advice and help in business matters, how to find jobs and the like. In this way they satisfactorily integrate the supranatural with the uncertainties and competitiveness of urban life. Against the background of the traditional world-view, which assumes a constant interaction between empirical reality and the spirit world, the prophets provide a simple, intelligible "system of reference" in which the Spirit of God acts as a protective power in a world fraught with uncertainties which many people experience as threatening. The mere fact of ordinary membership of some denomination encourages self-confidence. Here constant exposure to witness and proclamation, in which God's help, protection and healing in everyday life feature prominently, plays an important part.

(5) *Social supervision:* Due to the absence of the kinship structure and tribal authorities in urban areas, social control poses a real problem. The Independent Church leader supplies this need by setting up a set of behavioural codes, such as a prescribed marriage ceremony as a requirement for the church's acknowledgment of a marital union and a prohibition on smoking, liquor, dancing and extramarital sex. By maintaining a position of authority over his followers the Independent Church leader is able to enforce this code of

135

conduct. Discipline is administered by means of pastoral interviews or by a church council.

(6) *Inter-ethnic contact:* The Independent Churches in Soweto are not predominantly run on ethnic lines and thus provide an opportunity for people of different languages and cultural backgrounds to get to know one another and associate at a meaningful level. In the congregations such intertribal contact occurs on a concentrated but small scale. Nonetheless the churches' contribution in this sphere is extremely valuable in the large, impersonal urban community.

(7) *Information service and mutual aid:* For newcomers from elsewhere the Independent Churches provide useful information. At church services new members are informed of job opportunities, the workings of the transport system and where to apply for housing. In addition to spiritual assistance members are given material help, for instance food for the unemployed, help with funeral expenses or to a household stricken by sickness or bereavement. The women's associations within the Independent Churches are geared to seeking out those who need help and providing relief. West found that in Soweto the offer of material help in particular persuaded people to join some active Independent Church congregations.

(8) *Leadership:* In a system that offers few leadership positions the extensive leadership hierarchy of the Independent Churches offers a vital compensation. Stress and frustration are discharged through the exercise of authority, preaching, dancing and a vast range of expressions of ecstasy and inspiration by the Holy Spirit. Exercise of authority in the Independent Churches also provides an outlet for political frustration. Although the Independent Churches can hardly be described as political pressure groups that effect large-scale changes, one can nonetheless say that in a system that is a product of one-sided political control by Whites these churches provide scope for meaningful urban life and the defusing of racial tensions through a host of activities that acknowledge members' human dignity.

Martin West summarizes the situation in Soweto thus:

Soweto's independent churches provide a blend of old and new which is particularly attractive to the people who join them. These people are mostly elderly, poorly-educated, and first-generation townspeople. For them Soweto has few voluntary associations, other than sporting clubs, and few opportunities. Against this background the independent churches are very important as their congregations provide small reference groups in relation to the wider society. In them individuals are secure as part of a small community: they have their assigned places, each has an identity as a church member, and a ready-made group of friends. The group is able to give both moral and material assistance in time of need, and assists individuals in their adjustment to city life.[22]

22 Ibid., p. 199

CHAPTER 5

ORGANIZATION AND LEADERSHIP

A major key to an understanding of the Independent Churches
is their leadership. One of the great appeals of these movements
is the existence of structures which offer authority and prestige
— in other words, fulfilment of leadership ambitions. When
members of Independent Churches discuss their reasons for joining a group they rarely mention leadership as a prime consideration, yet the principal leaders are all aware of the importance of
leadership ambition as a powerful underlying motive for joining
their churches. Some of them exploit this need for status and
recognition by appointing new members to official positions without any training or trial period of membership; alternatively promotion in the leadership hierarchy is accelerated. Other principal
leaders are more cautious and first try to cultivate loyalty and
ability to perform a task effectively before appointing new
members to office.

Whatever its policy, the urge for leadership and the traditional
background of secessions and subdivision of tribal territory to
resolve tribal leadership conflicts mean that every Independent
Church is faced with the possibility of schism at some stage of its
development. Whenever a junior office-bearer defects with a
number of hard-won congregations the principal leader invariably complains: "This man sows uncertainty and confusion in
the church simply because he wants the leadership *(ukuru)."*

Hence a discussion of the various facets of leadership will reveal
both the strengths and the weaknesses of the Independent Church
movement. Apart from analysing the leadership hierarchies,
calling, appointment, training and succession of office-bearers,
we shall also deal with such matters as messianic leadership,
schisms and ecumenical co-operation.

5.1 *DIFFERENT TYPES OF LEADERS*

Observers frequently refer to the parallels between traditional and
Independent Church leadership. Sundkler remarked on the im-

print of the Zulu monarchy on many Independent Churches in South Africa:

> The leader whether 'Bishop', 'Overseer' or 'President' is a king, *inkosi,* and the Church is his bride.[1]

Wishlade pointed out the similarities between Independent Church leaders and rural village headmen.[2] Actually it is quite understandable that in rural communities the traditional authority structure would provide Independent Church leaders with a model in their attempt at establishing an indigenously acceptable form of church leadership.

For purposes of classification Sundkler distinguished between the chief-type and the prophet-type of the "Ethiopian" and Zionist churches respectively. The ideal chief-type leader would be an able executive official, bold in the struggle against the Whites; the prophet — whose leadership shows parallels to the traditional soothsayer or doctor *(isangoma, n'anga)* — must establish a direct link with the supernatural through his visions and dreams. Sundkler even distinguished the respective physical attributes of the two types of church leaders: the solidly built, taciturn "chief" of the church and the thin, nervous, highly strung prophet.[3]

Within the prophetic movement as such Sundkler makes a further distinction between the Zionist prophets who accept Jesus Christ as Saviour and the Bantu Messiah who has usurped the position of Christ. As pointed out earlier,[4] the basic point in this distinction is the question: "Who stands at the heavenly gates — Jesus Christ or the Bantu Messiah?" Sundkler classifies such leaders as Masowe, Edward Lekhanyane and Isaiah Shembe as Black Messiah figures who have taken over Christ's position as mediator at the gates of heaven. In his view the evolution of a prophet into a Messiah is marked by the following phases:
(i) the prophet's calling as a leader; (ii) his "death" and resur-

---

1 Sundkler, 1961, p. 102
2 Wishlade, 1965, p. 80
3 Sundkler, 1961, p. 109f
4 Infra, p. 41

rection"; (iii) revelations through dreams; and (iv) growing expectations among the group, marked by dream experiences as a result of which the leader is increasingly recognized as "custodian" of the heavenly gates, through which he will eventually conduct his followers.[5]

Sundkler's classification of leadership (chief — prophet — Messiah) radically influenced subsequent literature. Missiological observers such as Oosthuizen, Martin and Beyerhaus apply similar distinctions in respect of what they term messianic leadership and go even further than Sundkler, claiming that there is a total usurpation of Christ, a Black Christ, a deification of the Black Messiah and a Black Saviour.[6] It is a moot point, however, whether Sundkler offers a broad enough criterion for distinguishing between different kinds of messianism, this third category of Independent Church leadership, and whether the empirical data justify the categorically condemnatory theological judgments of the aforementioned missiologists. We shall dwell on this aspect in some detail later on.[7]

Sundkler's distinction between chief-type and prophet-type leaders is not easy to apply. Thus among the Shona Independent Churches there are so many prophetic leaders who fit the description of the "Ethiopian" category that this classification ceases to be applicable. Mutendi, a prophetic leader, offered greater resistance to the White administration than any of the Ethiopian-type leaders, so that among the Shona it would be more true to say that prophetic leadership is characterized by courageous struggle against the Whites than to attribute this quality to "Ethiopian" leadership. Conversely, there are too many Ethiopian-type leaders who can be described as thin, nervous and highly strung (attributes of the prophet), for instance Bishop Gavure of the First Ethiopian Church and the Revd Zvobgo of the African Reformed Church (Shonganiso), for Sundkler's classification of somatic types to hold water. The only distinction that can be consistently applied is that which refers to the prophetic leader's claims to direct contact with the supernatural by means of dreams, visions,

5 Sundkler, 1961, p. 323f
6 Daneel, 1982(a)
7 Supra, p. 179f

speaking in tongues and the like, whereas the Ethiopian-type leader makes no such claims.

In a sense both prophetic and Ethiopian-type leadership resembles that of a chief. Like the Shona chief, the Independent Church leader is at the head of a trichotomous legal system. The council of each individual congregation corresponds to the village court; the circuit or regional court of the church reminds one of the ward court (court of the *dunhu);* and the supreme church council at headquarters is similar to the chief's court which has jurisdiction over the entire tribal territory. In this latter context in particular the authority of the church leader or senior "judge" is determined by traditional patterns. Like the chief, the church leader is assisted by two kinds of officials. High-ranking clergy and overseers of circuits, like ward headmen, are fully fledged councillors *(makota).* Then there are the junior officials who act as messengers, spokesmen, intermediaries and assessors in the church court. They initiate a case, lay down the procedure and conduct the cross-examination. The court sessions and juridical system in Zion City were particularly reminiscent of those of tribal courts. Mutendi's clergy *(vafundisi)* were venerable councillors who listened while Mutendi's sons and sons-in-law conducted the proceedings. Like a chief, Mutendi said very little during court sessions until he eventually delivered his verdict, which usually reflected the general feeling of the court. Even though the ethical code on which Mutendi's jurisdiction was based differed from that of the chief, the approach to the accused and the conclusion of the case with a fatherly rebuke was strikingly similar to those in a traditional court case. As in the case of a tribal chief, Mutendi's judicial authority was final. It was accepted as the foundation for the welfare and order of the "new tribe".

Naturally leadership in the Independent Church is never wholly static, but is subject to change. Thus in the early days of the ZCC Mutendi personally acted as prophet and healer, but as Zion City grew and a central administration became necessary, clear trends of "chieftainship" and even (Rozvi) "monarchy" emerged. Even though by and large Mutendi continued to act as prophetic leader, he delegated specific prophetic tasks such as speaking in tongues, prophecy and faith healing to subordinate officials. His personal responsibility became increasingly confined

141

to counselling high-ranking church officials and traditional authorities, administration and lawsuits. Hence it is partly a case of integrating administrative and prophetic functions in the leadership of the principal figure in the movement, and partly of accommodating a church's leadership hierarchy to permit differentiation and effectiveness.

By contrast the leadership of Johane Maranke changed far less than that of Mutendi. Johane remained the itinerant preacher and faith healer, his cousin Simon was the senior prophet and his brother Anrod the organizer of the home congregation. Only after Johane's death did his sons and successors, Abero and Makebo, emerge more specifically as leaders of the "chief-type". They seldom preach but protect the interests of their father's church by counselling and controlling its administration through discussions in the supreme "courts" of the various church districts.

In the First Ethiopian Church, on the other hand, the leadership developed from the non-prophetic variety to one that includes faith healing and exorcism. Bishop Gavure assimilated some of the more popular Zionist and Apostle practices into his church so as to broaden his sphere of influence and offer a more comprehensive spiritual service to his followers. Thus changing patterns of leadership depend on changing needs within churches and the innovative insights of the leaders.

Martin West is doubtful about the value of an analogy between the traditional tribal system and Independent Church leadership in urban areas. In the absence of tribal structures in these areas church leadership has to be assessed on its merits. West maintains that Sundkler's dichotomy between chief-type and prophet-type leaders is not applicable in Soweto.[8] I feel that West may be under-estimating the aftermath of traditionally determined leadership concepts in urban areas, and that one can still demonstrate a correlation between the exercise of authority in traditional rural courts and in the church council of an urban congregation. More significant is West's distinction between the exercise of *charismatic* and *judicial* authority. He quotes Max Weber in this connection:

8   West, 1975, p. 49

... charismatic authority ... shall refer to rule over men, whether predominantly external or predominantly internal, to which the governed submit because of their belief in the extraordinary quality of the specific *person* ... Legal authority is based on an *impersonal* bond to the generally defined and functional duty of office.[9]

West believes that in some instances one can make a distinction between the charismatic authority of the Zionist leaders and the judicial authority of Ethiopian-type leaders in Soweto. More often, however, the pattern is a combination of the two. West says this is because most Independent Church leaders in the urban area have difficulty in keeping their members on the basis of purely judicial authority. When the two types of authority are not integrated in the position of the paramount leader, they are still maintained in the various offices of the leadership hierarchy. Thus in most Zionist churches one finds that judicial authority is vested in the bishop and charismatic authority in the prophet. Of course, this applies not only to urban prophetic churches but also to rural ones as soon as the informal phase of church development is followed by the institutionalization of leadership.

5.2 *APPROACH TO MINISTRY*

Harold Turner's comment on the Church of the Lord Aladura applies equally to most other Independent Churches in Africa:

> The mystique of the ministry is not attached to authority to celebrate the sacraments or to theological education, but is present in the anointed man of God who can perform the rituals of the Church and lead its worship, help his people in their everyday troubles through his gifts of healing or revelation or interpretation, and discipline them in their attempts to follow the pattern of Christian life laid down by the Church.[10]

9 Ibid., p. 49
10 Turner, 1967(b), p. 33

One of the most striking features of the ministry in the Independent Churches is the *continual presence* of the senior clergyman — whether he is known as bishop, overseer, minister or prophet — in his congregation. Pastoral contact with co-religionists is frequent and direct. Among the Shona the clergy of the Independent Churches rarely draw stipends and are as reliant on a subsistence economy as any lay member. This is conducive to solidarity between leader and followers at the existential level.

Since contact between clergy and laity is reciprocal, most Independent Church clergy have no systematic programme of parish visiting. The more common practice is for members to visit the senior office-bearer at his home. This reflects the traditional approach, namely that office-bearers, like village headmen and tribal chiefs, have facilities to receive people with problems at their homes. Like the tribal authority who has a "meeting place" where court sessions and interviews are conducted, the church official also has a special place for official or unofficial discussions (a special hut, lean-to or gathering place under a tree) next to his home.

In addition to a strong emphasis on mutual contact and pastoral care the ministry of the Independent Churches is marked by an intuitive sense of the threefold office of believers — those of prophet, priest and king.

5.2.1 *The royal office*

The royal office is expressive of the Christian's sanctified life and struggle against evil powers. It embraces a passive element of acceptance of sanctification through the work of the Holy Spirit and religious peace in Christ the King, as well as an active response in the form of a conscious struggle against the powers of darkness.

On the whole the clergy of the Independent Churches are aware of their royal office. In Spirit-type churches particularly the ministry is marked by a struggle against the destructive forces that imperil man's spiritual and material welfare. The prophets' ceremonies of faith healing, exorcism and countering sorcery create a constant awareness of involvement in the church militant. This is closely linked with traditional concepts of power and authority, with the result that some prophets and their followers tend to confuse the Christian's royal dignity and spiritual power with magical powers and the respect which in the kinship structure is vested in the principle of seniority. In cases of such confusion one usually also finds an imperfect perception of the kingship of Christ. The prophet may be inclined to monopolize and manipulate the divine power in his relations with his followers, with the result that they come to rely so much on his function as their representative that their own implication in the royal office is forgotten. This is the case when a patient prolongs his stay at a prophetic faith healer's colony after he has been exorcised in the belief that only this prophet can vouchsafe him against future onslaughts from the forces of evil. Here the grasp of Christ's kingship is imperfect and individual responsibility as an active agency of God's sovereignty over evil is superseded by the overriding activities of the prophet. Instead of receiving spiritual deliverance the patient becomes enslaved to the person of the healer.

In a church such as the *Chibarirwe* where there is a strong overtone of reaction against mission church policy in respect of traditional religious customs, the royal office is less clearly manifested in the ministry. One rarely hears confrontation-type preaching about ancient beliefs which might impair a proper grasp of Christ's kingship. The prevailing spiritual approach is rather a compromise and relativization of the exclusive character of Christian discipleship than radical resistance to the powers that undermine true discipleship. The Revd Zvobgo's African Reformed Church, a reform movement that broke away form the *Chibarirwe,* manifests a far more resolute and positive response to the kingship of Christ over the whole of human life.

5.2.2   *The priestly office*

The coming of Christ replaced the Old Testament priesthood, which implies human mediation between God and man through the bringing of sacrifices, with the perfect priesthood of Christ. Hence the New Testament reference to the Christian's "royal priesthood" implies a totally new concept. Firstly it implies *priestly dignity* which gives all those who believe in Christ free access to God; secondly it involves *spiritual offerings* of prayer, praise and the living sacrifice of the renewed self, which replaces all mediatory offerings on an altar, in response to the sin-offering of the high priest Jesus Christ; and thirdly, it implies a *service of sacrifice* expressed in a daily life of love and service as a manifestation of inward crucifixion and commitment.

The Independent Churches rarely apply the title of "priest" to any of its leadership positions. Probably this indicates a universal acknowledgment of the unique priesthood of Christ. True, the *vaPostori* referred to Johane as "high priest *(mupristi mukuru)* but this was a recognition of his exceptional leadership rather than of a specific priestly function.

Nonetheless the traditional concept of mediatorship does cause some confusion which prevents a proper grasp of the aforementioned priestly status of the individual Christian. This applies particularly to the Spirit-type churches. Some members regard the prophetic leader as being "closer to God" than they are. After all, he takes the place of the spirit medium *(svikiro)* who calls up the tribal spirits, the ritual priest who represents the kinship group in addressing the ancestral spirits, the cultic priest who beseeches the traditional Supreme Being for rain at Matonjeni, or the *n'anga* who represents a link with the supernatural. Against this background it is quite understandable that to some followers the prophetic leader would become a sort of "mediator", whose representative function goes far beyond the biblical concept of intercession and who interferes with the individual's free access to the presence of God.

Mutendi's ministry exemplifies this. The fact that some of his followers considered it spiritually sufficient to bring their problems to the "man of God" in Zion City for a solution, or that they brought gifts so that the leader could ask God for rain on their behalf, indicates a limited conception of the priestly status of the individual believer. Thus one ZCC member told me that he only took "trivial matters" to God himself, since "important issues" are "raised to heaven" by Mutendi. Such an attitude reflects the traditional concept of mediatorship. Only the officially sanctioned ritual mediator communicates directly with the supernatural. A ministry that places such emphasis on the mediation of the church leader could easily lead to neglect of individual prayer. We should add that in his ministry Mutendi did not consciously reserve the priestly office for himself alone. He saw his mediation on his followers' behalf as intercession, which had to supplement and not replace the individual's direct communication with God.

The priestly attributes of spiritual sacrifice and self-sacrificing service are manifested in the lives of many Independent Church clergy. Through regular periods of seclusion, fasting, meditation and prayer the prophetic leaders set an example, while Ethiopian-type leaders encourage perseverance in prayer and good works. In fact, the ministry of the Independent Churches consistently focuses on sacrificial service on an organized basis, so that the priestly office culminates in a goal-directed and lively diaconate. Examples include the pastoral service that prophetic leaders render along with their faith-healing activities; educational service through the establishment of schools; the *Ruwadzano* women's organizations which are particularly active in assisting people in times of illness or bereavement. In this latter regard the *Topia* (First Ethiopian Church) has gained some renown as "helper of the needy" through its widespread assistance to those in want. There is also Bishop Timithia Hore of the Zion Sabbath Church who, on his own initiative and at his own expense, erected a centre for the blind and physically handicapped at his head-quarters.

Hence the diaconate of the Independent Churches reveals a *comprehensive approach*. Christian and specifically priestly service implies more than just spiritual care. It includes agricultural, educational and "medical" facets.

5.2.3 *The prophetic office*

The prophetic office implies witness and preaching of God's Word. It is that ministry of God's Word for which the official clergy and lay members of the church are responsible, just as it was manifested in the "primitive church" through the preaching of the apostles and the testimony of believers. It is a task that implies inspiration through God's Spirit and knowledge of his Word.

In the Shona prophetic churches the prophetic office is mani-fested in a Protestant sense through proclamation *(kuparidza),*

147

and in the Old Testament sense in that divine communications are revealed through prophecies *(kuprofita,* to prophesy) to the community of believers by individuals with the gift of prophecy. *The differentiation of prophetic gifts does not supersede the kerygmatic task of prophets or lay members.* By and large it is accepted that preaching and witness are the task of *all* believers and not the prerogative of some office-bearer. Many prophets officially have the dual title of prophet and preacher (be it *mushumairi,* preacher; *muvhangeri,* evangelist; or *mufundisi,* minister).

Most Zionists and Apostles regard prophecy as an essential aspect of ministry. In their view it is the accepted way for the Holy Spirit to communicate his will for a particular situation. Prophecies are seldom considered canonical, but rather represent divinely inspired interpretations, the credibility of which depends on their concurrence with scriptural truths. Prophecies that deviate from Scripture are rejected as false. Hence prophets are expected to be thoroughly conversant with the Bible and to live "close to God".

Prophecies are usually closely bound up with pastoral work. Hence the Shona word *kuporofita,* to prophesy, means in the first place to reveal God's will for a "patient" (as regards getting a job, marital problems, success in a venture, diagnosis of an illness, sorcery, etc.), and only very rarely a prediction of the remote future. As a means of exposing destructive powers and expelling them the prophetic task represents a powerful *control* in the Spirit-type churches. As exercised by authentic and adult prophets, this form of ministry helps greatly to alleviate individual stress and promote harmony in congregational life.

Because of the similarity between prophecies and traditional divination one might well ask whether there is any essential difference between the two and whether prophecies in fact represent a truly christianized practice. After all, the need for revelation and the views on the causes of disease or mishaps are the same. There is no doubt that in some cases there are syncretist trends in this regard, but one must bear it in mind that the prophetic churches consistently reject traditional divination as unbiblical, that the prophets interpret their extraperception as deriving from the Holy Spirit and *not* from ancestral spirits, and that despite similarities in the diagnosis of illness, prophetic therapy always remains Christian in orientation and centres on God's saving power, as opposed to the traditional *n'anga's* activities to placate the spirits (through ancestor worship).

With reference to control over prophetic activities, Turner says that in the Aladura churches

> it is widely recognized that revelations may come from the devil and his evil spirits, as well as from the Holy Spirit and the angles, so that one must 'discern the spirits' ... Under the influence of evil spirits some utter false dreams, visions and prophecies deliberately; this 'lying against the Holy Spirit,' is a very great sin; and anyone so discovered must be excommunicated.[11]

He also points out that in the Aladura church strict control is exercised over the number of divinatory messages, the intensity of Spirit ecstasy and the interpretation of dreams and visions during church services.

In the Shona prophetic movement the control over prophecies is less systematic, so that it rarely happens that a prophet is suspended for "lying against the Holy Spirit". Some prophecies are accepted simply on the strength of the prophet's authoritarian personality or eminent rank and are not necessarily correlated with scriptural norms. Still, the tendency to "discern the spirits" is present in both the Zionist and Apostolic movements. Thus a junior prophet's revelations will be discussed by senior clergy during a service or a court session, especially if they affect the congregation directly or imply charges of sorcery or witchcraft. On occasion experienced prophets are even called in to cross-check. Prophets who disturb the order of a service are silenced or removed. This latter form of control is extremely important. There is no doubt that, no matter how much significance is attached to the revelatory function of the prophetic office in the Old Testament sense, *prophecy should not be allowed to interfere with the kerygmatic function of the clergy or lay believer*.

The Ethiopian-type churches recognize prophecy in terms of the ministry of the Word but not in a revelational sense. In

11 Ibid., p. 133

practice, however, members of these churches employ the services of Zionist and Apostle prophets. Some do so in spite of explicit scepticism, whereas others readily concede that nowadays "prophecy" could well be a legitimate channel for the work of the Holy Spirit.

5.3 LEADERSHIP HIERARCHIES

5.3.1 System of offices and ranks

In both the Ethiopian-type and the Spirit-type churches church government is structured hierarchically with a great variety of offices, often subdivided into various ranks. In addition to the position of the paramount leader, usually designated bishop, archbishop or "great bishop" (mubhishopi mukuru), the most common offices are those of minister (mufundisi), evangelist (muvhangeri), deacon (mudhikoni), preacher (mushumairi) and overseer (mutariri) — often ranked in this order. In Zionist churches any office below that of mufundisi may be held by a prophet, or a person who is purely a prophet may have a status equal to that of any of these offices, depending on his seniority in that group. A common development, already pointed out in the case of Mutendi, is that the paramount leader starts off as a prophet, but then largely delegates his charismatic authority to subordinate officials while he as bishop concentrates on administrative functions and judicial control. Such a division of authority contains a built-in danger of potential conflict since the charismatic influence of a prophet over the group can become so strong as to endanger the bishop's position.

Every group of congregational hierarchies in a circuit or church district falls under the jurisdiction of the local authoritative official. In practice the leadership hierarchy is often incomplete with an individual congregation. Mutendi's refusal to allow more than one minister per district meant that in most ZCC congregations direct authority is vested in the offices of one or more evangelists, with several preachers and deacons to help them. Instead of promoting evangelists to the office of minister when there are several evangelists in a congregation, they are ranked in order of seniority as first, second and third evangelist. If a congregation should have too many clergy it may request Zion City to divide the congregation into two, a custom reminiscent of the *traditional secession of kraals*. Just as internal strife and leadership problems in rural village communities are resolved by establishing a new village headmanship, so leadership ambitions in an overcrowded congregation are defused by subdivision into two congregations, each with its own place of assembly. In congregations where there are too few clergy, office-bearers often temporarily employ their children's services; for instance a deacon could easily allow one or two of his sons to act as deacons. If the congregation supports such a step the posts are eventually officially confirmed at headquarters.

By contrast with the ZCC, other Zionist bishops, for instance Bishop Andreas Shoko of the Zion Apostolic Faith Mission, insist on each congregation having its own pastor. Consequently the jurisdiction of a *Ndaza* Zionist minister is usually much smaller than that of a ZCC minister (who normally has control over a whole circuit comprising several congregations). In Bishop David Masuka's Zion Apostolic Church virtually every congregational leader is designated bishop, a distinction being made between "minor" and "major" bishops. No matter how impressive and psychologically significant these titles may be, the effective power associated with them is often equal to that attached to much lower offices in other churches. Hence there is no homogeneous pattern of titles applicable to all Independent Churches. The individual preference and standardization of each group decide the issue.

Johane Maranke's *vaPostori* have the most extensive leadership hierarchy of any Shona Independent Church. The four principal offices are those of baptist, evangelist, prophet and healer, in that order of importance. However, among the *vaPostori* there is some difference of opinion on this score. Some clergy regard these principal offices as equally important, whereas others place the office of either prophet or evangelist at the top of the hierarchy. Much depends on the local situation. If the "owner of the members" *(mwene wevatezvo)* in a district happens to be a prophet or an evangelist, his office inevitably carries greater authority than that of the baptist *(mubhapatidzi)* or healer *(murapi)*, and the hierarchy of that district is interpreted accordingly. In addition to these four offices there are the secretary *(munyori)* and the judge *(mutongi),* with the choristers and lay members below them. Senior tribesmen with experience of the proceedings of tribal courts are usually appointed judges. In addition to them there are usually a number of younger evangelists and/or baptists serving as judges, which eliminates the risk of domination by an older, traditionally oriented lobby in the church courts.

Each of the four principal offices are subdivided into five ranks, each with its own insignia appearing as a monogram on the official vestments. The symbol (e.g. a star for a baptist) is incomplete for the lowest rank, whereas for the three senior ranks the respective qualifications from top to bottom are added: LIEBAUMAH, L.U. and L. Opinions differ as to the meaning of this word (colloquially pronounced *rabaumah),* but the consensus is that Johane "saw" the entire hierarchy in a vision. This much at least is certain, namely that the sought-after post of a junior or senior *rabaumah* carries the connotation of important, great or purified — in short, it implies outstanding leadership in the exclusive true church of God.

In the Apostolic hierarchy an individual usually progresses up the various ranks of the office to which he is appointed, but there are instances where he may change his office altogether. Murphree believes that each congregation is represented by the senior incumbents of the four principal offices,[12] but this view does not accord with the facts. In the Chingombe tribal area there are many Apostle congregations where there are several clergy belonging to one category, whereas another category may be altogether unrepresented. In 1966 the *sabata* (literally, sabbath day — i.e. congregation) in Chingombe South had a *rabaumah* evangelist, a junior baptist (fourth rank) and three junior evangelists (fourth and fifth ranks); in Chingombe North there was a *sabata* with one baptist, two evangelists and a junior secretary. In the event of a congregation not having its own prophet the Apostles usually summon a prophet from a neighbouring congregation when problems arise.

Note that the *entire hierarchy* of each district is never complete either at a congregational level or at the monthly assembly of a

12 Murphree, 1964, p. 95

few congregations, but only at the annual gathering of the entire district (called a *Pendi*, from Pentecost) where all the associated units of the church foregather. In districts where the *vaPostori* are very numerous the *Pendi* gatherings usually swarm with representatives of virtually every rank of each office. However, the numbers pose no problem since each member knows exactly on what date he joined the movement and when he was first appointed an office. Consequently the positions of authority in each rank are easily determined.

In the "Ethiopian" churches the leadership hierarchy pro rata to the number of members in the congregation is usually smaller and simpler. The allocation per congregation is more constant, so that, as in the case of the *Chibarirwe*, each congregation has at least a preacher, an overseer, an evangelist and a few deacons. Both the *Chibarirwe* and the African Reformed Church *(Shonganiso)* follow the system of church government of the Protestant mission churches. One finds that an evangelist or minister has usually had at least some form of theological training. Hence it is not possible for a deacon to advance through the various offices to the top of a hierarchy, as may happen in the Spirit-type churches. In this respect Bishop Gavure's *Topia* (First Ethiopian Church) occupies an intermediate position, in that it permits an office-bearer to progress from the lowest rank to the top due to lesser emphasis on theological training.

When the number of office-bearers is correlated with that of lay adult members one finds that in the prophetic churches and the *Topia* Church between 60 and 80 percent of all adult males occupy some office or other. The two exceptions are the *Chibarirwe* and Mutendi's ZCC, in both of which only about 30 percent of the men are office-bearers. This is because the *Chibarirwe* has a number of qualified ministers who stress the importance of theological training for acceptable leadership, while in the ZCC central leadership is so dominated by the leader that the appointment of large numbers of office-bearers, especially to senior posts, is deliberately avoided for fear of schisms, rivalry or undermining of the central authority of Zion City.

The reasons why the Independent Churches on the whole have such large numbers of office-bearers and attach such importance to status include the following:

153

(1)   The need for recognition, status and responsibility was heightened by the colonial and mission church situations which in many respects restricted Black leadership. An analysis of the dream experiences of individuals illustrates this point. Revd Josaya Chikwama of the ZCC dreamt repeatedly of the responsibility that he was to have as a spiritual leader at the very time when he was undergoing the frustrating experience of being fired by one White employer after another in the Harare industrial area.

(2)   There is some reaction against the traditional tribal political structure which is based on lineage rather than ability and therefore offers no satisfactory solution for leadership ambitions.

(3)   An excessive number of schisms and large-scale group fragmentation resulted in the arbitrary appointment of office-bearers in an attempt to enhance the outward image of the new groups and make them more attractive to outsiders.

(4)   Roles of responsibility were allocated as in the kinship structure, in which every adult is either the superior or the subordinate of every other adult. Because of poor ecclesiology and a concomitant tendency to regard the church as a kind of extended family, the proliferation of offices became a natural expression of meaningful group involvement.

(5)   The profusion of offices is partly in response to the New Testament injunction that all members of the *ecclesia* should be involved in the activity of God's kingdom. Thus the appointment of individuals to even the humblest of tasks is aimed at inducing and activating them to be involved in the business of the congregation.

As for women occupying official positions, it is remarkable that (according to a survey in the Chingombe villages) only some 15 per cent of female members, as opposed to 50 to 60 per cent of males, hold such positions in the "Ethiopian" and prophetic movements. The majority of these women play a prominent part in the *Ruwadzano* women's associations and the lower ranks of the leadership hierarchy where they serve as deaconesses, prophetesses, healers and the like. Despite the impact of outstanding personalities one gets the impression that as far as authority, status and control are concerned the Shona Independent Churches offer scope primarily for male leadership.

5.3.2   Kinship factors

The importance of kinship is manifested in the phenomenon that most Independent Churches could be called "family churches". It is nothing unusual for a small *Ndaza* church to consist of a few congregations, each led by a younger brother, son or nephew *(muzukuru,* son of a sister) of the bishop. In Bishop Forridge's ZCC — a splinter group of Mutendi's movement — all congregations are controlled by kinsmen of the bishop, and in the central congregation both the evangelist and the prophet are his sons, while his wives and daughters act as choristers, drummers and dancers during services.

In the larger movements too key positions are reserved for relations. In Mutendi's Zion City his sons play an important part in a ritual, organizational and judicial-authoritative context. Although the ministers in remote circuits are not necessarily related to Mutendi, the custom is that when any of them becomes too independent, one of the sons of the "man of God" is transferred to that district to act as "advisor" to protect the interests of Zion City and where necessary avert schism. In Johane Maranke's widely dispersed movement the right to administer the sacraments is reserved for Abero and Makebo, his two sons and successors. This gives the principal leaders an additional means of control and they are able to prevent the initiative from passing into other hands.

The importance of kinship is manifested also in the Independent Churches' mode of expansion. They prefer to baptize entire families. The binding authority of the head of the clan is used to persuade all households to be baptized en masse without necessarily paying attention to the spiritual state or conviction of individual members. In the process official roles may be created for members of the clan even though they may lack the ability or spiritual maturity to fulfil them properly. Naturally some eventually "grow into" the office, whereas others drop out or try unavailingly to meet the requirements. Bishop Forridge's one son confessed to me that he, supposedly a prophet, could never get beyond speaking in tongues because in spite of years of persevering hope and spiritual preparation the Holy Spirit did not send him any revelations.

In the Independent Churches in Chingombe it was established that a network of kinship ties marks the relations between all office-bearers. In the Nyaganwa ZCC congregation there were only three office-bearers — a first prophet, a deacon and a preacher — who were not related to the "minister" (mufundisi). Of the other three prophets, one was his wife and two were younger brothers. His sister's husband (mukuwasha) was a deacon, his wife's brother (mukarabga) a catechist, and another younger brother, a son-in-law and a maternal uncle were all preachers.

The relationship of the sekuru (maternal uncle) and muzukuru (sister's son) features prominently in most leadership hierarchies. This is the only relationship that implies equality according to traditional norms and is therefore marked by a lack of friction and rivalry.[13] Senior office-bearers like to appoint their vazukuru (sisters' sons) to key positions and assign them leading roles in the proceedings of the church court. As a rule a church leader can expect his muzukuru to be loyal and co-operative. Just as the tribal chief's muzukuru usually acquires considerable influence in tribal politics by virtue of the relationship, so the church leader's muzukuru is well-placed to exercise his influence on church affairs.

A correlation between kinship and seniority in the hierarchies of 28 Independent Church congregations in Chingombe yielded the following results: 31 (19 per cent) out of a total of 166 office-bearers were not directly related to fellow office-bearers of either senior or junior rank. In the 19 father-son relationships, the 44 blood brother, 25 maternal uncle-nephew (sekuru-muzukuru) and 16 paternal uncle-nephew (babamukuru-mwana — here the nephew is called "child") relationships the predominant pattern was for seniority and subordinateness in church leadership to

13 Daneel, 1971(a), p. 50

coincide with the roles in the kinship structure. However, in each category of kinship there was also *inversion of the traditional order,* in that a son, for instance, occupied a position senior to his father's. The most striking feature here was that a son-in-law *(mukuwasha),* who traditionally occupies a clearly circumscribed subordinate position in relation to his father-in-law *(mukarabga),* would actually appoint his father-in-law and brother-in-law to positions beneath his own in the hierarchy of the church. Often a solution is to appoint in-laws to comparatively junior but honorary positions such as that of "judge" *(mutongi).* In this way in-laws or an individual's own father can secure considerable status, as in the case of Johane Maranke who appointed his father "judge", without in any way endangering the paramount leadership of the church.

Inasmuch as the kinship structure emerges in the Independent Churches one could say that the traditional patterns are perpetuated in the "new order". However, this is not a case of direct adaptation since in the context of an Independent Church congregation the responsibilities entailed by superior or subordinate positions acquire a new meaning in terms of Christian goals. Besides, the inversion of traditional patterns of authority illustrates that the hierarchical order of the Independent Churches can also radically *transform* the ancient codes by setting up new patterns of authority.

5.4 APPOINTMENT, TRAINING AND SUCCESSION OF OFFICE-BEARERS

5.4.1 *Vocation to the ministry*

In the prophetic movements the first step towards the ministry is the experience of a divine call or vocation, in the form of either a dream, a vision, prophetic revelation or physical transportation to heaven. The majority of prophetic office-bearers testify to dreams or visions which included direct encounters with God himself or his emissaries. They themselves appear in some sort of official apparel associated with the ministry. Thus a prospective office-bearer may dream about himself drumming on a hilltop to summon his followers, or healing the sick, or suffering tribulations as an itinerant preacher. A call is only corroborated when God himself or his emissary gives the injunction in a dream or vision that the time has come for action in everyday life.

A divine vocation is often accompanied by other manifestations of God's presence. It may be some form of possession by the Spirit, speaking in tongues, a period of "powerful prayer" with the assumption that this was inspired by the Holy Spirit, fasting, Bible study and periods of seclusion (usually on mountains). Particularly when a new movement is being launched it is important for the paramount leader to convince his followers that the initiative came directly from God. Consequently during the initial period there are frequent references to the leader's call so as to establish a direct link with the supernatural.

In the Spirit-type churches one can distinguish certain stereotyped vocational dreams and visions such as the Joseph theme and the Moses theme. Thus both Johane and Mutendi dreamt of wheat sheaves which had greater merit than the other sheaves. Johane also dreamt about himself as a Moses figure who led his followers through fire (some *vaPostori* still practise a symbolic walking on fire) and enemy countries by means of his sacred rod. By attaching almost canonical value to such dreams and visions in the books of their churches Johane and Mutendi set a standard according to which prospective office-bearers could be "measured". An endless variation on the same standardized themes can be found in the dreams of Zionists and *vaPostori* who aspire to some sort of authoritative position in their churches.

Dreams and visions can also serve as divine affirmation of appointments after they have been made. Especially in rapidly expanding churches many office-bearers are appointed on grounds of kinship, status in the community, natural leadership talent and so on. In such cases "affirmatory dreams" are important to show loyalty and consolidate positions, especially when there is a power struggle which threatens to undermine positions of authority.

Sundkler maintains that by contrast with the Zionist emphasis on vocation by the Holy Spirit, the Ethiopian-type churches regard "good character" and general leadership qualities as sufficient substitute for theological training.[14] This statement could create the impression that a divine call is less important in non-prophetic groups. We must stress that in most Ethiopian-type churches leaders and subordinate office-bearers also claim to have been divinely called. Here too dreams and visions play an important part. The difference is that among non-prophetic groups the focus is less sharply on dramatic encounters with the supernatural. Sengwayo, leader of the African Congregational Church *(Chibarirwe)* attested to the "voice of God" which led him to establish his own church. He claimed that his leadership and the accompanying growth of his church were a direct result of divine inspiration. At the same time there was a conspicuous lack of ecstatic manifestations of the Holy Spirit in the *Chibarirwe.*

5.4.2   Leadership qualifications

No matter how important dreams, visions and the accompanying spiritual gifts of speaking in tongues, prophecy and faith healing may be, the crucial qualifications for appointing an office-bearer are not necessarily his remarkable spiritual powers. When asked about the requirements they set, church leaders do not always mention commitment to God's work, spiritual ardour and strong faith. Among the exceptions were Bishop Andreas Shoko of the Zion Apostolic Faith Mission, who responded: "Educational standards are unimportant. We want the heart! Every office-bearer must have a friendly heart and be intent on serving God with his whole being." The Revd Zvobgo of the ARC *(Shonganiso)* maintained that a candidate for leadership should be a man of strong faith who knows his Bible well and observes the laws of the church.

In most instances the first reaction of Independent Church leaders was not to mention the spiritual dimension at all, but to associate qualification for leadership with one of the following character traits:

---

14 Sundkler, 1961, p. 125

tsika dzakanaka (good conduct), that is someone who leads an
   exemplary life;
moyo munyoro (a friendly heart) — a sympathetically disposed
   person who is not easily angered;
kubata vanhu (to control people) — someone able to exercise
   authority over people and influence them; and
kupa murairo (to "give" the law) — someone who can lay down
   the law and uphold it in daily living.

Along with these qualifications some leaders mentioned a long
period of membership. This meant that a candidate should have
had sufficient time to demonstrate group loyalty and become conversant with the practices of the church.

Bishop Forridge's comment is representative of the view of
many Independent Church leaders:

> I choose new office-bearers myself. In the first place I ex-
> amine the person's way of life. If his reputation is good and
> his life exemplary I will appoint him first as a preacher, then
> as a deacon, then as an evangelist, and eventually as a
> minister. I do not care much whether or not the person is
> clever. I am looking for a reliable person who is able to
> lead others. He must not be inclined to quarrel. I expect him
> to maintain discipline in the church.

This comment illustrates the sensitivity in prophetic circles
about the educational standard of office-bearers, which is naturally significantly lower than that required by the mission
churches. Interestingly, this same Bishop Forridge was the first
Zionist bishop to complete a two-year theological course successfully many years later, after the establishment of a theological
training centre for Shona Independent Churches in 1972. Conscious of the advantages of theological study he now stresses
biblical knowledge, effective preaching and general insight into
the essential features of Christianity as important qualifications
for leadership.

Despite this the continuing emphasis in the Independent
Churches on natural rather than spiritual leadership indicates
that, in the first instance, traditional leadership ideals are still
focal. Consequently some Independent Church leaders evaluate
"good conduct", "balanced behaviour" or "good character" in

ZCC drummer leading congregation during Church service

Elison Mutingwende of the Shinga Postora baptizing recruits after locating and destroying witchcraft medicine

Infant baptism by Maranke Apostles in 'Jordan'

Bishop David Masuka Jr. of the Zion Apostolic Church (Ndaza) addressing congregation during Sunday service

High Priest Abero Maranke of the African Apostolic Church
of Johane Maranke (Postori) observing Pendi (holy communion) procedure.

Barren woman consults Ndaza prophetic healers for cure

Preparation for entry of 'Jordan' by vaPostori baptizers

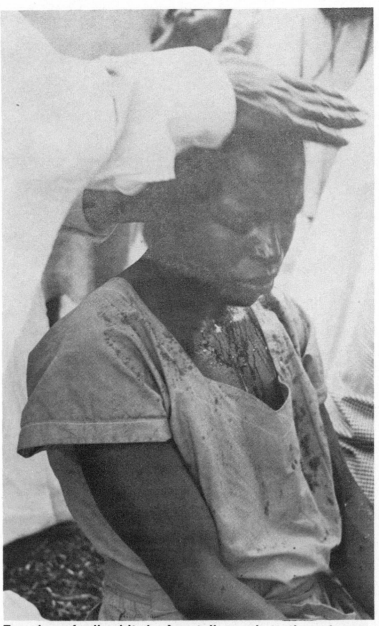
Exorcism of evil spirits by Apostolic prophets, through symbolic sprinkling of holy water and laying on of hands

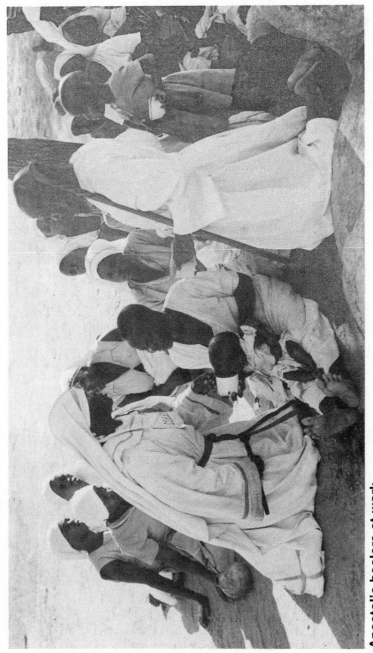

Apostolic healers at work

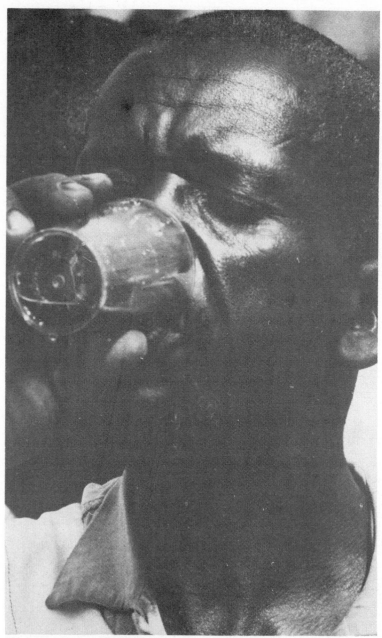

MuPostori participating in holy communion

Ndaza bishop leads followers in dance

Infant baptism by vaPostori baptizers

Baptized infant received on bank of 'Jordan' — symbolizing transition from old to new life.

Bishop Samuel Mutendi of the ZCC addressing chiefs during Sunday service

After the founding of the Zion Christian Church in 1925 Bishop Mutendi experienced great opposition from government authorities and tribal chiefs. However, as the bishop's popular image as "man of God" grew — one who could "pray down" rain, establish spiritual and material well-being for his followers and even consolidate the leadership of chiefs — the tribal dignitaries from all over the country started to flock to his Church. In this respect the ZCC bishop, himself a *muRozvi,* appealed to and in some respects revived the sentiments concerning the past glory of the old Rozvi dynasty.

**Bishop Andreas Shoko of the Zion Apostolic Faith Mission
(Ndaza Zionist Church) preaching**

Baptism conducted by ZCC minister

terms of traditional law and social norms rather than scriptural criteria. In the second place it faithfully reflects the basis on which many office-bearers in these churches were and still are appointed.

As for *age,* the traditional principle of seniority continues to play a major part, with the result that there is a marked preference for middle-aged and older people in positions of authority. Among prophetic churches the ZCC, and among Ethiopian-types churches the *Chibarirwe,* were particularly inclined to appoint older people to senior positions. In Chingombe a mere 12 per cent of ZCC senior office-bearers and only 5 per cent of those in the *Chibarirwe* were below the age of forty. In the *Chibarirwe* most evangelists and ministers were over fifty. Of course, this accords with the image of a church which is popularly known as "the church of the old people". A conscious attempt to assimilate ancestral customs into the church must inevitably lead to vesting power in those who are old enough to compel respect in the traditional sense of the word. Key positions in traditional ritual, for example that of addressing the tribal spirits in rain-making rites, are also held by older people.

The *Ndaza* Zionists, the *vaPostori* and *Topia* Church, on the other hand, tend towards younger office-bearers: 29 per cent of the *Ndaza* Zionist, 49 per cent of *vaPostori* and 42 per cent of *Topia* office-bearers were not yet forty. Nonetheless it was striking that the age group from 20 to 30 was largely confined to the lowest ranks of the leadership hierarchy. These were the junior prophets, evangelists and deacons often charged with church-expansion activities. Often they were also, as mentioned earlier, sons, daughters, nephews and the like of high-ranking officials.

The following data indicate that Western *educational standards* have virtually no influence on the leadership of the Independent Churches: 17 per cent of the Spirit-type and 14 per cent of the Ethiopian-type leaders among the Shona churches had *no* schooling at all. In Bishop Mutendi's ZCC this category constituted 24 per cent of office-bearers. The vast majority of all office-bearers in Independent Churches in Zimbabwe (and probably in the whole of Africa, if one considers the generally high educational standards in Zimbabwe) had only between one and five years' schooling. Of all the Zionist and *vaPostori* office-bearers only 13 per cent had progressed as far as standard three, while the Ethiopian-type churches are slightly better off with 22 per cent of their office-bearers in this category. It follows that there is little correlation between high educational standards and promotion to a high-ranking office such as that of bishop, minister, chief overseer or some such. Of course there are exceptions such as Sengwayo of the ACC *(Chibarirwe)* and Zvobgo of the ARC *(Shonganiso)*, whose primary school education was followed by a basic form of catechetical, evangelistic or even "teacher" training.

Some church leaders overcome the problem of illiteracy by memorizing large parts of Scripture. Others go to considerable lengths to acquire a basic knowledge of reading and writing. Bishop Gavure of the *Topia* church was taught to read and write by a member of his family. On church-expansion campaigns, he says, "I walked around with books in my hands to memorize new words." Without this zeal for learning it is unlikely that Bishop Gavure would have developed the insight to advance to the position of paramount leader of the *Topia* church and also the presidency of the African Independent Church Conference *(Fambidzano yemaKereke avaTema)*.

Some leaders stress their lack of education so as to illustrate their independence from the mission churches. Shembe regularly referred to the fact that his lack of schooling had made him a useful instrument in the hand of God.[15] Johane Maranke was inclined to denigrate his early contacts with the Methodist Mission Church. This he did by declaring that he could interpret the books he received in his visions only by the inspiration of the Holy Spirit and not by means of any mission school training. This same attitude, associated with a need to compensate in a world where educational qualifications are playing an increasingly dominant role, crops up frequently in the preaching of Zionists and *vaPostori*. A popular theme for sermons which I have often heard is that school certificates and university degrees will be no qualification for entering the gates of heaven one day.

15 Ibid., p. 125

Of course, this attitude is somewhat ambivalent, for the apparent rejection of education as an important requirement for effective church work is often accompanied by an unspoken desire for greater wisdom and efficacy through study. This is why theological training projects for the Independent Churches, such as the erstwhile AICA in South Africa and *Fambidzano* in Zimbabwe, were greeted so enthusiastically. One of the most profound motives for aspiring to theological training is the hope that it will earn respect and recognition from the historical churches.

5.4.3 *Leadership training*

Various forms of in-service training were developed in the Independent Churches from the outset. Among the Shona the first phase of church expansion between 1920 and 1935 was marked by the arbitrary appointment of many wholly untrained office-bearers. These people had to minister to their growing congregations by means of what advice they could obtain from their headquarters. Some could no doubt rely on a measure of experience gained in mission churches, but even a prominent leader such as Mutendi was originally despatched as an untrained "messenger" from Zion. As is commonly accepted in the prophetic churches, the main criterion was a powerful manifestation of the inspiration of the Holy Spirit. In the case of Johane Maranke it is clear that the first group of office-bearers appointed after the first mass baptism into the new church in July 1932 had no training other than a few days of preparatory discussions with the prophetic leader.

The standard pattern of "informal training" that evolved in most of the Independent Churches was as follows:

A new leader's popularity attracts people to his headquarters from a large territory. Through participation in faith healing and other religious activities the new member becomes acquainted with the new faith. He is then sent back to his home to proclaim the new religion there. During this phase the potential office-bearer's sole "training" consists in what sporadic advice he can glean from headquarters and the practical experience gained in the course of recruiting new members. As soon as a sufficient number of new members has been recruited a senior representative is summoned from headquarters to conduct the baptism, officially recognize the existence of the new congregation and confirm the appointment of the local office-bearer as its leader. Thus the new office-bearer's motivation to proselytize and start a congregation is stimulated by the knowledge that success is decisive for his appointment, status and future promotion in the leadership hierarchy of the church.

As soon as a local leader of one or a few congregations has been officially appointed he becomes personally responsible for training office-bearers in the expanding local hierarchy. In-service training of a group of relatives and close friends who have been appointed junior preachers, deacons or prophets consists in corporate religious activities such as preaching, fasting, prayer groups, parish visiting, proselytizing campaigns and disciplinary action in council sessions. Some local leaders start biblical instruction at an early stage, accompanied by discussion of the church's doctrines. However, in practice it often happens that a new office-bearer's sole "training" in this initial growth phase consists in rendering service to the congregation under the supervision of the local leader, who may well be a "novice" in the new church himself.

Shortcomings in the local "training programme" are remedied at the annual mass assemblies at headquarters. These enable the principal leader to teach his followers in private discussions, council sessions or sermons. Or, as is common among the *vaPostori* at their feasts, regular meetings are held for the various office-bearers, specifically to enlighten newcomers about the finer points of their office.

Bishop Mutendi summoned his leader ministers from the various districts to Zion City according to a fixed programme. Consequently there were always a few of these people in Mutendi's immediate presence so that he could enlighten them on biblical matters, church organization, tribal politics or whatever struck him as important. Their close involvement in the daily programme of Zion City during their stay there constituted an on-going in-service training.

For an example of how Mutendi "trained" his ministers we quote from one of his "tutorial" addresses. It was delivered on an occasion when the supreme court *(dare)* of the church was discussing a case of the disloyalty of a ZCC official who had refused to do duty in Zion City. Mutendi thereupon addressed the ministers and other officials who were present as follows:

Read us Micah 4! I chose this passage to concur with our decision. The minister we have dismissed will be trapped in a snare. He spurned the law of Zion [Mi 4:2] and then rebelled when it was used to call him to account. And yet all of us have decided to accept that law ... He will now try to lead others astray also because he has been relieved of his post. It will be like King Saul who let himself be consoled with a harp when his crown was taken from him ... We do not want a rebel who refuses to have his case heard by the church council. We are removing him because we do not want ZAPU people in our church. We did not decide to join that movement. Why then should he have done so? Remember that King George's soldiers did not open fire until commanded to do so ...

When I was in South Africa I with Lekhanyane meticulously observed the laws of the church. Some of my followers have broken away to try and build up a following of their own, but they were caught in a snare. It is my gift that many people follow me. Such a gift cannot be taken away. I, on the other hand, am unable to sing. That is why I sit and listen when others sing. You must know the law of Zion. Read Micah 4! We want people who will be true to their promises, whose yea will be yea and whose nay, nay.

In Micah 4:1 there is the prophecy that the people of the latter days will know peace. The prophet was referring to us, for we are the people of the end-time. The saying that the house of the Lord will be situated on the highest of the mountains means that Zion will be exalted above other churches. The cooking stones [other churches] are underneath the pot [Zion]! All people will come to Zion. As they increase Zion will be exalted. The people form part of and build Zion ... as Headman Ndanga did yesterday when he gave us money to build Jerusalem. It was an amount of $48 and will be used to build Zion higher than any church or nation ...

Out of Zion shall go forth the law, and the word of the Lord from Jerusalem [Mi 4:2]. Once in Johannesburg Zvenyika and others broke away from us, accusing us of error. But I said: 'That is impossible, for this law reached Zion first. When God comes he will certainly enter the house of the first wife.' When the Nyasa started to argue with us I quoted Zechariah 12 to them where it says that when God comes, he will come to Zion for it is the 'supreme court'. All nations will come to Zion for that is where God will be . . .

You yourselves have laid down the law that if a minister or high-ranking official were to commit adultery or err gravely he shall lose his position . . . I uphold the law in Zion. If you are condemned under this tomorrow, do not complain, saying 'Mutendi is wicked' and then go off to join Makamba, Joram or one of the other leaders. They are backsliders and weak in their faith. This place where we are is Jerusalem! There is no other home. Here we want faithful workers. We grieve when office-bearers break away and take people with them. If you labour and obtain God's forgiveness there will also be plenteous rains.

This is *Zionist in-service training par excellence!* No classroom is needed, for the principal leader employs any church occasion to teach his subordinate office-bearers. In this case the dismissal of a disloyal office-bearer led to a "lecture" on loyalty, the dangers of separatism and a statement on politics. Church dogma is not expounded systematically, but the essence of Zionist dogma emerges in the identification of the Old Testament Zion with Mutendi's Zion City. The uniqueness of the Zionist church among other churches is illustrated not only by means of a somewhat egocentric "exegesis" of biblical texts, but also with reference to the historical background of the ZCC — that is, Mutendi's own experiences. Interpretation of biblical texts and the history of their church are used to enhance group solidarity and reaffirm Mutendi's leadership. Hence training and consolidation of the leader's position go hand in hand. Loyal service to Zion and a proper attitude towards God are directly related to rain. It is another way of telling people who rely on an agrarian subsistence economy that prosperity and success are associated with willingness to render service according to the established norms.

5.4.4 *Appointment ceremonies*

Not all Independent Churches reserve the official appointment of office-bearers for court sessions during conferences at headquarters. When a *Ndaza* Zionist bishop is appointed the principal leader usually journeys to that district to conduct an official ordination ceremony. *VaPostori* appointments are made at the level of district conferences *(Pendi),* and are confirmed during the July "Easter festival" at the church centre in Maranke. In the ZCC, *Chibarirwe* and ARC *(Shonganiso)* the appointment of office-bearers is the prerogative of the church's supreme "court" *(dare)* at conference level.

At Zion City the "court" (or church council) sits at least once during each of the three great annual conferences to deal with the nomination and investiture of office-bearers. All the representatives of congregations or church districts where new office-bearers are required gather with the *dare.* The existing office-bearers of the congregation concerned appear before the councillors, standing up while lay members sit down next to them. Mutendi himself used to remind his followers at this point of the importance of appointing people who can carry responsibility and who have already given proof of spiritual talents and abilities. The ensuing discussion is conducted by the office-bearers and members of the relevant congregation, with the councillors acting as a sort of jury. Several people may be nominated for junior posts, and proposals for promotion within the existing hierarchy may be made. From the discussion it is evident that seniority in the group, leadership potential (also in the spiritual sphere) and popularity are the deciding factors. The talents and weaknesses of office-bearers who are up for promotion are discussed quite frankly. At one such gathering in April 1965, the qualities of Ezekiah, who had been nominated for the senior post of minister, were being discussed. His exceptional fervour during evangelization campaigns was commended, but there was some doubt and the question was explicitly raised whether Ezekiah's restless nature would permit him to see to the needs of the Zaka congregations at home who would fall under his care.

After voting by such members of the congregation as are present the elected parties remain standing for the final affirmation by Mutendi and his councillors. The *dare* as the supreme authority of the church has the right to veto the choice of church members, so that the appointment of every official is subject to both *democratic election* and *hierarchical authority*. The veto is rarely exercised but members are reminded of the overriding powers of the church's supreme council. Each of the elected officials is given an opportunity to deliver a short speech. It is pre-eminently an occasion to express their loyalty to the "man of God" and the church. It has binding force, for Zionist office-bearers fear the humiliation of public charges before the *dare* of poor co-operation or disloyalty.

Finally all the newly elected office-bearers are consecrated by laying on of hands and prayer by Mutendi and his councillors (mainly ministers). This ceremony is greeted with jubilant cheering from the spectators and speaking in tongues to symbolize the sanction of the Holy Spirit.

The Revd Sibambo of the ARC *(Shonganiso)* has drawn up an elaborate list of questions with appropriate answers so that a new minister can prepare himself for the ordination ceremony. Ordination *(kugadza ufundisi)* takes place at the annual session of the General Assembly. Some of the prescribed questions and responses for this ceremony are as follows:

Q: Do you wish to become a minister?

R: I am not able to do this work, but if God calls me, so be it.

Q: What are the conditions for ministry?

R: I must be called by God.

Q: How many wives are you permitted to have?

R: Only one.

Q: What is your commission?

R: To record the important events in my congregation; to teach people; to preach God's Word; to baptize; and to celebrate communion.

Q: What do you teach others?

R: Firstly that they must be rid of their sins, and secondly that they must obey the injunction in Mark 16: 15 and go out to proclaim the Word to others.

Q: What will you eat?

R: Paul says: "The owner of cattle uses milk." Christ says: "Leave your blankets and purse at home when you set forth on your way."

Q: How will you promote God's work?
R: I will encourage people to contribute generously.
Q: What do you teach with regard to divination, prophecies and murderers?
R: Church members are not permitted to take note of such things. Those who are involved in such things may not take communion.
Q: With which denominations do we refuse to co-operate?
R: Roman Catholics, Zionists and Apostles.

Important points to note are that the questions and responses during the ordination ceremony revolve around the basic doctrines of the church (only one wife!) which distinguish it from other Ethiopian-type churches; the classic mission injunction as an essential point of teaching, placing the emphasis on church expansion; and a direct correlation between the advancement of God's work and financial contributions. Because the church's attitude towards traditional practices and towards other denominations (which clearly reflects the Protestant tradition) is explicitly stated one could say that the ordination ceremony in itself constitutes instruction for members of the General Assembly and reaffirms their group identity.

5.4.5 *Succession in the leadership hierarchy*

Sundkler maintains that

> the Independent Bantu Church tends to have its leadership passing from father to son, this being one of the characteristic ways in which the Independent Church adapts itself to the African heritage.[16]

This is true also of the Shona Independent Churches, particularly the prophetic ones. Succession to leadership on hereditary lines indicates the strong influences that traditional customs continue to exercise. The traditional custom of linking the succession

16 Ibid., p. 118

to the headmanship to the leading house or houses of the politically dominant kinship group is paralleled by the tendency among founder-leaders in the Independent Churches to reserve the future leadership of their followers for their immediate relations, preferably their sons. Church headquarters and the nucleus of each outlying congregation show similarities to the extended family, which accepts and affirms hereditary leadership. Just as the eldest son of a deceased head of a family in the traditional context inherits both property and religious authority by means of the *kugadzira*[17] rite, so the son of a bishop inherits his property and position of authority in the church during the ceremonies that follow his death. In both the traditional context and in the Independent Churches such inherited responsibility — whether for the family or the church — is seen as a lifelong commitment.

A major factor in inherited leadership is the intimate tie that grows between a founder-leader and his followers. In a concerted attempt to achieve continuity in the face of a constant threat of schism the leader is elevated by his followers to the "lifelong presidency" of the church. Leader and church are identified in the minds of members to such an extent that one could expect his name and even his influence to continue after his death. On his demise the close tie is perpetuated through the deceased's appearance to his followers in dreams and his continuing presence in the person of his successor-son(s). The interaction between a deceased leader and his church unmistakably reflects the aftermath of traditional views on the relationship between the living and the "living" dead. Just as an ancestral spirit protects his living descendants, so the deceased church leader — even if he is considered to be "with Christ" or "standing at the gates of heaven" — continues to be actively involved in his church. The church responds by honouring his name and meticulously obeying instructions given in dreams.

Even the ceremony of succession to the leadership manifests some features of the traditional *kugova nhaka* (division of the estate) rite. When Johane Maranke died his cousin Simon Mushati, chief prophet of the movement, tried to keep church affairs

17 Daneel, 1971(a), p. 101f

170

and family property separate, but Johane's brother Anrod applied
certain aspects of the traditional *kugadzira* ritual, thus incorporat-
ing Johane's entire "property", which included the church, in the
distribution of his estate. As in the traditional ceremony of trans-
ferring a name, Johane's eldest sons Makebo and Abero had to
sit on the customary mat *(rupasa)* to inherit their late father's
name and his sacred staves. The staves symbolized Johane's
charismatic and judicial authority, so that this ceremony was
quite unmistakably a transfer of church leadership.

A striking feature in discussions on the succession to leadership
is the heavy accent on the son and successor's right to inherit
his father's clerical vestments, staves and other symbolic
emblems. This could be a relic of the fetishist mentality whereby
ownership of such heirlooms would in itself guarantee some measure of success in church leadership. I was frequently struck by
the fact that in the Independent Churches office-bearers tend to
prefer discussing biblical grounds for hereditary leadership rather
than the spiritual powers, organizational experience and leadership potential of the son(s) succeeding the father. Office-bearers
in the pophetic churches felt that the Holy Spirit, who had instituted this kind of succession (*kutevera ropa*, literally "the blood
of the late leader succeeds"), will enable the successor-son and
new leader to act competently. This left little scope for any hypo-
thetical measures that could be followed should the eldest son
prove to be wholly unfit as a successor. However, Torera, a
senior healer in the Apostle movement, claimed that "if my
eldest son who must succeed me is a fool people will desert him.
He will not follow God's will and in that case God will choose
someone else ... It does not matter if my son is ignorant to
begin with. He will be permitted to wear my official dress and
other healers will instruct him. Only if he should prove a total
failure will someone else be chosen in his place."

In the prophetic movements hereditary leadership is often
justified on the grounds of the Jewish monarchy and/or the transfer of Aaron's function to his son Eliezer. Such references rarely
make a distinction between the royal and the priestly leadership
in the Old Testament, or between the religious leadership of the
Jewish temple and the New Testament *ecclesia*. It is more a

matter of Bible texts selected to justify a traditionally oriented and hence acceptable notion of leadership.

The fact that inherited leadership is the Achilles heel of the Independent Churches is borne out by the crisis that almost invariably follows the death of a founder-leader. The greatest schisms in the churches of Johane Maranke and Mutendi followed very soon after the death of these leaders. The conflicts that ensue are usually between high-ranking officials whose positions are affected and the sons who succeed the leader. The appointment of Johane's sons directly affected the influential position of their uncle, Simon Mushati, who protested openly in these words: "The heritage of God's Word cannot be passed on to children." At council meetings his supporters quoted Joshua 1: 1 as grounds for their argument that ecclesiastic office cannot be inherited. As often happens, arbitrarily selected biblical texts, backed by the "correct" interpretation through dreams and visions, were used by the opposing parties. In the course of the dispute Mushati was accused of unlawfully laying claim to the leadership, whereupon he and a substantial number of supporters broke away to continue the "true" Apostle church of their own. The leadership of Abero and Makebo was consolidated by means of dreams and visions which accentuated the continuing control of the deceased leader. In the case of Mutendi, as in Lekhanyane's ZCC, the conflicting claims of sons, who were already in leading positions prior to his death, resulted in schisms.

In such succession crises it often happens, as in the case of Bishop David Masuka's Zion Apostolic Church, that latent tensions and leadership frustrations come to the surface. Senior office-bearers in outlying circuits, who had been largely responsible for the expansion and consolidation of the church in their home districts and therefore could lay "claim" to converts of their own, feel less bound by loyalty to the successor-son than to the founder-leader. If he has sufficient support such an office-bearer could well break away and set up his own church after the demise of the paramount leader. These schismatic leaders usually oppose the principle of hereditary leadership and insist on a ballot in the church council. It was in such circumstances that Willi Sharara and Makamba broke away, taking many congregations with them, shortly after Peresu had succeeded his late father, Bishop

172

Masuka.[18] This schism led to large-scale disintegration of Masuka's church, at that stage one of the largest Zionist churches among the Shona. Ironically, schismatic leaders who initially oppose the principle of hereditary leadership begin to insist on it the moment their own leadership of the "new church" has been entrenched.

In the Ethopian-type churches among the Shona the principle of hereditary leadership has been less rigidly applied than among the prophetic movements, probably a result of adherence to mission church practices. The supreme council of the church is supposed to appoint a successor by ballot. This is how Bishop Gavure of the First Ethiopian Church came to be appointed after the death of the founder-leader Chidembo. Gavure was the son of Chidembo's sister *(muzukuru)* and was elected on the strength of his key role in the expansion and organization of the church in 1952. On the death of Sengwayo, founder-president of the *Chibarirwe,* he was succeeded, not by his son Pauro, but by Makaya, a former member of parliament from the Bikita district. Hence the ensuing schism did not result from a struggle between the kinsmen of the deceased and office-bearers over the issue of hereditary leadership. Instead the objection was that an outsider with political status had been imported — because of Sengwayo's request before his death — to take over the leadership of a church in which he had played no role previously.

These examples should not lead to the conclusion that in the Ethiopian-type churches hereditary leadership has been consistently replaced by the principle of democratic election. The fact that Chidembo's eldest son could return after many years' absence as a migrant labourer in South Africa and lay claim to his late father's position with some measure of success in opposition to the influential Gavure is evidence of the continuing influence of deeply entrenched traditional values. Prior to his death even Gavure, despite the fact that he himself had been elected, expressed the wish that his eldest son Ishmael (at present a theological tutor in the *Fambidzano's* training programme) should succeed him as president of the FEC. In this case Ishmael's

18 Daneel, 1982(a)

173

virtually unanimous election as successor to his father was a confirmation of the deceased's wish and of hereditary leadership.

Hereditary succession affects not only the highest positions in the Independent Churches. Especially among the prophetic groups the entire leadership hierarchy is swayed by an intermingling of traditional and biblical norms. It is fairly commonly accepted that when any office-bearer who is head of a family passes away, his son inherits not only his possessions but also his church vestments and religious responsibilities, even if these pertain to a comparatively humble position in the hierarchy. If the son who is to inherit is too young and inexperienced, his religious task is reserved until a later date. However, instead of a paternal uncle acting on his behalf, as would have been customary in the traditional kinship pattern, the deceased's subordinate fellow office-bearer is promoted in the hierarchy to fill the vacancy. In effect therefore, there is a *dual succession*. Lazoro Mahere, an Apostle evangelist, had this to say in this regard:

> Joshua and I worked together as evangelists. He was my senior and therefore in charge of evangelization campaigns. When he died his firstborn son Elia received his name by sitting on a mat and being addressed as Joshua. In this way Joshua's son inherited his vestments with the monogram APE on it. This son sits among us wearing his father's vestments when we gather in the wind shields [*misasa*]. We honour him greatly, as we honoured his father. He attends the evangelists' meetings because he must still be instructed. I myself succeeded his father. When he grows up he and I will work together, just as his father and I had done. But I will be the senior even after he has grown up.

Such a dual succession to the deceased's office could culminate in co-operation, but essentially it contains the *seeds of separatism*. When the son of the deceased grows up and plays an increasingly important part in the church a power struggle often results — even schism, when he and the office-bearer who had been moved up the hierarchy both lay claim to the same position. This is a clear case of old and new norms of leadership which continue to play a part. A lack of integration of these norms contributes towards disharmony. Traditionally a son who has inherited his father's possessions also expects to benefit by the father's position in the community and in the church. Indeed, the way in which he is admitted to the ranks of the office-bearers leads to expectations of eventual succession to the office his father had once held. But there is also the junior office-bearer who is promoted on merit to the office of the deceased. Ultimately both have "legitimate" claims and a power struggle ensues. It happens quite often that conflicts of this nature are resolved by the principal leader permitting the secession of new congregations, in much the same way as a village headman allows for segmentation, that is, the formation of new villages, with the obvious retention of their tribal political allegiance in spite of the measure of autonomy afforded them.

5.5 LEADER AND OFFICE-BEARERS

5.5.1 Control over followers

As in any organization, control in the Independent Churches can pose formidable problems when expansion results in a vast following dispersed over a large geographical area. The leader is no longer able to exercise direct control as in the early days when he journeyed from village to village on proselytizing campaigns with his small, manageable following. To control his followers he has to rely increasingly on office-bearers representing outlying congregations.

Essentially the hierarchical leadership system in most Independent Churches is *autocratic*. The principal leader delegates authority to office-bearers and controls their appointment. Autocratic principles are most clearly manifested in the prophetic churches of Mutendi and Johane Maranke, where the supposed mystical powers of the principal leader enhance his authority and ensure a greater measure of direct control. More ZCC members and *vaPostori* than adherents of any other Shona church stressed the *total subjection* of office-bearers to the principal leader. To 93 percent of the ZCC members that were interviewed Mutendi's authority was absolute. The "man of God" had to be honoured in every way and his position as lawgiver was virtually "unassailable." Among the *vaPostori* only 53 percent of the respondents spoke of Johane's absolute authority. This disparity in the approach to two of the most outstanding prophetic figures among the Shona relates to the fact that during his lifetime Johane had failed to evolve as powerful a centralized base for his church as Mutendi had done. He was the itinerant prophet and preacher, more involved with expanding his church than with its organizational control. Besides, at the time of my field study he had been dead for some time, whereas Mutendi was at the height of his career, so that one could expect differing accents in the approach to their leadership.

The direct contact between the prophetic leader and his followers through faith healing and exorcism enables him to exercise greater control over the church as a whole than is possible through control over and instructions to office-bearers. Thus Mutendi made all serious "cases" from neighbouring ZCC congregations come to Zion City where he could attend to them regularly during morning prayers. He also exercised so much personal control over the communion that all his followers had to visit Zion City regularly to receive this sacrament. In this way he maintained constant prominence among his followers, which enabled him to augment, modify or neutralize as he saw fit the built-in control he exercised through the official hierarchy which he headed. By establishing something in the nature of a personality cult he could relativize the authority vested in the ranks of ZCC office-bearers.

Autocratic leadership is less strongly developed in the Ethiopian-type churches. Here too the principal leader exercises control with the aid of a hierarchical system of office-bearers, but he has less direct, intense contact with his followers than the prophetic leaders. At a congregational level he is far more dependent on his office-bearers to implement his decisions. Hence group control relies more on a balance in the play of relations between senior and junior leaders. This was borne out by the interviews that were held: 78 percent of the *Topia* Church members interviewed, 83 percent of the *Chibarirwe* and 62 percent of the African Reformed Church *(Shonganiso)* made no mention of the absolute authority of the paramount leader, but tended rather to emphasize brotherly co-operation and common belief in the leader-follower relationship.

One of the most pressing problems constantly besetting most Independent Church leaders is the ambition of junior office-bearers for more power. Sundkler maintains that South African "separatist" leaders are forever confronted with the dilemma that virtually every local preacher is an aspiring "superintendent". Unless newly appointed office-bearers are given an opportunity to extend their own influence and authority within reasonable limits the chances of frustration and schism are considerable. It is moreover all but impossible for the paramount leader to gratify the ambitions of all his office-bearers. Firstly, wholesale appointment of office-bearers very soon presents the problem of over-staffing. Secondly, the traditional tendency to appoint people to "lifelong" offices results in stagnation in the promotion of junior office-bearers. Consequently in an overcrowded leadership hierarchy juniors have to wait for the demise of seniors, the secession or dismissal of such people, or for the subdivision of congregations which creates new senior vacancies. To the principal leader, however, such subdivision entails a risk of promoting office-bearers to senior ranks before they have acquired the necessary experience or loyalty to the church. Accordingly some leaders prefer to strengthen group cohesion in existing congregations, and possibly forfeit a few office-bearers, rather than take the risk of wholesale fragmentation and subdivision of congregations. Because of these irreconcilable forces that continually beset leadership hierarchies there is a perennial fear of schism that undermines the leader's authority, compelling him to devote considerable attention to control strategies.

5.5.2 *Duties and work schedules of office-bearers*

In most Independent Churches the duties of each office are spelled out in the constitution or on the certificates issued in respect of the various offices. Thus the ZCC constitution lays down that the duties of a minister are: preaching; laying on of hands and prayer for the sick; blessing children; baptizing believers; and burying the dead. A ZCC deacon has much the same responsibilities, but is not permitted to baptize. As any church grows it arrives at consensus about the duties of its office-bearers. This process depends on the stage in the development and institutionalization of offices, nature of the central authority, size of congregations and availability of office-bearers. Usually the prevailing consensus is flexible and often deviates from the written rules. Obviously much will depend on the relationship between the principal leader and the office-bearers. Mutendi had no difficulty in introducing changes without any opposition from office-bearers. Thus he was able to appoint a chief as deacon and grant him greater powers and privileges than usually inhere in the office. In 1965 Chief Mazuru in fact helped to baptize new ZCC members immediately after his own baptism and appointment as deacon in this church. In such a case honouring a chief was put above rigid observance of the constitutionally laid down duties. Sengwayo, leader of the *Chibarirwe,* did not have the same power as Mutendi, yet he too permitted some improvization at local level to resolve problems. Thus in Chingombe leading evangelists were allowed to take the part of "minister" in a congregational context owing to a shortage of senior office-bearers. However at major church conferences such evangelists were not accorded the treatment given to ministers in deference to the ideal of properly qualified clergy.

The leader's control over the work schedules of his office-bearers depends largely on his ability to motivate his followers to upbuild and expand the church. Johane Maranke's ability to inspire people to travel around like the early Apostles resulted in large numbers of *vaPostori* devoting a large part of their lives to protracted evangelization and proselytization campaigns without any form of financial support. Bishop Mutendi also aroused his ZCC followers' enthusiasm to continue building Zion City and to undertake "missionary campaigns" several times a year so as to expand the church over an ever greater geographical area.

In 1966 I analysed the work schedule of a ZCC minister, the Revd Bracho, to form some impression of the ratio between church activity and participation in a subsistence economy. In addition to taking church services and conducting pastoral work in the Chingombe tribal area every week, he had to travel around for four to five months of the year. These absences included attendance of four church conferences at Zion City, each of which was followed by evangelization campaigns in various parts of the country and then reporting back personally to Zion City. These campaigns involved lengthy journeys, including a visit to

178

Gweru to conduct the establishment of a new congregation and baptize eight new ZCC members at Bulawayo after preaching there. He also travelled to Triangle in the Lowveld where three new members were baptized, to Buhera (four baptisms), Enkeldoorn (six baptisms) and the Mazungunye tribal area in Bikita (three baptisms). On these journeys Bracho did not concentrate purely on church expansion, but also stayed with ZCC members of outlying congregations and in this way provided an information link between church headquarters and people who were unable to attend the big conferences. The reports he brought to Zion City dealt with both the welfare of existing congregations and the addition of new converts.

If one considers that, apart from contributions from local churches towards the Revd Bracho's meals and travelling expenses, he received no stipend, and that his livelihood depended on the subsistence economy run by his wives and children at home during his absence, one cannot but regard his motivation and service to the church as remarkable. In fact, this is true of the majority of Independent Church office-bearers: *much of their lives is devoted to church activity and they receive no stipends.*

Obviously there is a close correlation between the endeavours and self-sacrificing service of individual office-bearers and the inspiration provided by the paramount leader, but there are other factors too. Often the ambition of proving their own powers, to acquire power and prestige in the community or establish their own sphere of influence are strong if unspoken motives. No matter how influential the paramount leader is, there is usually a profound conviction that the basic impulses inspiring Christian service emanate directly from God. Thus most office-bearers regard self-sacrifice and service as their own direct response to God's commission and not simply as obedience to the injunctions of their paramount leader.

5.6 "MESSIANIC" LEADERSHIP?

Following Sundkler several missiologists (G.C. Oosthuizen, M.-L-Martin and P. Beyerhaus) distinguished a third category of Independent Churches, namely messianic movements. In some respects these researchers judged such movements far more harshly than Sundkler had done, thus creating the impression that so-called "Messianism" was a *radical distortion of prophetically oriented Christianity, as a result of which the Christ of the Bible was more or less superseded.*[19] Such terms as "messianic", "nativistic", "post-Christian" and the like were bandied around, enough to make one ask whether this was in fact an accurate and fair assessment of the empirical phenomenon. In this section we shall first glance at these researchers' approach to "messianic" leadership and then consider some supplementary perspectives from the Shona churches. The importance of this whole subject is plain if one considers that the outstanding examples of so-called "Messianism" cited are in fact the most prolific movements in Africa, namely Kimbanguism in Central Africa, Lekhanyane's Zion Christian Church and Shembe's Nazarene Baptist Church in South Africa. According to the set criteria the two largest movements in Zimbabwe — those of Mutendi and Maranke — would also fall in this category.

5.6.1 *Biblical Christ or Black Messiah?*

As stated before, Sundkler originally maintained that the key question behind the fundamental distinction between Zionism and "Messianism" is: who stands at the gates of heaven — the Jesus of Scripture, or some Bantu Messiah in the person of Shembe, Lekhanyane, Khambule or Masowe?[20] Whereas Zionists would settle for Jesus Christ as Saviour, the messianic movements would opt for a Black Christ. The obvious implication is that Christ's *mediatorship,* especially in relation to life after death, is totally usurped by the Black Messiah. Sundkler categorically described Shembe as a mediator, the one who holds the key to heaven.[21] This function of the Black Messiah is *exclusive,* relating inter alia to the Zulu's reaction to the political colour bar, so that Shembe will turn Whites away from the heavenly gates and admit only his own followers. After all, the Whites will have received all their blessings in this life.[22]

19 Sundkler, 1961, p. 323
20 Ibid., p. 290f
21 Ibid., p. 291
22 Martin, 1964, p. 127

Martin also refers to the role of the Black Messiah as the "controller of the keys" to the gates of heaven, who will admit only his own followers to Paradise.[23] She points out the connection between the former monarchy of the Zulu and the Black Christ ideology. Just as the Zulu king had traditionally acted as *mediator* between his people and God, so the Black Christ has become the mediator effecting the salvation of his people. One of the most powerful reasons for this development is the Black man's great longing for a concrete revelation *here and now,* a visible God who will be his own.[24] The result is that such leaders as Shembe and Lekhanyane are elevated as "kings" in their colonies, mediators in their own new Jerusalem, and that Jesus Christ as head of the church fades into the background.[25]

Apart from the mediator's role, other facets of Christology are at issue. Oosthuizen claims that in nativistic movements (which include Zionist and messianic movements) the *authority* and *kingship* of Jesus are denied by a one-sided emphasis on man's personal powers.[26] Man gains control of God and God is seen as the personification of human needs. The traditional accent on magic and obtaining enhanced vital force is very much in evidence. This makes it possible to control and monopolize Christ's authority.[27] In Oosthuizen's view such a pragmatic, magically oriented religion leaves little scope for self-negation for Christ's sake. Ultimately it boils down to a selfish morality which seeks greater vital force for the self and one's community.

Martin in particular stresses the usurpation of the *cross of Christ* in Messianism.[28] She traces this trend to the traditional magical approach which focuses on the realization of God's kingdom here and now, the successful miracles of the Black Messiah and deliverance from forces that endanger the vital force, so that religion becomes a matter of faith healing and the satisfaction of material needs instead of the biblical concept of redemp-

23 Ibid., pp. 125-127
24 Ibid., pp. 165-166
25 Oosthuizen, 1968(a), p. 101
26 Ibid., p. 89
27 Ibid., p. 103
28 Martin, 1964, p. 158

tion. Thus, in keeping with his followers' expectations, the messianic leader wants a *theologia gloriae* at the expense of a theologia *crucis*,[29] but the Black Messiah is a *Messiah without a cross*,[30] a false Christ who cannot effect reconciliation in respect of the curse invoked by man's rebellion against God. To substantiate the messianic evasion of the cross, Martin cites the Zulu minister who stated that these sects are South Africa's attempt at evading the cross.

Like Martin, Beyerhaus points out that the cross is rejected, not only because of the Western foreignness of the gospel, but because of the negative response to the proclamation of the Christian message of salvation. In his inaugural lecture at Tuebingen Beyerhaus put some searching questions to the messianic movements: Has the cross of Christ become a stumbling-block because of the self-glorification and self-deification of the Messiah figure? Is this not essentially a case of irritation in natural religion caused by the *theologia crucis*?[31] If Oosthuizen is right in contending that the gospel's summons to a new life is transformed into a summons to a *force vital,* then one cannot but answer Beyerhaus's questions affirmatively, and one would have to concede Oosthuizen's point that there is no question of a true theology of the cross.[32]

Among the above observers there is in the final analysis no doubt as to the *total usurpation* of the evangelical Christ by the Black Messiah. Sundkler quotes some hymns from Shembe's hymnal to demonstrate the absence of *Jesu Krestu.* Hymn number 154 reads:

> I believe in the Father
> and in the Holy Spirit
> and in the communion of saints
> of the Nazarenes.

From this Sundkler concludes that the doctrine and life of Shembe's followers had no room for Jesus Christ.[33] As Jesus had

29 Ibid., p. 160
30 Ibid., p. 160
31 Beyerhaus, 1967, p. 516
32 Oosthuizen, 1967(a), p. 89
33 Sundkler, 1961, pp. 283-284

once effected salvation for the Jews, so Shembe will effect it for the Zulu. Beyerhaus is more generally condemnatory. He finds little in either Zionism or Messianism that has anything to do with "authentic" Christianity. Christ becomes purely pseudonym for the messianic leader. He writes: "This complete substitution is especially notorious in the messianic movements."[34] The entire Christian concept of God is unrecognizable, Christ is ousted, the Holy Spirit is usurped by traditional spirit manifestations and God the Father is equated with the traditional deity.[35]

The usurpation of Christ's place is accompanied by two parallel developments: the *deification of the Black Messiah,* and the *replacement of Scripture* with other norms. With reference to the first of these trends, Sundkler cites Shembe's omnipresence, his work of creation along with God the Father, and his identification with *uMvelingqangi,* the traditional Zulu deity.[36] Some of his disciples in fact refer to him unquestioningly as God himself. That this is not an inevitable development is clear from Martin's reference to Edward Lekhanyane's explicit denial of any claims to Messiahship or deification. Nonetheless she believes that some of his followers regard him as God and Saviour. One observes, however, that she does not quote statements of ZCC members to substantiate this qualification, but cites the views of members of other churches.[37] Beyerhaus is less cautious and states categorically that the Black Messiah is pretentious in encouraging his own glorification and deification among his followers and in the process becomes a beguiling threat to Christians from the traditional churches.[38] Because of this messianic distortion Beyerhaus believes that to members of these movements the God of the Bible is no more than an "unknown God".[39] Oosthuizen, again, claims that the deification of the prophetic leader is not purely a reaction against the "White Christ" of the White man, but also an attempt to keep in touch with the traditional concept of the

---

34 Beyerhaus, 1969, pp. 74-75
35 Beyerhaus, 1969, pp. 74-75; Beyerhaus, 1967, pp. 503-504
36 Sundkler, 1961, pp. 283-286
37 Martin, 1964, p. 131
38 Beyerhaus, 1969, p. 78
39 Ibid., p. 79

supernatural. This is why the preaching of the Black Messiah consists in a subjection of the old supernatural forces.[40] Here we touch the very nerve of Oosthuizen's approach, namely that the African Zionist and messianic movements are a radical, syncretist transformation of Christianity into the traditional religion which gives the ancient forces and ancestral spirits crucial significance.

Evidently there is no doubt about the *elimination of God's Word* either. Oosthuizen writes with almost monotonous regularity that in the ZCC the Bible has lost its value;[41] that in "nativistic" groups the traditional religion, not Scripture, forms the basis;[42] that both the Bible and Jesus Christ are pushed into the background.[43] The word of the prophet "Messiah" takes the place of the Bible because this satisfies the Black man's desire for a concrete revelation. The prophet's sole authority is his own inspiration.[44] In the same vein Martin and Beyerhaus respectively refer to the Bible as a pushed aside[45] and a closed[46] book in Black Messianism, so that the traditional cultural heritage becomes the norm for biblical interpretation. Beyerhaus generalizes when he discerns in Zionism, and by implication in Messianism as well, a syncretism which still makes use of Christian terminology but sacrifices *all* the biblical concepts underlying these terms and replaces them with pagan ones.[47] If all these statements were true and the movements of Shembe, Lekhanyane, Kimbangu and similar Zionist groups offered no more than a distorted or degenerate Christology, a denial of the cross, a deified Black Messiah and a vanished or radically modified gospel, then one would have to agree with Beyerhaus and Oosthuizen that one could not but call them a "post-Christian" phenomenon.

40 Oosthuizen, 1968(a), p. 78
41 Ibid., p. 37
42 Ibid., p. 73
43 Ibid., p. 91
44 Ibid., pp. 126-127
45 Martin, 1964, p. 158
46 Beyerhaus, 1969, p. 79
47 Ibid., p. 75

5.6.2 *Radical criticism and a changing approach*

The initial evaluation of messianic leadership by all these observers is radical and largely condemnatory. Sundkler speaks of
a return of pagandom. The syncretistic sect, he writes, "becomes
the bridge over which Africans are brought back to heathenism
— a viewpoint which stresses the seriousness of the whole situation". [48]

Martin maintains that there is *no genuine conversion* in the
messianic movements.[49] In a syncretistic degeneration one is
dealing with "African Christianity" and not with Christ.

> This *African Christianity and African Christ* are utterly
> opposed to the *revelation of the unique Messiah, Jesus of
> David's house,* who is the Saviour *of all races and na-
> tions* . . . [50]

Oosthuizen and Beyerhaus in particular pursue a line of consistently negative criticism which ultimately amounts to a verdict
that there can be *no return to true Christianity* from Messianism.
The absence of the church of Christ is described with utter conviction:

> Christian sects have often developed into churches, but
> where nativism is basic this will not happen because contact
> has been lost with the Word and with Christ's work on the
> Cross.[51]

Beyerhaus mentions an explicit, existential contradiction *(Widerspruch)* of the gospel message in Messianism,[52] and a concomitant
self-deception whereby the Zionists fail to realize that their concept of God bears no relation to the holy, mighty God.[53]

48 Sundkler, 1961, p. 297
49 Martin, 1964, p. 162
50 Ibid., p. 163
51 Oosthuizen, 1968(a), p. 96
52 Beyerhaus, 1967, p. 510
53 Beyerhaus, 1969, p. 75

When one examines the method of these theologians one gets the impression that they set about their work in terms of Western categories and that the ideal of a logically consistent line of thought and the construction of a coherent system in describing "Messianism" had stood in the way of balanced reflection on a multifaceted phenomenon. Certain trends which the researcher had either observed personally or which had been mentioned by other observers are constantly isolated and then generalized or even absolutized in a practical application which lacks logical, convincing proof that these trends in fact apply to the religious group as a whole.

When Martin quotes statements by Black leaders from mission churches to substantiate her view that the Independent Churches evade the cross or that Lekhayane is invoked as God himself in prayer, one at once wonders whether she has ever really studied this movement. Anyone who is familiar with the relations between 'historic' churches and Independent Churches is aware of conflicts and jealousies bred by their polarized group loyalties. Hence one cannot expect an objective view if it is based on statements made by antagonistic members of rival groups. Anyone who knows the ZCC at all well will know that Lekhanyane is *not* addressed as God himself, but that the introduction to most ZCC prayers usually address "the God of Lekhanyane".

Oosthuizen's approach creates the impression that data from the literature were selected in such a way as to overaccentuate negative aspects at the expense of positive ones, resulting in a caricature so as to substantiate a preconceived characterization of prophetic and messianic movements as "post-Christian". Any Western Christian who keeps in close touch with the Independent Churches and observes and experiences their weaknesses as well as their truly Christian attributes should appreciate that one cannot speak of a total degeneration.

My implicit objection to the work of these researchers is therefore that the empirical basis in no way justifies this harshly condemnatory criticism. Beyerhaus's emphasis on Christology is important, but he does not provide sufficient evidence for his categorical rejection of Zionist customs as unchristian and a mere return to traditional religion. One's impression of this method is that what is being theologically evaluated is a caricature rather than the empirical facts. We shall return to this in our concluding chapter.

The theological importance of empirical studies is borne out inter alia by the changed approaches of Sundkler and Martin after many years of continued contact and involvement with the initially much criticized "messianic" groups. Practical experience led both these researchers to alter their views quite distinctly. Sundkler probably realized that his initial categories in his first study, *Bantu Prophets,* had helped to induce radical and one-sided views among certain authors. At all events, he gives a very different appraisal of "Messianism" in his subsequent study, *Zulu Zion and some Swazi Zionists,* published in 1976. Here he objects to the way in which Oosthuizen categorically defines Shembe as a Messiah on the basis of his hymns.[54] At bottom Shembe's followers had nevertheless maintained a fundamental distinction between God and his Zulu servant Isaiah Shembe.[55] He acknowledges that it was misleading to regard "nativistic Zionism" as a bridge leading the Black man back to his traditional religion. Zion was far rather a bridge to the future.

> To those in the movement, Zion meant newness of life, health and wholeness, a new identity. If it was a bridge, it appeared to them a bridge to the future.[56]

Now it is Sundkler's turn to warn against the misconceptions to which the term "Messiah" can give rise. He admits that his initial deductions from the information about Shembe had been too Western and dogmatic,[57] and suggests that the term *iconic leadership* might be more appropriate than "Messianism". The biblical conception of Christ as *EIKOON TOU THEOU* (image of God) suggests a reflection: to his followers the ironic leader is a reflection and concretization of Christ without necessarily usurping Christ's place.[58] One observes a totally changed state of mind

54 Sundkler, 1976, p. 190f
55 Ibid., p. 196
56 Ibid., p. 305
57 Ibid., p. 309
58 Ibid., pp. 193, 310

when Sundkler comes to the following conclusion about Shembe and Khambule, both of whom he had previously classified as Messiah figures:

> There is *no* conscious attempt to minimize the revelation of Jesus. Sermons and testimonies underline that Jesus is the Ultimate Authority and Final Judge.[59]

Martin's changed approach is even more dramatic. Whereas in her dissertation she was negative and rejected Kimbanguism,[60] as we have shown, her field study and personal participation in the movement led her to totally new insights. She admits the limitations of her original approach which had been based mainly on a study of documentary sources,[61] and in an enthusiastic first article she claims that the Kimbanguist movement is a truly Christian church representing the complete Christian life as portrayed in the gospel according to Luke.[62] Now she rejects the charge that Kimbangu as "Messiah" replaced the biblical Christ and asserts that through this leader Jesus Christ has for the first time acquired existential reality for the Congolese.[63] Kimbangu is held up as an outstanding example of Christian discipleship, rejecting ancestor worship and leading people to Christ.

> Simon leads them to Christ (he is the instrument of Christ) and is not a new Messiah, not the Saviour, but the chosen servant through whom Christ has revealed himself to the Africans.[64]

These shifts in emphasis in the work of Sundkler and Martin mark a new theological evaluation of what had originally been branded "Black Messianism" — one which portrays these movements as a legitimate, contextually effective, christianizing process, and does not merely for the umpteenth time point out their syncretism or unchristian degeneracy.

59 Ibid., p. 310
60 Martin, 1964, p. 163
61 Martin, 1975, pp. vii-xi
62 Martin, 1968, p. 12
63 Ibid., p. 10
64 Martin, 1975, p. 146

5.6.3 Reinterpretation of the "mediatorship" of the Black Messiah

Among Shona Independent Churches the ones that would pre-eminently qualify as "messianic" according to the original classification of Sundkler and Martin are Mutendi's ZCC and Johane Maranke's *vaPostori*. Like Shembe and Lekhanyane, both Mutendi and Maranke were credited with a *mediatory function at the gates of heaven,* which at once raises Christological questions. If one moreover considers that both leaders played a dominant part in the preaching and thinking of their followers, this would be sufficient for the casual observer to start yet again applying such labels as "messianic", "syncretistic distortion" and the concomitant usurpation of the role of Christ. But what is actually real and alive in the minds of these Shona Zionists and Apostles? I shall cite just a few of the cardinal points that have some bearing on Christology.

There is no doubt that *Christ's mediatorship* is sometimes misconstrued in the Shona Churches, or that it might function only partially in the religious experience of individuals. Mutendi's pervasive influence during his lifetime meant that some of his followers had only a hazy notion of the exclusive nature of Christ's work of salvation. Mutendi was certainly a sort of "mediator" to some people because of his mystical powers by which he controlled all faith-healing activities in his church. *He* was the emissary, the "man of God" in the City of Zion, who listened to the problems of his followers and was expected to convey all these problems to God in heaven. That this exceptional role of Mutendi's could cause misconceptions about the accessibility of God can be seen from the following comment by a ZCC deacon, Ammon Norumedzo:

> Mutendi is the one who speaks directly to Mwari. We do not address *Mwari Wokudenga* [the God of heaven] directly, but we speak to the God of Lekhanyane and Mutendi. Minor problems are resolved by us, the office-bearers, without referring them to God. The big problems we bring here to Moriah and our leader then presents them to God. We cannot ourselves raise matters to heaven.

In his attempt to define Mutendi's mediation Norumedzo went so far as to distinguish between the accessible God of the Zionists, the One of Lekhanyane and Mutendi who is always mentioned in Zionist prayers, and the more remote God of the heaven. Here one can discern the traditional concept of a Supreme Being who has only indirect dealings with individuals. To Norumedzo, Mutendi in a sense takes the part of a chief, who will in any event after his death be a great ancestral spirit and act as mediator between God and his living descendants.

However, this example is *not* representative of the views of all ZCC members and in no way proves an absolute usurpation of the mediatorship of Christ. To many Mutendi is no more than an emissary or messenger of God who teaches and guides them and *intercedes* for his people.

But what about Mutendi's function at the gates of heaven? The Revd Matevure's viewpoint is representative of the prevailing belief among the ZCC during Mutendi's lifetime:

> When judgment comes Mutendi will stand at the gates of heaven and point out to God all those who had been his followers here on earth. This will happen *before* the actual judgment.

Countless interviews on this matter with ZCC clergy and lay members revealed that this was certainly not regarded as an *exclusive function* fulfilled by Mutendi, in the sense that it would ensure access to heaven for ZCC members only or replace the mediatorship of Christ. Only a very few people believed that Mutendi would as it were pass judgment with Christ on the last day. In this regard the distinction between Mutendi and Christ was usually maintained and there was no mention of a Black Messiah or a Black Christ. The standard responses to the question of Mutendi's relationship to Christ went something like this:

— Mutendi is *like* Jesus but cannot take his place. Mutendi is our 'foreman', but Jesus is above him.
— To us Mutendi is like the Pope is to the Catholics and the Revd Louw (pioneer missionary to Mashonaland) to the DR Church. He is subordinate to Jesus but in him we see the likeness of Jesus.

— We venerate Mutendi because he is *like* Jesus, but he himself warns us *not* to compare him to Christ.

In strict theological terms there is some misconstruction among the Zionists. There are *no* biblical grounds for the leader's function at the gates of heaven, which implies some measure of mediatorship to some people. Yet there is adequate proof that the Bible remains focal in these movements and acts as a powerful corrective. Mutendi himself continually warned against any form of deification and never questioned the Trinity of the God he proclaimed. Neither he nor his followers interpreted his leadership as a form of "Black Messiahship". Hence his function at the heavenly gates must not be seen as an attempt to supersede the biblical Christ. Far rather it must be regarded as a *projection of a common social usage onto the unknowable realm of life after death, namely the custom that an ordinary man must never approach an eminent person except through the agency of an officially sanctioned intermediary.*

Thus it is an attempt to conceive of the confessed but unknown reality in terms of traditionally oriented images. Mutendi was sent by God. It follows that, to a mentality that is not fundamentally versed in Western theology, Mutendi would be the one who would eventually present them to the "Great One". *Mutendi's role at the gates of heaven is therefore largely that of introducing his people, which in no way inteferes with exclusiveness of Christ's mediatorship or the judgement of God.* The important distinction is that his role as intermediary at the heavenly gates does *not* imply automatic access to heaven for his followers. Zionists are universally agreed that the final judgment of acceptance or condemnation rests with God, and that the deciding factor is not membership of the church, but the individual's faith and life in direct relationship with God.

Viewed thus the charismatic leader's function as "custodian of the gate" is far too *scanty a basis* for Sundkler's original definition of Black Messianism. At most one could speak of *messianic tendencies.* The term "iconic leadership" is far more appropriate. The above quotations also indicate that, in the case of Mutendi, the leader is seen as an image or reflection of Christ.

Another important point is that the function of "custodian of the gate" is far more widespread in the Shona Independent

Churches than one would be inclined to expect. Even among the less prominent Zionist leaders it is fairly widely accepted that the leader will be awaiting his followers at the heavenly gates. Bishop Forridge, who ministers to a handful of small congregations only, was firmly persuaded that every church leader, no matter who he is, is in duty bound to appear at the gates of heaven after his death and there await his followers. This belief in no way undermined Forridge's preaching, which was highly Christ-centred, and required personal faith in the biblical Christ as a qualification for conversion and baptism. Hence among the Shona churches Sundkler's question ("Who stands at the gates of heaven?") cannot serve as a criterion for messianic classification.

In the case of prominent prophetic leaders there is a real danger that in the period after their death there may be some degree of *deification*. Counter to Beyerhaus's contention that the so-called "Black Messiah" encouraged such deification, both Mutendi and Johane warned their followers against it. Yet among some *vaPostori* there were signs in the period following Johane's death of an extra dimension being added to his leadership. He was regarded as omniscient, at least as far as events in his church were concerned, and it was believed that he continued to control his church by means of dreams.

One extreme case, the Apostle evangelist Amos Haire, said:

> On the day of judgement Johane will put me in heaven. You people of the Reformed and Catholic churches will be judged by Moses. Those who were taught by John and Jesus will be placed in heaven by John. But we Blacks are represented by Johane.

Here Johane's function as mediator in the hereafter goes beyond that of performing an introduction. Christ's work of salvation is obscured, if not totally eclipsed, by Johane's role. To the Black man the leader is equal, not subordinate, to Christ. But this view is *not representative of the vaPostori movement* as a whole, nor does it represent the interpretation of an existing doctrine. What it in fact indicates is a mentality which is more flagrantly nationalistic, militant and anti-White than that of the Zionist groups. The *vaPostori* consistently proclaimed that the Whites' period of grace has expired because they killed Jesus and suppressed the biblical message of the Holy Spirit. The time has come for Africa to be blessed. The oppressed house of Ham has been called to continue the task of Jesus Christ. The banner which the descendants of Shem and Japheth had trampled underfoot, has been seized upon by Johane who now marches triumphantly at the head of the once oppressed race, the house of Ham.

In this case one could speak of a nationalistically inspired, partial deification, but a more representative trend may be seen in statements such as those of the Apostle office-bearers Onias Muchinge and Muteiwa. The former averred: "Johane is not the Christ of the Blacks, but a messenger who taught the Black man much about God's Word." The latter believed that Johane did not have the power to initiate his followers into heaven: "Johane gives his people to Jesus and in that sense he is a mediator. But he himself will also be judged by God according to his sins." Thus by and large a fairly balanced view on the relationship between the prophetic leader and Jesus Christ is typical. Of course, this does not mean that doctrinal patterns concerning the biblical Christ have stabilized in these churches. Owing to dynamic processes which may be engendered by political pressure or group conflict there is always a possibility of change, either towards degeneracy or towards spiritual enrichment. This calls for caution in any theological evaluation and also for an on-going evaluation.

How does the leadership of a figure like Mutendi or Maranke affect the *kingship* and *authority* of Christ? Is it true that Christ's authority, kingship and cross are rejected through a "selfish morality" which manipulates Christ? Once again we must acknowledge that there is no question of a properly worked out Christology. Nonetheless it is remarkable that Mutendi in particular should frequently have spoken of the authority of the healing Christ and his redemptive power over evil spirits. It was Mutendi too who thrice every year after the "Easter festivals" in Zion City mobilized his church in a country-wide missionary drive *in explicit recognition of the kingship of Christ*. This acknowledgment was always expressed in his sermons on Christ's classical missionary mandate as recorded in Matthew 28: 19.[65] His vision of conversion and church growth was based on this. Undoubtedly there was some misinterpretation in Zionist ranks. Involuntarily

65 Daneel, 1980

some of them must have identified the expansion of God's kingdom with that of a Black Zion. But there are innumerable similar examples of such a narrow interpretation of God's kingdom in church history, as if its frontiers coincided with those of a particular denomination. And who can judge whether those Zionists who spend several months each year doing pastoral and evangelical work in strange villages are motivated by purely pragmatic or selfish considerations?

A study of the preaching during Zionist campaigns revealed that although Mutendi occupied a key position, he was never held up as a Black Messiah with exclusive mediatory or redemptive powers exercised on behalf of his followers. On the contrary: he was always held up as a remarkable example of Christian discipleship.[66] The central theme of the sermons of the Revd Ezekiah (whom I accompanied on his campaigns) were: Mutendi as "messenger of God", the work of the Holy Spirit as manifested in prophecy and faith healing, the kingdom of God, the coming judgment and the need for repentance.[67] Under all these themes he constantly referred to the life and work of Christ.

As for the Trinity, Ezekiah's sermons shared a general trend in the Independent Churches — that of referring more readily to God the Father than to the Son. Mwari, the Father, is easily conceived of as Judge, Protector and Law-giver. In terms of the traditional kinship structure, Jesus the Son occupies a subordinate position. Along with God the Father the other consistent focal point is the work of the Holy Spirit. But this does not mean that Christ's ministry is completely pushed into the background. Indeed, the work of the Holy Spirit presupposes acknowledgment of the ministry of Jesus as Mediator and Saviour. *In my view one must therefore concede that there is an imperfect or unobtrusive but at the same time a presupposed Christology which in no way denies either Christ or his cross.* This idea of a presupposed Christology accords with Sundkler's concept of "iconic leadership". After all, the ministry of Mutendi, Johane and other prophetic leaders was designed to translate and interpret the work of Christ in concrete terms to render it intelligible in their own indigenous

66 Ibid., p. 111
67 Ibid., pp. 110-116

context. Such concepts as "presupposed Christology" or even "contextualized Christology" certainly do not imply completeness or even absolute correctness, but they are far truer to the empirical facts than the aforementioned verdicts which are more like one-sided theological projections — to make an all but incomprehensibly vast phenomenon theologically manageable and manipulable — rather than attempts to do justice to the facts.

5.7 LEADERSHIP, SCHISMS AND ECUMENICAL CO-OPERATION

There is a vital connection between leadership in the Independent Churches and the ever continuing process of schism and fragmentation. The ordinary human aspiration to power, recognition and status results in constant leadership conflicts, a basic cause of schism or the defection of individuals. Virtually all Independent Church leaders who lose members as a result of this process refer to the inability of their *vaduku* (juniors, i.e. junior office-bearers) to assume authority and their ambition to exercise greater authority. The schismatic leaders for their part tend to conceal their deeper motives and cite doctrinal differences or the faults of their paramount leaders to justify their launching of a new church.

5.7.1 *Causal factors*

Leadership conflicts in the Independent Churches are caused by both external and internal factors. *External* causes include the influence of Western culture which stimulated leadership on the basis of ability or education, but at the same time limited the scope for exercising leadership within the colonial framework. Thus this relates to the sort of *socio-political* situation which Sundkler and Balandier have mentioned as a cause for the establishment of Independent Churches.[68] The tribal political system with its accent on hereditary leadership and limited jurisdiction moreover provides insufficient scope for leadership over a broad

68 Daneel, 1974, p. 7f

spectrum. The Independent Churches with their multifarious and differentiated leadership hierarchies to a large extent provide an outlet for frustrated individuals who are reacting against these circumstances. This explains the attractiveness of the Independent Churches with their heavy concentration of office-bearers, but also generates *internal* factors within the church structure which are conducive to schism.

Among the internal factors one can distinguish between theological and non-theological causes.

Theological causes: The *diversity of Western denominations* has meant that Africans were confronted with a bewildering multitude of divided churches from the outset. They associated these churches with nations and concluded that if it is possible to have an "English", a "German", a "Dutch" or a 'Swedish' church, then a Black church for Africa was also justified. The importation of a divided church created the impression that everyone was entitled to interpret the Bible in his own way without a definitive tie with some doctrine or tradition. As Martin points out, Protestant theology did not in every respect lay a firm theological foundation for the doctrine of the church as the one body of Christ on earth, a body which transcends the bounds of tribe, race or nation.[69] This created an atmosphere which promoted rather than counteracted further division of churches. Besides, owing to their lack of, or at most very elementary theological training, many of the clergy of the Independent Churches possess a *very sketchy concept of ecclesiology.* Thus to many Shona Independent Church members the church is primarily an association of people who "belong" to some leader. Hence the formation of a new church or switching from one church to another is often not seen as a retrogressive step, detrimental to the body of Christ, but as progress, an improvement on the previous church's rules and therefore something that has God's blessing.

A third point to remember is that most Independent Churches have only a hazy perspective on the development of Christianity since the days of Christ. Not surprisingly, therefore, they distinguish between churches as groups who either approve or con-

69 Martin, 1964, p. 166

demn the use of alcohol, who pray with their eyes open or shut, who "have" or "do not have" the Holy Spirit, and so on. This focus on *external attributes* and the *rules of churches* has contributed to the fact that the formation of new churches is seen as a perfectly legitimate institution of a new set of rules by another leader. Apart from deeply rooted factors such as leadership ambition, divergent personalities and the like, the Independent Churches themselves define and experience schisms in terms of doctrinal differences — about the day of rest, use of alcohol, polygamy, etc.

Another highly significant theological facet is the *process of individualization*. Protestantism has always insisted on individual decision, both in conversion and when distinguishing between good and evil. Although theologically correct, this emphasis has sometimes been misconstrued in the process of acculturation, resulting in some undermining of religious authority. The fact that it is the individual's right and duty to decide for himself on the grounds of the biblical data was sufficient cause for some members of Independent Churches to drastically question both the codes of their respective churches and their application. Thus although the Independent Church leaders introduced Christian values in lieu of the traditional codes in their churches, the new message in fact bred a critical attitude which could easily result in schism. Within the context of the church as a new sort of "tribe" there was a far stronger tendency towards individual thought and action than in the ancient tribal context.

Non-theological causes: However important the theological causes for schism and individual defection may be, non-theological influences remain crucial. Far more important than the diversity of Western denominations and an inadequate ecclesiology is the influence of traditional community life on the people's conceptualization of the church. The continual fragmentation of churches reflects a characteristic typical of indigenous tribal structures, which amounts to a grafting of traditional customs onto the church. In the same way that a kinship group will break away and set up on its own on the death of the patriarch of an extended family, a bishop or senior office-bearer may defect with a number of followers after the death of a church leader. Just as an overriding bond of kinship between the different groups continues to exist in the traditional family context, so one finds in the Independent Churches that, despite their autonomy, schismatic groups retain their links with the "family of churches".

The traditional custom of *subdividing villages* after the death of a headman or when numbers grow too great is also transferred to the church. Village subdivision always occurred in the context of a *dunhu* (ward, subdivided tribal territory). To the Black man the *dunhu* with its chief and component villages has the connotation of "home". Hence village subdivision was an acknowledged custom within the overall context of "home" to permit the solution of village conflicts and divide authority in an ever changing situation in a way that would not harm the stability of the community as a whole.

By applying this practice to the church (i.e. subdividing congregations and circuits when promotion of office-bearers is restricted through excessive demand for clerical posts and other problems), Independent Church leaders were able to solve internal problems by redistributing authority. In this regard Bishop Gavure of the First Ethiopian Church said: "When one of our congregations grows too large and the clergy are at loggerheads, we divide the congregation. It always works. In this respect we are like village headmen who subdivide their villages."

However, this practice is not always a real solution to internal strife because it is not always sufficiently associated with the biblical concept of reconciliation. The bishop does not always manage to keep the subdivided congregations within the denomination in the same way that the *dunhu* chief kept the divided village within the boundaries of his territory. As a result the traditional pattern of village subdivision has a twofold effect on the Independent Churches. On the positive side it offers a tactful leader an opportunity to resolve conflicts in his church's ranks, sometimes in the face of imminent schism. On the negative side this custom is perverted by schismatic leaders to justify breaking their ties with their former church.

Nonetheless it is remarkable that even in cases of radical defection the traditional concept of continued involvement with the broader family group — like the newly established village that remains part of the *dunhu* — always resurfaces in interchurch relations. There were numerous schisms in Bishop Masuka's Zion Apostolic Church, leading to the establishment of such churches as Mutema's Zion Sabbath Church, Zacheo's Zion Protestant Church, Mtisi's Zion City, Kuudzerema's Zion Apostolic Church of Jesus Christ and Komboni's African Zion Church of Jesus.[70] Each of these churches is fully autonomous with its own headquarters and internal organization, yet the various leaders still feel kinship with Masuka, call him "father", sometimes send him contributions and attend major church festivals at his headquarters. At large conferences Zionist solidarity is accentuated to the extent that there is little sign of the background of friction and schism.

A major internal cause of schism is the combination of well-nigh incompatible norms of leadership — both biblical and traditional — with no clear policy for deciding claims to leadership. This is manifest in the appointment of office-bearers, the way they are promoted in the leadership hierarchy and the inheritance of leadership.

The aforementioned prominence of the kinship structure in the *appointment of office-bearers*[71] can be traced back to the nature of church expansion, manifested particularly in the baptism of kinship groups. The decision of the head of the clan is final, regardless of the beliefs of his family. Consequently kinsmen are baptized and posts are created for them without their necessarily possessing the leadership talent or spiritual maturity for these tasks. In this way the importance of the kinship structure in fact obscures the biblical norms for church leadership, and relatives of local leaders are appointed to key positions without necessarily possessing sufficient knowledge of the Bible or proper knowledge of the character of the Christian church. Naturally to such office-bearers schism would mean exactly the same as subdivision of a village, and they will not have many scruples about accepting it, or even causing it if they deem it necessary.

As for the *way office-bearers are promoted,* here too there is a built-in potential for conflict caused by the heavy concentration of kinsmen in the leadership hierarchies. Just as key figures in the traditional order have certain lifelong religious duties, so there is a tendency to appoint office-bearers for the whole of their lives. This inhibits promotion on grounds of spiritual matur-

70 Daneel, 1971(a), p. 300
71 **Infra,** p. 155f

ity, experience and service in the church. Sometimes junior officials have to wait for their seniors in the hierarchy to die before they can be promoted. To be sure, the frustration caused by this kind of delay may be resolved by splitting congregations and creating new offices, but often the frustrated office-bearer will simply defect and join another church or set up his own.

As explained earlier, the succession of a deceased paramount leader by an eldest son who *inherits the leadership* of the church is a major cause of schism.[72] Hereditary leadership, as we have said, is the Achilles heel of the Independent Churches. In virtually all the larger churches the death of the paramount leader triggers off a major crisis and leads to schism.[73] What usually happens is that senior clergy in outlying circuits who have done much to expand the church lay direct claim to their "own" congregations. They experience the leadership of the deceased leader's son as a type of meddling and contest his religious authority. This was what happened when Willi Sharara and Makamba broke away from David Masuka's Zion Apostolic Church during the transfer of the leadership to Masuka's son Peresu,[74] and when the prophet Simon Mushati publicly contested the succession procedure following Johane Maranke's death.[75] Ironically, the same schismatic leaders who initially quarrelled with hereditary leadership, expect their own sons to succeed them after their death. Thus the rejection of the principle of hereditary leadership in one phase does not necessarily provide a permanent solution to the inherent problems.

We have also referred to the *dual succession* that occurs when office-bearers die[76] — that is, the inheritance of the deceased's position by his son and the simultaneous promotion of a junior office-bearer to that same post. The fact that this practice is based on a combination of traditional and biblical norms, thus placing two parties in a conflict situation, largely explains the constant defection of individual office-bearers. As long as the son and heir can gain the support of his co-religionists in his claims to the

72 **Infra**, p. 169f
73 Daneel, 1982(b)
74 Daneel, 1971(a), p. 302f
75 Ibid., p. 331f
76 **Infra**, p. 174

religious authority of his late father in the church hierarchy, and as long as this custom is not resolutely replaced with biblical norms, the unity of Independent Churches will remain vulnerable and schisms will continue.

5.7.2   *The process of schism*

Sundkler analyses the "dynamics of fission" in three phases:

(a)   the first schism, that is defection from a mission or Independent Church;

(b)   integration of the new church, marked by a sort of centripetal rigidity and even social isolation in order to consolidate the main group; and

(c)   fresh crisis and renewed schism.[77]

Sundkler admits that this is an oversimplification of an often highly complex process. Thus the third phase is not always a *terminus ad quem,* but could be a transition to fresh possibilities.[78]

With reference to the initial schism, Sundkler distinguishes between conscious and unconscious preparation for schism. The latter refers to background factors such as the aforementioned Western denominationalism and traditional division of villages which creates a climate that is conducive to schism. Conscious preparation is when this climate is exploited by a schismatic leader who teaches a faction in the church according to his beliefs and then confronts them with a radical alternative. This crisis results in schism and the construction of a new organization for the defecting faction.

To the new church the period of integration and growth (Sundkler's second phase) is one of conscious moulding according to a preconceived type. The schismatic leader exercises control with

77 Sundkler, 1961, p. 170
78 Ibid., p. 170

growing rigidity and radicalism. His conformist followers respond by imitating his actions, whereas those who do not agree with his actions break away to form yet another group or return to their original church. After a while the leader becomes more moderate because his initial radicalism now proves to be disruptive and if unmodified could lead to loss of membership.

In the fresh crisis and renewed schism of phase three the background factors remain the same, but the rationalization introduced by the new leader demands either even greater radicalism or a "return to the old ways". Sundkler maintains that this is usually the phase of decline, stagnation and indifference.[79]

Sundkler's three-phase model is particularly important to understand classical schisms, that is, when the new church is born from a defecting segment of the original church. But the model fails to explain the process of schism in every respect.

Thus the three pioneers of Zionism in Zimbabwe were not in a position to organize schism from a mission or some other church. Bishop Masuka never belonged to a mission church prior to joining Zionism. Bishop Mutendi and Andreas Shoko were originally DR members, but they defected (1) as migrant labourers, so that they were relatively isolated from their church at the time; (2) as individuals, without initiating substantial numbers of co-religionists into their new movements; and (3) as people impressed by the indigenized customs of Black churches and therefore only indirectly reacting to their own mission church backgrounds.

Hence the growth of the Shona Zionist movement was marked by a gradual increase in numbers drawn from various religious backgrounds in response to the missionary activities launched by the Zionists. The same pattern may be seen in the continuing process of schisms and regrouping. Classical schisms do occur, but then mainly in the succession crisis following the death of a principal leader, as explained earlier.

In view of the profound influence of traditional custom on Independent Church leadership it is understandable that the dominant feature of the fragmentation process would be the *change in congregations through defecting office-bearers* — call it a "fluidity of leadership". In an attempt to secure more in-

79 Ibid., p. 177

fluence or render a more effective service some clergy continue to "roam" from church to church, or even make successive attempts to establish new churches. Bishop Hazael Mudyanadzo's story is no exception:

> After leaving the mission church in 1932 I became a Zionist by joining the Church of Pilate. Their law did not permit beer drinking, so I defected and joined Makamba's [Zionist] church which permitted the drinking of sweet [unfermented] beer. After a short while I left and became a member of Kuudzerema's [Zionist] church. By this time I realized that beer drinking had become very important to me. Consequently I joined Peter Mutema's [Zion Sabbath] church where one can drink openly without subterfuge. At present I belong to Bishop Nehemiah Gotore's [Zion Sabbath] church.

Mudyanadzo's narrative indicates a limited conception of the church. It would seem that to him joining a new church was equivalent to joining a society or a club, with the rules governing beer drinking as his first priority. If one considers that each time he moved to a new church he must have taken at least a few followers with him, and left others behind in his old church in a state of doubt and disillusionment, it is clear that this constant flux in congregations through the coming and going of clergy must be conducive to *spiritual insecurity and instability*. The effect this has on congregations is not altogether harmful. In some cases it may result in a spiritual revival, a constructive regrouping of congregations that have lapsed into a decline, and a positive evangelistic outward orientation which promotes church growth.

In 1965 and 1966 the activities of two defecting office-bearers were observed in the Gutu district, a study that did much to clarify the process of schism and regrouping. The two men were a senior baptist, Sauro Garanuako, of Johane Maranke's African Apostolic Church, and the prophet Elison Mutingwende of Johane Masowe's Apostle Church. The two were friends who lived in Kono's village in the Chingombe tribal area.

203

(a) *Preparatory phase*

In both cases leadership ambition played a major part. Elison was frustrated because his church was in a decline and his prophetic activities therefore could not earn him promotion in the church hierarchy. Sauro's pomotion was continually postponed owing to a surfeit of office-bearers in Maranke's Apostle Church. In addition both men had difficulty in adhering to the strict prohibition on beer drinking in their churches.

Once it became known that Elison and Sauro were contemplating a change there was a marked increase in religious activity in the surrounding villages. Bishops of various churches invited the two to their services and periodic conferences were held in Kono's village in an attempt to persuade these two prominent figures to join their churches. Several churches held combined services and conducted lengthy discussions with the two office-bearers. One may therefore conclude that the *mere hint of possible defection by two prominent individuals gave rise to diverse ecumenical interactions among Independent Churches*. After a year of intensive religious activity the two friends decided to join Bishop Nehemiah Gotore's Zion Sabbath Church.

(b) *Defection and the formation of new church groups*

In neither case was there any large-scale conflict or schism, only a gradual loosening of ties with the original church and the defection of a mere handful of people. The very absence of a crisis situation makes this type of defection highly misleading as regards its destabilizing influence on the original church. Thus Sauro's "departure" from the ranks of the *vaPostori* had no immediate impact worth mentioning, but in due course it triggered off a series of individual defections with grave consequences for the congregation.

When Bishop Gotore consecrated Sauro as bishop, Elison, who was to occupy a lesser post, decided to start a new church of his own — further evidence of the importance of leadership ambition. At the consecration service the sermons of both Bishop Gotore and Sauro reflected great dependence on God and the conviction that they were making an important contribution within the framework of God's kingdom on earth. Hence it was clearly a matter of far greater import than merely switching from a church that prohibited beer drinking to another that permitted it.

Elison for his part founded the *Shinga Postora* (Courageous Apostles) movement which concentrated on the "courageous" combating of witchcraft. The accent was mainly on service to the community by destroying evil, destructive forces in the name of the overriding power of the Christian God and thereby effecting deliverance. This was at the same time a useful recruitment technique since those who had been helped by the prophet Elison were eventually baptized in the "Jordan" and initiated into the new church.

Early in 1966 both these office-bearers were ready for church expansion — the one in a new congregation of an existing Zionist church, the other launching a new movement.

(c) *Expansion and consolidation*

Sundkler's second phase concerns the integration of the new group in keeping with the radicalism of the schismatic leader. In the absence of a defecting faction from the original church on whom the defecting office-bearer can concentrate, his primary aim is to recruit followers and then consolidate the expanding group under his leadership. This is precisely what both Elison and Sauro did. Although in neither case radicalism featured very prominently — for instance, the beer-drinking issue faded progressively into the background — there was some degree of "centripetal rigidity", as Sundkler puts it. In Elison's case the *Kushinga Postora* centred their activities on combating witchcraft. Members identified with the group by testifying to their deliverance from evil forces through the ministry of their prophetic leader. They travelled with Elison to neighbouring villages to help solve problem situations, to destroy witchcraft medicine and to initiate new members into the group. In this case the cohesive rigidity lay in non-acceptance of anyone who questioned or criticized Elison's activities.

Because of Elison's concentration on witchcraft he was constantly on the move so that organization and pastoral work were to some extent neglected by his clergy. Despite this eight congregations were established in the course of a single year and he was beginnig to exercise a strong influence on village life in Chingombe. His "prophecies" during baptisms helped to clarify village conflicts and bring antisocial personalities to justice. At the same time he admitted undesirables to his church, thus effectively proclaiming a message of reconciliation and helping to resolve local conflict. Hence Elison's activities had a remarkably healthy impact and the overriding connotation was certainly not one of schism with adverse implications for the original church.

By contrast with Elison's anti-witchcraft campaign, Sauro preached individual conversion. Group integration was effected by giving new members short-term goals such as communal agricultural projects to raise funds for the first great conference of the Zion Sabbath Church in the Chingombe tribal area.

After the village headman Kono and some other prominent villagers had joined the ZSC Sauro soon mobilized the entire village community to work together. Within six months he had expanded the congregation to over a hundred members and his authority in Zionist circles was established.

To the new congregation the conference in August 1966 was extremely important. It represented their official integration into Bishop Nehemiah's ZSC, and was to be the occasion for the appointment of new office-bearers and a test of Bishop Sauro's leadership. An outstanding feature of the conference was its *ecumenical character*. All the mission churches, Ethiopian-type churches and especially the prophetic movements in the area were represented, so that there were some 500 participants. Leaders of the various churches were permitted to take an active part in the proceedings by preaching, prophesying, song and dance. In this way the various denominations contributed positively to recognize, encourage and establish the new congregation. For the time being group interests were shelved as Apostle prophets of Sauro's former church and *Shinga Postora* prophets collaborated to expose evil forces, purify delegates, confess sins and perform faith healings.

Such a conference is typically an all-round festive occasion. It included sermons on church law and group identity. Calls to repentance culminated in baptisms in a nearby dam. Prophetic consultations were presented throughout. Office-bearers were consecrated and faith healings performed towards the end of each service. *Ironically the outcome of schism was not disintegration and conflict, but ecumenical co-operation and spiritual renewal!*

The August conference not only successfully concluded the first phase of Sauro's church expansion effort, but provided the impetus for further growth. Six months later Sauro was still operating from Kono's village, but already his congregation(s) extended beyond the neighbouring villages into the surrounding tribal areas. Thus only one year after the establishment of the ZSC the time had come to reorganize and subdivide congregations.

The different contexts in which Elison Mutingwende and Sauro Garanuako proselytized and expanded their respective churches illustrate the diversity and flexibility of the Independent Churches. For Elison schism had resulted in service to the community at large, but not in an open-minded approach to other churches. Although members of other churches were involved in his anti-sorcery activities, they were more in the capacity of observers in the exclusive "prophetic specialist" group than participants making a relevant spiritual contribution to the occasion. Sauro's proselytizing, on the other hand, expanded in an ecumenically open situation in which the initiative was shared by a great many prophetic churches, not merely to affirm Black Christian solidarity, but to help with the creation and shaping of a new congregation. Instead of reacting negatively to Sauro's defection the Maranke *vaPostori* participated in the proceedings in a spirit of identification with the establishment of a new Zionist congregation. Hence the ZSC congregation officially emerged, not in an atmosphere of isolation, but in the midst of a multidenominational situation with considerable exposure to kindred and even rival groups.

5.7.3 *Evaluation of the process of schism*

One can quite definitely assert that schism will remain an inherent feature of the Independent Churches in the future. The two case studies of Sauro and Elison represent a process of defection and fusion that recurs with the regularity of the tides. While the socio-political and religious factors that engender the need for security and leadership continue, and while the Independent Churches remain rooted in African culture which includes village subdivision and hereditary authority, the process of schism, grouping, regrouping and rejection of old ties in favour of new ones will likewise continue.

It is essential that one should evaluate both the negative *and* the positive implications of schism. Theologically one cannot deny the disruptive element which undermines the unity of the church, the body of Christ. Constant schism essentially promotes a superficial ecclesiology, which dilutes the special nature of the church to that of a sort of school (among the Shona the word *chikoro,* school, is quite commonly used for the church) or association. Fluidity of leadership may also shake the stability of the lives of individual Christians and cause spiritual retrogression.

But there are also positive aspects to schism and regrouping. Even though the motives of the clergy may not necessarily be pure, the stimulation of church growth and concomitant conversions and/or spiritual renewal are indisputable. There is no doubt that many of the people who joined Elison and Sauro had genuine conversion experiences. Elison's activities did not constitute a breakthrough of the magically oriented mentality in every respect, but he did manage to introduce the Christian message of God's sovereignty over evil powers at an existential level in an area where the Black man feels his most profound need for deliverance and security. Sauro's ecumenically oriented activities did not end with the August conference, but culminated in continued ecumenical interaction between the ZSC, Elison's *Shinga Postora* and Maranke's Apostle movement. The fact that schism and regrouping had not led to isolation and stultifying exclusiveness is partly a reflection of the traditional concept of home as the *dunhu* (subdivided tribal area) with its villages. Despite subdivision of villages the basic loyalty to the headman, the *dunhu* and the politically dominant kinship group remains unchanged. In terms of the Independent Churches, the basic loyalty — despite schism and church establishment — towards the spiritual "home", the church family, or in this case more specifically the prophetic movement, remains unchanged. Once the schismatic leader or defecting office-bearer has consolidated his position in the new group he is inclined to look for meaningful co-operation within the broader, to him familiar church framework. This natural solidarity provides a basis for more comprehensive, institutional attempts at ecumenical co-operation.

5.7.4 Ecumenical co-operation

The Independent Churches' striving for recognition from the historical churches, for greater unity among themselves and particularly for better theological training has led to several attempts at advancing ecumenical co-operation in various African countries. As far back as 1919 the Revd Mkhize, a Zulu minister, organized a meeting in Bloemfontein to unite Black clergy and laity. During the twenties the African National Congress tried on behalf of the "separatists" of South Africa to launch the United National Church of Africa. However, no attention was paid to denominational and doctrinal problems and the venture soon proved abortive. In 1939 the African Methodist Episcopal Church tried to establish a federation of churches. This venture was supported by such influential leaders as the Revd J. Nhlapo and Prof. Jabavu.[80] In 1937 the Bantu Independent Churches Union of South Africa was set up among the Zulu; it consisted of Zionist and Ethiopian-type churches with a congregationalist background. A strong motive for this striving for unity was the conviction that it would improve the "separatist" churches' chances of official recognition from the government. During discussions with the government's advisory council mutual differences crystallized. The Zulu Zionists' objections to associating with church members who used medicine and ate pork illustrated the apparent impossibility of unity among such widely divergent groups.[81] In his description of these ecumenical attempts Sundkler created the impression that he too believed that the venture was predestined to failure.

However, in 1965 some Independent Church leaders negotiated with members of the Christian Institute. Previously they had eschewed contact with the mission churches, but the multiracial, interdenominational character of the Christian Institute posed no threat to the individuality of the Independent Churches and they therefore decided to co-operate with this body. In June 1965 the African Independent Churches' Association (AICA) was founded at a conference in Queenstown, which included delegates from

80 Sundkler, 1961, p. 52
81 Ibid., p. 52

the Christian Institute. Within a very few years (1965-1972) the number of member churches shot up from 100 to 400. With the Christian Institute in charge of fund raising and effective administration of funds, the AICA was able to recruit members, arrange conferences and launch a theological training programme. As a result of leadership conflicts a faction of 46 churches under the Revd Mthembu, first president of AICA, broke away in 1970 and in conjuction with the Revd N. van Loggerenberg of the DR Church proceeded to establish the Reformed Independent Church Association (RICA). Like the AICA, the RICA placed the emphasis on theological training.

West gives a sound survey of the origin of the AICA, its leadership conflicts, theological training projects and the eventual collapse of this ecumenical body directly after the Christian Institute had transferred full financial control to the AICA president, the Revd E.V.M. Maqina, and his executive committee in 1973.[82] The activities of the AICA clearly demonstrated that the *Independent Churches are able to overcome doctrinal differences* if the motivation to co-operate is sufficiently strong. Unlike the earlier attempts at unity described by Sundkler (which floundered on the Zionist churches' prejudices) the downfall of the AICA was not due to general religious differences, but to a constant struggle for leadership, for the status of controlling a financially viable organization, the financial benefits of occupying some office and financial mismanagement. What enabled the divergent member churches — which covered the whole spectrum from Spirit-type to Ethiopian-type — to overcome their profound religious differences so effectively? West maintains that the desire for better theological training, arising from a sense of inferiority to the mission churches, was the main cohesive factor. He writes that

> the theological education programmes of AICA and the increased standing they gave to member churches as well as the advantages of the education itself, constituted perhaps the single most important cohesive factor within AICA. The college and correspondence course, for example, were cited

82 West, 1975, chapter 8

regularly by informants as evidence of the effectiveness of their organisation and the excellence of its aims.[83]

In addition the AICA gave the Independent Churches some status and a measure of recognition, an important psychological gain. The small, relatively unknown churches in particular benefited by their association with a body which was recognized not only in South Africa, but also internationally as a result of fund raising and mutual visits.

Similar motives featured prominently in the establishment in 1972 of the African Independent Church Conference (*Fambidzano yamaKereke avaTema*) among Shona Independent Churches — an ecumenical "experiment" which today numbers some 50 member churches and runs one of the most successful theological training programmes of its kind. In addition to the aforementioned natural solidarity as a basis for ecumenism, the need for recognition and more effective leadership through theological training was a major motive. Once it became evident that these churches could uphold their identity, and as ties of friendship were forged through co-operation, the Zionist leaders were able to modify their critical attitude towards the Ethiopian-type churches, which had really been a condemnation of the latter's alleged neglect of the Holy Spirit. This did not in itself resolve the doctrinal differences, but it became easier to abandon group prejudices through the establishment of common goals, greater recognition and status and especially the absence of an involved dogmatic-historical background such as besets Western churches. Unity in Christ as defined in John 17: 21,23 was made a cornerstone of the Shona ecumenical movement from the outset. The fact that in the early years the Zionist churches were prepared to tolerate a preponderance of leaders of Ethiopian-type churches on the administrative board despite their own numerical superiority indicated an amazing sense of solidarity.

The main contribution of *Fambidzano* has been its Theological Training by Extension programme, which has enabled hundreds of office-bearers from many Independent Churches and even a number of bishops to do a two-year diploma course. The substance of the courses focuses mainly on Old and New Testament

83 Ibid., p. 165

studies, ethics, homiletics and especially church history. This has opened up new perspectives on the development of Christianity — something that had been lacking previously. It has helped to promote self-knowledge and self-criticism in relation to other churches and Christianity generally. Although the overall impact of *Fambidzano* on the Independent Churches still has to be researched, it is evident even at this stage that the schismatic trend in the groups concerned has declined significantly since 1972. Guruveti, a senior official in Makamba's Zionist church was able to avert schisms in his church by means of insights gleaned from his theological course. At a *Fambidzano* conference he explained how he was able to reach a compromise solution with prospective defecting office-bearers by paying serious attention to the non-theological background factors.

The greater stability since the establishment of *Fambidzano* is remarkable, for there have been no major schism or defection by individual office-bearers from any of the member churches since then. Naturally there were regular conferences and member churches obtained membership of the then Rhodesian Christian Conference and the Zimbabwe Christian Council, all of which strengthened the will to co-operate. The former isolation of the scattered "reserve churches" has ended totally, not only in terms of mutual relations between Shona churches, but also in relation to the universal church. Regular contact with overseas donors and mutual visits have created a strong sense of real involvement and therefore greater responsibility towards the church of Christ throughout the world.

As in the case of the AICA, *Fambidzano* also had a guiding influence from outside. I personally prepared the ground for the establishment of *Fambidzano* and, at the insistence of the member churches, acted as "director" of the movement for nine years. Fortunately it was possible to apply a modified form of the principle of inherited leadership on my departure in Dec. 1980 when Peter Makamba — an adopted "kinsman" of mine and son of the Zionist Bishop Makamba — took over my responsibilities.[84] At present he is principal of *Fambidzano's* theological training institute.

84 Currently my position is that of "lifelong honorary director" of **Fambidzano**

Gradual transfer of financial and administrative responsibilities some time before my departure contributed to the present stability. The growing number of extension centres over a wide geographical area and over 400 students enrolling for the theological course annually have meant that the demand is greater than the lecturing staff of some twenty staff members can actually handle.

Apart from contributing to the theological moulding of Independent Church leaders or potential leaders, the *Fambidzano* "experiment" has proved that through ecumenical co-operation — based on the inherent ecumenical trends within these churches — constructive measures can be instituted to counteract the constant process of schism and individual defection.

CHAPTER 6

LIFE AND FAITH OF THE INDEPENDENT CHURCHES

It is all but impossible to give a picture of religious life in the Independent Churches without lapsing into misleading generalizations. Nevertheless an attempt will be made to describe some of the more striking features, once again citing the Shona churches by way of illustration. Naturally the presentation in this chapter is very cursory. The aim is not to discuss the various topics exhaustively, but merely to furnish a provisional background which is very important for a theological evaluation of this phenomenon. For a clearer picture of this multifaceted field we shall use Molland's scheme for a comparative presentation of Christian churches as our guideline.[1] He describes churches in terms of the following four basic aspects: church polity, doctrine, worship and ethos. Although the order of importance of these aspects varies in different churches, it is still an acceptable scheme to systematize the data.

6.1 CHURCH POLITY

The nature of church polity in the Independent Churches was outlined in chapter 5. What emerged particularly in the case of the Shona churches was the hierarchical order of leadership, with the exercise of authority manifesting distinct traditional tendencies. Observers have arrived at similar conclusions about Independent Churches elsewhere in Africa. Thus Baeta writes about the churches he studied in Ghana that on the whole they

> followed the basic pattern of organization of African communities ... it centres round the strong personality of its leader, who is its real pivot, though use is made of all sorts of councils as well; above all it gives more scope to individuals to express themselves freely.[2]

1 Molland, 1959, p. 6
2 Baeta, 1962, pp. 128-129

Particularly in the case of church leaders such as Mutendi and Maranke among the Shona, Shembe and Lekhanyane in South Africa and Kimbangu in Zaire, the movement as a whole revolves around the leader to such an extent that there are clear signs of the traditional organization of a sacral kingship (especially among the Zulu) or of a tribal chief. However, when one considers smaller churches (even groups formed around such figures as Sauro Garanuako and Elison Mutingwende) the basic tendency to orient church polity and organization mainly to the principal leader remains the same. As pointed out earlier, this person-orientation is in fact a weakness which can result in grave problems over succession to the leadership and may end in fragmentation.

Exercise of authority in church polity manifests features of traditional tribal organization. In the latter the judicature operates at three levels — the village court, the ward *(dunhu)* court and the chief's court. In the same way decisions on organization and disciplinary measures in the church are taken at the level of the congregational court, the circuit or ward court and the court of the principal leader at church headquarters. Among Shona Independent Churches the common use of the term *dare* (court) for the church council — whether at congregational, circuit or headquarter level — and the procedure, especially in disciplinary cases, are further indications of the traditional influence of tribal organization and traditional judicature.

In addition to the traditional aspects, church polity has also adapted Western church forms. Possibly the traditional background features particularly strongly in the Shona churches because so many of their prominent leaders never held important positions in the historical churches and a large percentage of them never belonged to historical churches at all. Clearly in such a situation Western models of church polity will be followed less consciously than in the South or West African situation where churches were formed more as a result of classical schism and therefore adhere more closely to the models of Western Christianity. Turner maintains that in the Aladura church in West Africa, which draws 70 percent of its members from mission churches, Western patterns of church polity are at least as important as the traditional order of authority. At the procedural level the use in the Church of the Lord of programmes, agendas,

215

reports, motions and minutes (all of them virtually unknown among Shona Independent Churches) clearly reflects customs in the historical churches and government departments.[3]

Anglican influence is discernible in the hierarchical episcopal structure of the church and in such terms as "primate", "bishop", "orders of the clergy and the laity" and "parochial council". In the three-tier structure of church councils, composed of clergy and laity, one observes a *Presbyterian influence*. There is also the *Methodist influence* to be seen in the annual clergy conferences, terms such as "conference", "church districts" and "circuits", and the role of the laity in preaching and prayer. Thus the Church of the Lord incorporates a variety of historical church influences into a single system to adapt to indigenous circumstances. Turner uses this example to demonstrate the impossibility of simplistically adapting African church polity to the traditional authority structure. He refers to the somewhat idealistic suggestion of Hess, namely that where the indigenous government was basically local, a Congregational form of church polity should be used, where it was regional a Presbyterian system should be applied and in cases where there were territorial rulers the Episcopalian system should be followed.[4]

On the basis of the Aladura example Turner finally presents the following illuminating summary of the traditional and Western character of church polity:

> The African features we have described are therefore not expressed through a structure that closely mirrors traditional society, but rather through a polity that continues the hierarchical system inherited both from traditional society and from the Anglican Church, and modifies it by the addition of elements from the Presbyterial and Methodist forms of government. It could be regarded as a mixed Western polity operating in a characteristically African way, and with considerable emphasis on the authority of the leader.[5]

---

3   Turner, 1967(b), p. 26
4   Ibid., p. 27. Turner is referring to Mahlon M. Hess, "Political systems and African church policy," in **Practical Anthropology**, iv, 5(1957), pp. 170-184
5   Turner, 1967(b), p. 27

Among the Shona differences in the church polity of Ethiopian-type and Spirit-type churches are less dramatic. On the whole, however, one could say that the Ethiopian-type churches adhered more closely to the system inherited from the historical churches than the prophetic movements did. Thus the annual calendar and conference procedure of the African Congregational Church *(Chibarirwe)* and the African Reformed Church *(Shonganiso)* resemble those of the American Board and the DR Mission Church more closely than is the case in the Zionist and Apostolic Churches. But here too the trend — whether the background is Congregational, Reformed, Methodist or Presbyterian — is progressively towards episcopalianism.

In most Spirit-type churches there is a greater variety of official positions and titles than in the "Ethiopian" groups, such as archbishop, bishop, junior bishop, priest, minister, baptist, prophet, evangelist, preacher, deacon, overseer and the like. The significance attached to these titles varies from one group to the next and usually differs greatly from the meaning attached to them in Western Christianity. The same may be said of certain theological qualifications. To demonstrate the tremendous difference between the two ecclesiastic worlds, one need merely point out that the majority of Shona Zionist bishops have had no more than two or three years of primary schooling. Of course, this does not remotely imply that the Zionist bishop is inferior to his Western counterpart. He ministers to his own people according to the prevailing norms and has the status and authority to exercise a profound influence over large numbers of followers.

The emphasis on hierarchical order does not rule out lay activity. Whether through integration into the lower ranks of the hierarchy or simply by imposing various duties, the fact is that virtually every church member has some form of responsibility. Here too the traditional kinship structure is reflected in that every relationship between kinsmen is structured according to superiority or subordination with concomitant duties. In some cases this is a result of Methodist influence which, according to Sundkler, laid the foundation for efficient church organization in Africa.[6] Because of this division of responsibility — often in-

6   Sundkler, 1962, p. 164

dicated by distinctive emblems or monograms for even the most minor function — the pride and self-esteem of individuals are so stimulated that personal identification with the church develops far more strongly in Spirit-type churches than in the historical one. The integration of the laity is a result of *the heavy emphasis on corporate life*. In these *'institutes of belonging'* everyone belongs to everybody else and all people are responsible for one another, with everything revolving around the prophetic leader who acts as intermediary. Sundkler points out quite rightly that he is always the leader, but a leader-in-community. He does not monopolize leadership but exercises it in a framework which gives all his followers opportunity for active participation.[7]

An important facet of church polity is the prominent role assigned to women, although in some Independent Churches the emancipation of women lags behind. Some *Ndaza* Zionist churches confine the woman's role to the lowest official positions. But by and large the trend is to give women scope to develop their own potential and evolve their own leadership hierarchy within their women's associations *(Ruwadzano)*. Prominent female office-bearers are permitted a major say in court sessions, particularly in disciplinary cases. Others can advance to senior positions in the ordinary leadership hierarchy as faith healers and particularly as prophetesses. It is nothing unusual to find entire communities of patients with a woman, either a prophetess or a faith healer, dispensing her services to some church. In certain outstanding cases one finds a woman at the head of the church, such as the Ndebele prophetess Ma Nku in Johannesburg, Alice Lenshina of the Lumpa Church in Zambia, Miriam Ragot and Gaudencia Aoka in Kenya, and Mai Chaza's City of God in Zimbabwe.

6.2   DOCTRINE OR "FAITH"?

Most Independent Churches do not have much in the line of doctrine in the Western sense of an elaborately worked out, systematic credal document containing the crux of the dogmatic

7   Ibid., pp. 127-141

guidelines laid down by that church. *Since religion is not a matter of meticulous formation but rather of expression in preaching, dance, song and festivity it is probably better to speak of "faith" rather than doctrine.*

The Ethiopian-type churches do have some form of doctrine inasmuch as they have adopted the credal documents and catechism books of mission churches. This is why "Ethiopians" are usually more orthodox than Zionists or Apostles. However, because of their reliance on the traditional ethos and their accent on experiencing their faith rather than reflecting on it rationally, these borrowed "documents" on doctrine *function only partially* and in some cases fade into the background altogether. Here the history of each church group plays a major part. When the African Reformed Church *(Shonganiso)* was established it was a conscious attempt at reforming the excessive adaptation of the *Chibarirwe* to traditional culture. Consequently the outspoken rejection of polygamy — in agreement with DR Mission Church policy — became a major bone of contention which left its mark on the reforming group. However, it was more a matter of maintaining their new identity than of reverting wholly to the doctrine of the DR Mission Church. Despite the obvious relation between the Mission Church and the "Ethiopian" church (at present both are using the same name — African Reformed Church) in both name and doctrine, here too "doctrine" functions only partially and the term "faith" is actually more apposite.

As for the Zionist and Apostolic churches, one could say that on the whole they have reached a New Testament position. The historical person Christ as Lord and Saviour is consciously accepted, even though this key facet of the faith is sometimes crowded out by a host of religious activities. God the Father also occupies a far more prominent place in the lives and faith of church members than he held in the pre-Christian view. His more direct involvement in the lives of individuals is evident from regular references to him in sermons and invocations in prayer of "God the Father" *(Mwari Baba),* "God of power", "living God", "God of miracles" and "our Protector". However, remnants of the ancient faith remain perceptible in the approach of individuals, who still place the emphasis on the "God of the heavens"

219

(Mwari Wokudenga), accessible only through the mediation of the church leader on very important matters.[8]

The Holy Spirit, on the other hand, is manifestly focal in the minds and experience of members of the prophetic movements. This is underscored by the fact that they commonly refer to their churches as "churches of the Spirit" *(makereke dzoMweya).*

As Bosch points out, the focal importance of the presence of the Holy Spirit in these movements is evident from two dominant trends which may be described as *soteriological* and *prophetic.*[9] Essentially both are the result of the Holy Spirit's direct involvement with human life.

6.2.1 *The prophetic trend*

The basic presupposition in all these movements is that the Holy Spirit himself — whether through dreams, visions or some other form of emotional inspiration — calls the prophetic leader and instates him in office. The original experience of Pentecost is repeated in an African context. Virtually all of the great prophetic leaders (Kimbangu, Johane Maranke, Lekhanyane and Mutendi) experienced some form of outpouring of the Holy Spirit and then consciously built a Pentecostal element into their churches, inter alia by calling their headquarters: Jerusalem, Moriah or Holy City. In the case of Kimbangu the new Pentecost dawned with the outpouring of the Holy Spirit on Nkamba — Jerusalem in 1921. Johane Maranke experienced an outpouring of the Spirit near Mount Nyengwe on 17 July 1932. So crucial is this event that the great Apostolic conference is held in July every year to experience Pentecost anew. Gatherings have been held on Mount Nyengwe to commemorate the calling of Johane. Another expression of the central position occupied by the Holy Spirit is the fact that both the conferences and regional centres of the church are known as *Pendi* (from Pentecost). By using these biblical terms the people are confessing that total renewal through the Spirit has begun once more, as happened in Jerusalem long ago. It is also expressive of a yearning for the continued manifestation of the Spirit.

8 Daneel, 1971(a), pp. 380-385
9 Bosch, 1973, pp. 60-62

220

What has been said about the Spirit-type churches in Zimbabwe applies to most of the prophetic movements in Africa:

> The Spirit always manifests His presence through speaking in tongues and through prophetic revelations. The Spirit cleanses the water of 'Jordan' for baptism — virtually all these groups practise baptism through immersion in 'Jordan' — the Spirit reveals the hidden sins of novices about to be baptized and He possesses and inspires the novice during or after baptism. In the name of the Holy Spirit, Church laws are upheld and through His revelations the inner sanctity of church members are determined before their participation in the all-important Communion service during *Paseka* festivals. Thus the whole control system within these movements hinges on the professed work of the Holy Spirit.[10]

Obviously the prophet possesses all the various gifts of the Spirit, but his followers also share in these through their constant contact with the leader and their own experience of the work of the Holy Spirit. The signs of possessing the Spirit are usually speaking in tongues, inspired revelations, dreams, visions and the like. In every group there are accepted, standardized patterns of speech in tongues which are regarded as authentic, but which permit individual variations.

6.2.2 *The soteriological trend*

The approach to Christian salvation is primarily pneumatological in terms of an implicit, less pronounced Christology. It is the Spirit that sets man free. In the prophetic churches soteriology is much more comprehensive than in many of the historical churches, where it is often reduced purely to the salvation of the soul hereafter. Salvation, healing and sanctification are inextricably linked in an outlook that makes little distinction between the

---

10 Daneel, 1971(a), pp. 347-348

sacred and the profane, between earthly and eternal salvation. However, it never lapses into a Western type of "social gospel" or merely a realized eschatology. *It is simply that the gospel is related much more realistically to the whole of human life than often happens in the historical churches.* As opposed to an impoverished, spiritualized gospel that did not always penetrate deeply enough into the existential world of the African — beset as he is by disease, infertility, sorcery and evil powers — salvation is experienced in terms of the protection of God's Spirit against such powers and not necessarily as deliverance from sin.

Against this background the focal positions of faith healing in the prophetic movements becomes understandable. Through the prophetic healer the Spirit himself reveals the cause and nature of the disease or temptation and prescribes the required therapy. Through the power of the Holy Spirit as expressed in prophetic exorcism the evil powers are expelled and protection against future threats is obtained. In all of this the prophetic healer is the key figure. Remember in this connection that the prophetic leaders of the major movements who, in the early phases of church establishment, had acted almost exclusively as prophet-healers, later became so wrapped up in administrative duties that the task of healing was performed by subordinate prophet-healers. Hans Juergen Becken, who conducted a valuable in-depth study of faith healing in Zionist churches, stresses the healing function of the prophetic leader. In the articles of faith of senior office-bearers, intercession and laying on of hands for the sick are stated as basic functions. These are regarded as every bit as important as preaching, baptism, administering the sacraments and burying the dead.[11]

Ritual acts, drinking of or sprinkling with holy water, burning of holy paper, anointing with oil, tying with sacred ropes, laying on of hands, purifications rites and the like are all directly related to the soteriological aspect, but are secondary to and symbolize the work of the Holy Spirit. Despite this it sometimes happens that some members may attribute an inherent power to these objects, an aftermath of the fetishist approach. When the sym-

11 Becken, 1972. Cf. also Daneel, 1970(b)

bolic value of ritual acts is susperseded by fetishism to a considerable extent one could speak of syncretistic distortion in a non-Christian sense.

6.3 FORMS OF WORSHIP

6.3.1 *Liturgy*

The pattern adopted by the Ethiopian-type churches in many respects resembles that of the historical churches. Sermons focus on a specific theme and with minor variations the liturgy is clearly an imitation of that of some historical church or other. Among the Shona the presence of trained evangelists, preachers and even school teachers from the various mission churches — even though proportionally they are not very well represented — leaves a mark on the form of worship. Thus there is a marked difference between the African Reformed Church *(Shonganiso)* — where the Congregational and Reformed influence dominates the liturgy — and the First Ethiopian Church, which occupies a position somewhere between the more orthodox and the Zionist approaches. Both Bishop Chidembo, the founder-leader of the FEC and his successor, Bishop Gavure, underwent hardly any influence in a mission church context. Thus they were able to evolve their form of worship spontaneously according to the needs they sensed. They therefore introduced faith healing with laying on of hands and prayer, as practised in the prophetic churches, as an integral part of public worship — but without adding the prophetic-diagnostic aspect.

In the Spirit-type churches *every service is an "event"*, usually lasting an entire afternoon. Preaching remains central, but there are a number of sermons (eight to ten on one afternoon are normal) which may range from messages of repentance, witnessing, historical accounts, expositions of aspects of the traditional cult, reports on evangelization campaigns and controversies on "doctrinal" differences to church consolidation aimed at inculcating the church's characteristic codes and rules into members. Thus there is considerable flexibility which permits the preaching to be suited to the circumstances. As far as content is concerned there is great variation, from coherent messages which propagate biblical truths realistically and fairly undiluted, to extreme fragmentation of texts, used out of context and manipulatively to proclaim stereotyped ideas. Throughout the accent is *not* on systematized, rational preaching, but on mobilizing God's people by testifying to experiences of God's presence, salvation and protection, culminating in festive rejoicing. Even didactic preaching is presented in an emotionally rousing rather than a logically informative way.

Of course, the sermons are interspersed with dance, song, clapping of hands, drums and other traditional musical instruments, ecstatic experiences, prophecies, communal prayer in which everybody prays aloud in unison, and the like. In this way the entire congregation is involved in some kind of active participation in the liturgical event. During services prophets are engaged in pastoral and diagnostic sessions in the immediate environment. Consequently those with problems can seek professional aid as it were "in between acts" and rejoin the congregation to listen to a sermon. Thus faith healing is actually part of the liturgy, as is confession of sin which, with prophetic encouragement, is fitted in between the sermons. Sometimes a prophet may interrupt proceedings to announce some message that the Spirit has revealed to him. Especially in cases where sorcery in the village is suspected a service may be dominated by prophetic revelations about this threat and the combating of evil powers. Despite the endless variation of prophetic services, which strike the Westerner as chaotic, certain limits are set and strictly maintained by the authority of senior office-bearers.

Church services are marked by a colourfulness in total contrast to everyday life, especially in tribal areas. Brightly coloured robes with monograms indicating the wearer's position in the leadership hierarchy are worn, or — as in the case of the ZCC — the congregation dress in neat uniforms wearing distinctive emblems. The wearing of crucifixes, sacred staffs, banners, sacred cords, beards, shedding of shoes at the place of meeting, the positioning of men and women during services and a variety of ritual acts such as washing of feet, anointment with oil, use of candles, exorcism and so on all contribute to a rich diversity which helps to determine the identity of each group and pschologically permits an experience of uniqueness, self-esteem, newness and release from daily drudgery.

In most prophetic churches *Easter* is the great religious event of the year. The great annual Easter conferences of Lekhanyane and Shembe are well-known in South Africa, as are those of Mutendi and Johane Marange in Zimbabwe. If one examines the annual Pentecost conference of the *vaPostori* in the Maranke communal lands one is at once struck by its *comprehensive nature*. For seventeen days people fast in preparation for receiving the sacrament; men and women live in separate quarters in the "holy city" (shelters spread over a large area); singers *(hakirosi)* continually chant spirituals, night and day; services are held in the mornings and afternoons, always accompanied by prophetic activity; the various orders of office-bearers stay together and hold meetings sometimes before dawn or in the late evenings, to hear reports on congregational work, get to know one another, encourage one another and pray together; sorcerers and witches are hunted out in a massive prophetic drive to purge the community of the church before God's face; the "judges" are constantly engaged on disciplinary cases in a number of "courts" where people sit through the night so that each case can be minutely thrashed out before a verdict is arrived at; and so on. This is the context in which preaching is used, in both Mutendi's and Maranke's church, partly to encourage group loyalty through historical accounts of the origins and development of the church, and partly to activate the whole church for further expansion. Towards the end of each Easter festival Mutendi usually preached one or more mission sermons by way of launching country-wide campaigns on which office-bearers were sent to visit congregations and preach repentance.[12] Thus it would be true to say that during the annual climax when Christ's work of atonement and salvation is commemorated, in conjunction with the birth of that church, when liturgy, ritual and spiritual purification mount to a crescendo with the taking of the sacrament, the impulses for church expansion are generated and co-ordinated anew for a fresh wave of missionary action.

12 Daneel, 1980

6.3.2 Use of the sacraments

As a rule only the two Protestant sacraments are used, with baptism featuring far more prominently than communion.

Baptism: Baptism is usually an adult affair involving immersion in any dam, pool or river called a "Jordan" for the occasion. In Ethiopian-type churches sprinkling is considered sufficient and it is rare for lapsed members to be rebaptized if they return to the flock. In prophetic groups, however, baptism may be repeated several times, although after the first occasion it is usually more of a purificatory rite than an initiation into God's kingdom.

All that is necessary for baptism is to confess the Christian faith. In some prophetic churches such as the ZCC there is fairly elaborate oral instruction in the faith and codes of conduct of the church as a preliminary to baptism. Sins have to be confessed under prophetic supervision. In cases of spirit-possession baptism may even be used as a form of exorcism, the tormenting spirit being called out and expelled by forceful immersion. The symbolism is very moving in river baptisms: the transition from the old to the new life is depicted by a group of singing church members standing on the bank to welcome the novice, entering from the opposite bank, to the "new dispensation" (sometimes called "heaven"). Sometimes young girls swathed in white are led from the "Jordan" to stress their virginity. Some prophet healers insist on baptism as a qualification for diagnostic and therapeutic attention. Hence many patients or other sufferers undergo baptism for the sake of prophetic help rather than out of a need to belong to a church. When baptism is followed by a prolonged stay in a prophetic colony it often happens that a temporary member becomes a fully fledged one. When an entire family is baptized and the motivation of individual members is meagre, it can happen that gradual integration into the life of the church will ensue so that baptism only becomes meaningful at a later stage.

There are always misinterpretations when symbolism lapses into magic. Thus some church members may take some water from the "Jordan" during a baptism to use as medicine. The power of God's Spirit is identified with the baptismal water to such an extent that the water itself is considered intrinsically powerful. It is then drunk or sprinkled to secure a state of health, salvation or protection. Prophets specializing in combating sorcery often use "baptisms" to bring village crises to a head.[13] These involve public confession of sins in the "Jordan" under the watchful eye of the prophet as representative of the Holy Spirit. Entire village communities are "baptized" in hour-long ceremonies and all manner of sins affecting village life come to light. This effects a sort of catharsis and witches or sorcerers are identified — often on the strength of their own confession. The guilty parties subsequently appear in the village court to account for their misdeeds. Leaders of the prophetic churches admit that such "baptisms" are not in accordance with the essential purpose of baptism. However, they are not inclined to condemn them because of their obviously beneficial social effect from the traditional point of view.

Communion: Although administered much less frequently than baptism, communion is in no way considered less important. The Kimbanguists who celebrated their first official communion on 6 April 1971, fifty years after the birth of this movement, are exceptional. One of the main reasons why communion is celebrated only at the large annual feasts, or otherwise only sporadically in outlying church districts, is the tendency to reserve the celebration of the sacrament as the special prerogative of the paramount leader. This tendency is common to both Ethiopian-type and Spirit-type churches. Motives influencing this are various. Firstly, the leader's mediatory function is associated with a sacrament which is specifically directed at a mystical union with the body of Christ. In other words, by presenting his followers with the elements of bread and wine the leader indicates his *mediatory responsibility* for his people. Secondly, confining communion to special occasions when the principal leader is present accentuates the *rare, exclusive, even mystical significance of the sacrament*. Thirdly, there is a purely *pragmatic* motive: communion draws followers to church headquarters at least once a year to receive the sacrament, and this contact between leader and followers *strengthens his control over* the movement as a whole.

Preparation for communion is vitally important. Sermons and ritual acts in the course of the great Easter and other festivals gradually mount to a crescendo culminating in the celebration

13 Daneel, 1974, p. 278f

of the sacrament. Among Maranke's Apostles the final build-up to the sacramental climax may continue for a full twenty hours. It starts with a number of sermons calling on people to humble themselves and be sanctified. This is followed by public confession of sin with thousands of Apostles running around great fires, loudly proclaiming the sins they have committed. The next "round" of confession proceeds throughout the night: thousands of people move past prophets guarding the "gates of heaven" (twelve entrances into a grass palisade, representing the heavenly gates), so that the Holy Spirit can exercise control to ensure that all secret sins are confessed. Sorcerers, witches, adulterers and other sinners are led to the "judges' fires" for discussion and a verdict on whether or not they may partake of the sacrament. This prophetic check on sinners is not meant as a discriminatory measure, but as a means of purifying God's people so that they may be worthy to enter the sanctuary behind the grass palisade. Then comes washing of feet after the example of Christ, followed by the final liturgy and celebration of the eucharist. As in the Zionist churches, the appearance of the principal leader and his communion sermon are a climax — as if the *praesentia Dei* had become palpable and added a new dimension to the proceedings. There was something tremendously moving about the effect when Bishop Mutendi appeared in his pulpit and the murmur of thousands of voices subside, or when Abero Maranke appears at the communion table where twelve Apostles (the twelve most eminent office-bearers of the church) await him and silence gradually falls on the vast host of worshippers. Here at the very heart of the ritual life of the church, the climax of the church calendar and of weeks of preparation, the principal leader alone can officiate to initiate his people anew into the body of Christ.

There is no fixed formula for the final sermon and the leader may use this occasion to broach virtually any subject, whether it relates directly or less directly to the sacrament. In 1965 and 1966 I heard Abero Maranke use the occasion for a message of repentance, Bishop Mutendi for an attack on the traditional cult of the Supreme Being and ancestor worship, and Bishop Gavure of the FEC for a plea for church unity in Christ.

The consecration of the bread and wine by laying on of hands and prayer may cause individual communicants to interpret it as magic. This is indicated by women who take home scraps of bread

228

to give to relatives at home because of its potential medicinal value. Similar misconceptions arise among members of the historical churches. However, most leaders of the Independent Churches stress explicitly that the bread and wine have purely symbolic value. Although it is not expressed in so many words, one of the cardinal features of the communion is that it is a *total experience.* Everyone who has legitimately entered the sanctuary — adults, infants, children — *participate together,* singing, speaking in tongues, sharing the renewal in Christ from the mystical experience of God's presence (with the arrival of the principal leader) to the exuberant festive rejoicing (after receiving the sacrament). In the Independent Churches *this climax is a crucial cohesive factor to counter fragmentation,* and to individual members one of the most inspiring parts of their religious life.

6.4 ETHOS

Ethos, in both Ethiopian-type and Spirit-type churches, is the area where they depart from the historical churches. Their ethos is born of an interaction between their own peculiarly African indigenous approach to Christianity and traditional mores. It is in this sphere, where the exposition of the *new* message as opposed to *ancient* customs occurs and the polarity between two worlds is experienced in countless ways, that one comes up against the special character and identity of the Independent Churches. The great attraction of the Black churches is their *deliberate association with the traditional ethos.* In some respects this adaptation is carried to a point where one cannot but speak of syncretistic distortion. In other ways this adaptation leads to an imaginative transformation of ancient customs so that it amounts to a *legitimate christianizing* or *Christian indigenization.* Whatever the eventual theological evaluation of this process may be, I am convinced — on the strength of my findings among the Shona churches — that *this* is where one must look for the fundamental causes of the growth of the Independent Churches. The dominant theme in my study of church growth and recruitment techniques is summarized as follows:

Indigenization, it seems, is a major pivot around which much of the successful recruitment of Independent Church members revolves ... it implies that Christianity appears in a typical African guise, that traditionally conceived needs are met with traditionally orientated answers and solutions ... and that herein lies the secret of the unique appeal of the Independent Churches to Africans. On the basis of the quantified answers given by numerous Independent Church members and an analysis of their own accounts of their reasons for joining these Churches, and also on account of observations in the field, I conclude that *this process of adaptation, in all its richness and variation, largely explains the rise and continual growth of the Shona Independent Churches.*[14]

Actually this topic covers the entire field of traditional religion and traditional customs. It is also one of the most fascinating, without which no representative theological evalution of the formation of Independent Churches is possible. Unfortunately it is a field which many observers have merely skimmed over, insufficiently fathoming the subtleties of the interaction between Christian and traditional values. Too often the outcome was merely an impressionistic description and an evaluation in terms of Western categories, taking far too little account of the dynamics of an on-going transformation process based on the gospel. However, in this study we can only mention a few facets of the indigenized ethos of the Independent Churches.

6.4.1 *Cult of the Supreme Being*

In the traditional Shona religion the *Mwari* cult with its headquarters in the Matopo Hills near Bulawayo was directed at securing plentiful rains for good crops, the fertility of women and harmony in tribal politics. Every year messengers *(vanyai)* were

14 Ibid., p. 309

sent with gifts to the cultic centre to ask for rain and discuss tribal politics, for instance the succession of chiefs.

Although the mission churches consistently condemned this cult, in practice their members continued to give contributions to the *vanyai*. Hence the dependence on the traditional deity — especially in rural areas where rain was vital to the peasants — continued. The Ethiopian-type churches made no conscious attempt to replace this ancient custom, but the prophetic churches did try to transform it. Bishop Mutendi in particular was noted for this.

He adopted the strategy of launching a frontal attack on the ancient cult in his sermons. Not only did he reject the traditional Supreme Being's ability to provide rain outright, but he forbade his followers to give gifts to the *vanyai*. However, he gave them an alternative. Instead of relying on the *vanyai,* Zionist delegates from the various church districts had to come with gifts to the October conference in Zion City and direct their requests for rain directly to the "man of God". He would then act as "mediator" by asking the Christian God for rain. Thus the Zionists in fact adopted the traditional way of asking for rain at the cultic caves — through dancing and the bringing of gifts — and filled it with new meaning. During a midday service the Zionist delegates would dance around a table where Mutendi was sitting, giving him their gifts with the request that he should pray for rain on their behalf.

One immediately wonders whether this is in fact a total transformation of the old custom, or whether there is not some residue of the traditional causality which linked the bringing of gifts with reward in the form of God's counter-achievement. Is it not essentially a matter of human merit in the face of God's free grace? The fact remains that by providing this substitute for a time-honoured custom Mutendi drew many chiefs into his church and triggered off a radical transformation process. The entire ritual of asking for rain was so effectively and totally brought into the context of the Christian church that traditionalists reacted sharply. This reaction, which neither mission nor Ethiopian-type churches ever provoked to any great extent, indicates that the Zionists had probably intervened far more profoundly at the level of the traditional ethos, and therefore posed a graver danger to traditionalists than the other churches did.[15]

6.4.2 *Ancestor worship*

Various observers of the Independent Churches have concluded that in reaction against the historical churches' rejection of the ancestor cult, the new churches had assimilated this traditional religious custom more or less intact. Oosthuizen maintains that the emphasis on the work of the Holy Spirit in the Zionist churches is the loophole for the traditional focus on the ancestors. In his view the result is a "resurgence of the old in a new form", "a world ruled through and through by the ancestors" and a "calling upon the ancestors".[16] Oosthuizen bases his assertions on Pauw who established that among some Tswana Zionist groups the doctrine of the Holy Spirit is actually used to strengthen and justify ancestor worship.[17] Sundkler cites Zionist prophets who in cases of barrenness prescribe conciliating the ancestral spirits through sacrifice. He believes that the angel who reveals the patient's ailment to the Zulu prophet is confused with the ancestral spirits:

> The Angel's main reproach in churches of Zionist type is that the ancestral spirits have been neglected ... The Angel not only brings a message from the ancestral Spirit, the Angel *is* the spirit, the ancestral spirit.[18]

Beyerhaus and Martin both feel that spirit activities in Zionist churches involve a syncretism which is a direct offshoot of the old *idlozi* possession (Beyerhaus)[19] and an equation of the Holy Spirit with the ancestral spirits (Martin).[20] It is against this background that Bosch refers to a conscious concurrence with the

---

15 Daneel, 1971(a), p. 103f; Daneel, 1970(a)
16 Oosthuizen, 1968(a), pp. 102-103, 123
17 Ibid., p. 122
18 Sundkler ,1961, p. 250
19 Beyerhaus, 1969, pp. 74-75
20 Martin, 1964, p. 162

232

traditional ethos, more specifically ancestor worship. To justify this, he maintains, the Independent Churches use biblical arguments, for instance the fifth commandment which is applied to the dead as well.[21]

All these observers create the impression that the old ethos survives largely unchanged or merely appears in a new guise in the Independent Churches. However, the approach to ancestor worship is far more complex, even within the framework of a single church, and adaptation is directed far more at a *christianizing transformation* than the casual observer would suspect. If one turns to the Shona Independent Churches, for instance, there are major differences between the "Ethiopian" and Zionist churches. Officially both the *Chibarirwe* (here cited as an example of an "Ethiopian" church) and the Zionist churches condemn ancestor worship *(kupira midzimu)*. This rejection is not formulated dogmatically, but arises from an intuitive belief that the traditional reliance on the ancestors contains elements that are incompatible with worship of the Christian God. Ideologically the two churches differ vastly. The *Chibarirwe* (derived from *kubereka,* to give birth to, hence "place of birth", referring to a conscious "return" to the customs of the fathers), who were more specifically reacting against mission policy than the prophetic groups, tends to compromise when it comes to members who take an active part in traditional rites. The Zionists, on the other hand, take a serious stand against the ancestor cult, but more by way of substitute rites which they use to replace the old order. Individual *Chibarirwe* members will still cite the fifth commandment to try and justify *kupira midzimu,* whereas Zionists consistently regard heathen *midzimu* as "evil spirits" *(mweya yakaipa)* from whom they must break away. Despite these ideological differences, the practice of both churches reflects concern with the Shona's need to maintain the association between the living and the dead. This concern goes much deeper than a purely syncretistic reversion to ancient customs, as is evident from the following examples.

21 Bosch, 1973, p. 65

(a) *Rain rites (mukwerere)*

Here one observes the greater tolerance of the Ethiopian-type churches.[22] Although the church leaders personally abstain from the *mukwerere* rites (both in a village context and in honour of senior tribal spirits), their sermons never contain a confrontation with the mediatory powers of the senior spirits of the tribe and no disciplinary measures are applied to affiliated village headmen who take the initiative in arranging such rites. This tolerance which enables tribal authorities to cope with their responsibilities in both the church and the traditional context has meant that in a tribal area like Chingombe (comprising 110 villages) the majority of village headmen have joined the *Chibarirwe*.[23] When I asked a *Chibarirwe* headman about the relation between Christ and the tribal spirits after he had participated in a *mukwerere* ceremony, his response was this:

> Jesus Christ has no connection with these rites, but we could not ignore the tribal spirits for the villagers have asked for rain. Makomo, our local evangelist, will not condemn me for the people have asked him to leave me alone so that I can approach the spirits and ask for rain.

This response illustrates the dilemma of people who try to reconcile traditional religious and Christian duties. This village headman still believed in the power of the tribal spirits to intercede for rain. At the same time his views were in many respects so permeated with Christian concepts that it seemed as if two religious worlds were co-existing side by side without much conflict. He did not regard the invocation of the ancestral spirits as contradictory to praying to the Christian God. This approach is a result of the compromise attitude of the *Chibarirwe* church leaders who add to the uncertainty, so that the exclusive nature of the Christian message fails to be appreciated.

In the Zionist churches the preaching is far more directly opposed to the rain-making function of the ancestral spirits. Just as

22 Daneel, 1971(b), p. 161f and Daneel, 1973, p. 65
23 Daneel, 1974, p. 114f

234

Mutendi had replaced the Supreme Being cult with a Zionist alternative, so the mediatory function of the tribal spirits, on which the local *mukwerere* rites are based, is replaced by the action of the Zionist church leader who intercedes for rain on behalf of his group.

The Zionists and Apostles followed up their rejection of the *mukwerere* rites by introducing imaginative church rites showing certain parallels to the ancient customs. When towards the beginning of the rainy season the traditionalists "climb the mountains" *(kukwira makomo)* to communicate with the tribal spirits, the Zionists and Apostles too ascend the hills to ask the Christian God for rain by means of prayer, fasting, preaching and prophecy. The prophetic leaders found sufficient biblical references to holy mountains to justify their adaptation to the essentially traditional association of rain-giving powers (of the tribal spirits and Mwari, the Supreme Being) with mountains. But there can be no doubt that the prophetic leaders have invested these mountain rites with a totally new meaning.

There are still some residues of the old belief in some causal connection between human behaviour and the absence of rain, but in the prophetic context this is no longer attributed to neglect of the ancestral and tribal spirits, but to individual man's sins against God. Consequently the Zionists and Apostles attach great importance to the many days they spend humbling themselves on the hilltops where, through sustained fasting and confession, they may avert the possible wrath of God which brings drought and disease.[24] Communication with and dependence on tribal spirits have been largely superseded by a church rite which centres on the omnipotence of the Christian God.

(b) *Family rites*

The key rite in the family context is the *kugadzira* (to set right, set in order), in which the reciprocal relationship between the living and the dead is paramount. The duty of the kinsmen is partly to bring the spirit of the deceased "back home", and partly

24 Ibid., pp. 112-113

to raise it to the status of a true ancestor *(mudzimu)*. During *kugadzira* ceremonies the estate of the deceased is divided and his or her name transferred to the relative (eldest son or daughter) who will henceforth represent the deceased. By virtue of being a fully fledged *mudzimu* the deceased is now expected to protect the family or, if they should neglect him or her, withdraw that protection, thus leaving the family exposed to dangers of witchcraft or sickness to punish them.

In the prophetic churches the *kugadzira* has been replaced with a ceremony of consolation *(runyaradzo)* which retains the traditional roles of both the living and the dead in much modified form.

The role of the living: In the *runyaradzo* the responsibility is borne, not by the deceased's kinship group, but by the relevant group of Zionists or Apostles. Relatives prepare the food, but the priestly function, which used to include addressing the *mudzimu,* has been taken over by the official clergy. Instead of initiating the spirit of the deceased into the hierarchy of the ancestors the aim is now to 'accompany' *(kuperekedza)* him or her to heaven. In lieu of the traditional reception at the grave and the eating of a ritual meal the *kuperekedza* occurs in the course of a church service. The following excerpts from sermons preached at a Zionist *runyaradzo* reflect certain typical features:

— There are two kinds of funerals: the one with no hope of ever seeing the deceased again, and the other — the Christian kind — where there is hope of seeing one another again in heaven. Choose which kind of funeral you want! Even the traditionalists dream about their dead returning from somewhere where they have seen Christ. Therefore seek God here and now, for to await death without him is hopeless.

— The deceased rehabilitated himself during his lifetime for it was his desire that his spirit should be preserved safely in Zion. Now he is being demanded from us. We showed him the right way. He will be conducted to heaven, for we are responsible for him.

— We all have to die one day. That is the will of God.

What is crucial is whether we die *in* Christ or not. If you people (referring to the traditionalists present) want to die heathen, have it your way. But you heathen cannot properly accommodate the spirit of a deceased person. The spirit has his conductors — the leaders of the church. We Zionists accompany our deceased member, who has been awaiting us here at the grave for the past few days, directly to heaven.

These excerpts highlight four significant trends:

(1) awareness of the urgency of a choice for or against God, resulting in a call for repentance ("seek God now");

(2) awareness of the deliverance effected by the risen Christ: Christ is the basis for hope, and dying in him is prerequisite for entering heaven;

(3) heavy emphasis on the church's role as the "'conductor" of the deceased to heaven — something which coincides with the tendency to propagate both church and faith among the non-Christian kinsmen of the deceased; and

(4) direct or indirect attacks on the traditional initiation ceremonies in an attempt to clarify the difference in the mediation of the living on behalf of the dead.

Note that the deceased is not addressed, as happens for instance in adapted Roman Catholic rites.[25] Zionists consciously *reject addressing the deceased as a form of veneration (kupira)* which they consider counter to true worship of God. In their sermons they frequently speak *about* the Christian life of the deceased in an attempt to offer those present spiritual inspiration. This point illustrates the prophetic churches' conception of the "communion of saints".

Another major innovation is that the *runyaradzo* is held for *all* believers, irrespective of age or status, whereas the *kugadzira* was intended only for adults (usually ones with progeny). The naming

25 Daneel, 1973, pp. 60-64

ceremony is stripped of traditional religious connotations in that the bearer of the name is not addressed as if the spirit of the deceased dwelt in him. The inheritance of ritual functions acquires new meaning (as pointed out earlier with reference to the succession to leadership) in terms of the position the deceased occupied in the church.

The role of the deceased: It is assumed that the faithful departed who have been "conducted" to heaven are "with God", provided they were accepted by God himself. Instead of becoming a *mudzimu* who can only attain to the Supreme Being via a whole hierarchy of ancestors, the deceased is much closer to God and his mediatory function is much more direct. Instead of standing at the doorpost to protect kinsmen, as was the traditional belief, the faithful departed intercedes for living believers. The task of a Christian ancestor is more or less to prepare a place in heaven *(kugadzira nzvimbo kudenga)* for the faithful that still have to follow him. The traditional approach is broadened in that the mediation of the deceased is not confined to kinsmen but to all brothers and sisters in Christ.

Remarkably, this mediatory function of the deceased is rarely mentioned in *runyaradzo* sermons. This reticence is probably due to the prophetic leaders' intuitive awareness that any emphasis on such mediation would be unbiblical. Besides, preparing a place in heaven does *not* obviate the living believers' responsibility towards God. The shift in emphasis in the prophetic churches to God's direct protection through his prophetic representatives is in any case so drastic that the desire for ancestral protection — and concomitantly the supposed dependence of the believers on the preparation of a place in heaven by the faithful departed — has faded into insignificance.

Clearly then — despite theological flaws — the *runyaradzo* is in keeping with a christianizing renewal and cannot be casually dismissed as syncretistic preservation of the old faith in a new guise.

(c) *Ancestors and faith healing*

Because of the striking parallels between the ancestor cult and prophetic faith healing practices one may easily get the impres-

238

sion that the old ethos is preserved and that, as Sundkler would have it, the prophetic healer prescribes ancestor worship. But is this in fact so? A study of prophetic activities in both the Zionist and the Apostle churches among the Shona leads to very different insights. The *diagnosis* of the prophetic healer resembles that of the traditional *n'anga* in that both concentrate on the personal causes of the sickness or mishap. If the patient's condition is not caused by a living enemy making use of magic, it is attributable to an evil, alien or ancestral spirit. If the spirit of an ancestor is involved, it is usually appealing to the patient to continue in his "profession" — for instance, that of *n'anga,* hunter or black-smith — or claiming a legitimate indigenous right such as a sacrificial animal which has not yet been provided or not yet offered.

The parallels between prophetic and traditional diagnosis have caused the historical churches to regard prophetic practice as a covert continuation of *n'anga* activities, yet there are consider-able differences. The prophet regards and experiences his in-spiration as deriving from the Holy Spirit, *not* from throwing bones or an ancestral spirit. More important, the prophet's con-cern with the spirit world is not designed to concede to the de-mands of the tormenting spirit. On the contrary: the prophetic healer tries to explain the Christian message to the patient at a vitally personal level of his existence. By taking seriously the patient's tradition oriented experience of threat and his need for protection he effects a confrontation between the besetting evil power and the liberating power of the Christian God.

Prophetic therapy also differs significantly from that of the *n'anga.* Whereas the latter insists on compliance with the de-mands of the spirit — implying ancestor worship if a *mudzimu* is involved — the prophet *rejects the claims of the ancestral spirits.* Hence there is no question of a Spirit-inspired charge of neglect of the ancestors. The prophet might make a compromise only if non-Christian kinsmen are putting pressure on the patient to provide a sacrificial animal. In such a case he may urge the patient to provide the animal for the sake of peace in the family. But the patient is explicitly forbidden from attending the tradi-tional ceremony and the prophet exorcises the demon in the name of the triune God. The need for exorcism is brought about be-cause the prophet calls the tormenting spirit — whether an ancestral or alien one — a demon or evil spirit. The emphasis on the work of the Holy Spirit in the diagnostic and therapeutic procedure could create the impression that Christ's kingship over the spirit realm is partly superseded, but in fact it is the implicit, presupposed fact on which the Shona prophets base their activities.[26]

6.4.3 *Magic and witchcraft*

The ethos of most Independent Churches is marked by a rejection of magic and fetishist customs. The Spirit-type churches in particular are vehemently opposed to the use of traditional amulets, medicinal fetishes, other magical objects such as knobkerries or blankets that represent the ancestors and the like. Some prophets specialize in "prophetic hunts" in which they publicly expose any secret "medicine" church members may have concealed on their persons at church gatherings. This springs from a desire to continually purge the church and exercise constant control in the firm belief that the Christian God will not tolerate any object that interferes with his own power. Once fetishes have been discovered they are publicly destroyed, usually burning them. As in this case of exorcism the visual act symbolizing victory over and deliverance from evil destructive forces (sorcery) or deceitful ones (magic) is of great significance.

As was pointed out with reference to Elison Mutingwende's church expansion activities, the prophetic struggle against sorcery and witchcraft *(uroyi)* is undertaken with fervour and great commitment. It can serve as principal recruiting technique (as in Elison's case), or form a major part of the task of any Zionist or Apostle prophet, whatever his position in his particular leadership hierarchy. Sorcery and witchcraft are associated with satanic forces and as such are combated. Witch-hunts remain closely linked with the need to find a scapegoat for an inexplicable accident or threat to social harmony. The prophet's action is not always free of discrimination either. However, evangelical impulses are in evidence when the prophet preaches a *message of*

26 Daneel, 1970(b), pp. 36-49

reconciliation about the exposed sorcerer or witch and takes the convicted party into his church as proof of the hope and grace extended to the socially unacceptable. This practice is not always innocent of prophetic exploitation of *varoyi,* yet by and large the attitude of Zionists and Apostles towards the "convicted" contrasts dramatically with the traditional approach, which could go as far as the death penalty.

The use of symbolic objects to counteract magic sometimes manifests traits of a new magic. To such leaders as Mutendi the use of all manner of objects — such as his consecrated staff, holy water, newspaper, needles and the like[27] — for the exorcism of malignant spirits and the maintenance of security and prosperity (spiritual and material) did not pose much of a problem. He always stressed the symbolic value of such articles. Yet there is no doubt that some church members are confused by this and that they fail to get beyond the traditional magical approach which continues to look for intrinsic power in the holy water, paper or whatever. In this sense emancipation from the old forces may imply a new sort of enslavement to the "symbols of the church" which supersede rather than clarify the essence of deliverance in Christ.

6.4.4 *The law and disciplinary procedures*

In most Independent Churches the ethos is strongly legalistic. This relates to tribal laws that had to be upheld for the wellbeing of the tribe and the principle of reciprocity in the kinship structure according to which all human relationships are governed by certain rules. Life in the traditional order was very much conditioned by the observance of special days of the week in honour of the ancestors (Shona: *chisi*) and abstinence from certain meats as laid down for specific tribes and clans.

In view of all this it is understandable that churches are primarily interpreted in terms of their various codes of conduct that distinguish one group from another. It also follows that the Old Testament with its multitude of religious laws will have a special

27 Ibid., p. 46

appeal for Africans. They feel a close affinity with the Old Testament and, because of an imperfect distinction between the Old Testament and the New, certain guidelines — such as sabbath observance, purificatory rites, a taboo on pork, times of fasting and the like — were taken from the Old Testament and laid down for the Independent Churches. The Old Testament also provided justification for *polygamy,* a practice most Independent Churches still adhere to. Let me add at once that acceptance of polygamy in no way condones immorality in the sense of loose living, but is subject to moral norms and church control that are strictly enforced. The most common argument in this connection is that the Old Testament contains some prominent characters who were polygamous and who were not rejected by God. Monogamy is considered a Western rather than a biblical custom.

Undoubtedly there is some element of traditional pragmatism and reciprocity in the Independent Churches, as is evident from the way in which they endeavour to cleanse the congregation by means of all sorts of ritual acts so that they can as it were appear before God in an acceptable way, and the way rain is requested by means of gifts in the adapted Shona rites. Salvation too is obtained through faithful observance of certain behavioural codes. This raises the old issue of the connection between merit (or works) and grace. *The question is whether the legalistic approach based on merit in many of the Independent Churches permits a sufficiently unbiased view on the grace of God.*

Observance of church law and the application of disciplinary measures are to a great extent adapted to the traditional legal procedures with the emphasis on "setting matters to rights" *(kuenzanisa mhosva).* The following are fairly common features:

(1) As in traditional legal proceedings, *enough time* is devoted to every case so that both accuser and accused can state their opinions fully. The tight schedules of mission churches simply do not permit time for this.

(2) Both accuser and accused are always *present.* Both parties are allowed to call witnesses so that the case can be put from every angle before a verdict is given. Because the guilty party is present the risk of reaction and defection is

less than if he is convicted *in absentia,* as sometimes happens in mission churches.[28]

(3) The minute description of every circumstance, which "brings matters to light" *(mashoko anobuda)* affirms the common guilt of the parties, which makes it easier for the accused to accept disciplinary measures. The court proceedings also serve as an outlet for pentup feelings.

(4) Disciplinary measures are usually realistic, for instance a prohibition on preaching for a number of weeks, prohibition on wearing official robes for a few Sundays, abstaining from the annual celebration of the sacrament and so on. These measures are rarely counterproductive, as sometimes happens in the mission churches, because the sentencing is experienced as less drastic and is based on emotionally assimilable, traditionally familiar proceedings.

6.4.5 *Other characteristics*

In conclusion we should point out a few other striking features. Members of Independent Churches often *behave* in exemplary fashion because it is stressed that they must witness to their faith. This is the reason for the often stringent rules for behaviour and moral standards. Traditional behavioural codes are consciously replaced by a Christian code with the emphasis on sexual self-control, industry, asceticism and human fellowship. The attention devoted to spiritual strengthening, renewal and responsibility for others, especially in the prophetic movements, gives meaning to life and imparts self-respect.

Another important characteristic is *mutual support and service* within the group. This generates a sense of security, making the church truly "a place to feel at home".[29] Outsiders are often struck by the fellowship. Thus in the First Ethiopian Church I

28 Daneel, 1971(a), p. 256
29 Welbourn & Ogot, 1966

observed how women of the *Ruwadzano* (women's association) regularly decided who had to assist with laundry, cooking and other household chores in cases of illness. There was also great supportiveness in terms of bereavement so that the bereaved were relieved of the trouble of funeral arrangements.

As for the *churches' involvement in the community* at large, the bigger movements co-operate constructively in various ways to promote not just the welfare of their own ranks, but also those of the community as a whole. The Kimbanguists concern themselves with institutions for neglected children, help to widows, the unemployed and the sick, and run schools which welcome children from other groups. Mutendi was intimately involved in tribal politics, schools and agricultural schemes. He and his sons were themselves master farmers and tried to encourage modern agricultural techniques in their neighbourhood.

Other modern trends that are increasingly emerging are *ecumenical awareness,* resulting in membership of the National Councils of the World Council of Churches and the All African Council of Churches, and attempts at improving *theological training.* As indicated in the case of *Fambidzano,* in many churches these developments are resulting in a breaking down of former barriers.

CHAPTER 7

THEOLOGICAL REFLECTION

Theological reflection on the Independent Churches in Africa and an evaluation of the different trends are by no means easy matters. The incredible wealth of nuances, contradictions within one and the same church, data that are not always reliable, one's reliance on observers who are themselves outsiders and can only partially fathom what is going on in these churches, the lack of documentation for analysis, etc. combine to make this an extremely delicate and complex undertaking.

Nonetheless reflection on and evaluation of the Independent Churches is one of the main tasks facing missiologists today. There are various reasons for this, as set forth in chapter 1.

(1)   The rapid growth in the number of groups since the beginning of this century has produced a massive Christian-oriented movement that simply cannot be ignored.

(2)   The focal importance to missiology of communication between the Christian gospel and non-Christian religions is another reason for reflection. The Independent Churches provide a unique opportunity to observe how the African handles his traditional religion when he is outside the immediate sphere of influence of the Western-oriented historical churches.

(3)   Interchurch relations make a theological evaluation of this movement imperative. Such an evaluation will be decisive for the policy determination of the historical churches when it comes to rejection of or possible ecumenical co-operation with the Independent Churches. Inescapable questions include whether one is dealing with Christian churches, sectarian groups or even neo-pagan movements. Do the Trinity of God and the key message of reconciliation and redemption come across adequately? Or is the distortion such that these movements should be regarded as "objects for mission"?

When one examines the literature one observes that such researchers as Sundkler and H.W. Turner who have had prolonged contact with the Independent Churches, evaluate them very positively without disregarding their less favourable tendencies. G.C. Oosthuizen, Marie-Louise Martin and P. Beyerhaus adopt a far more stringent, condemnatory approach. Oosthuizen bluntly refers to the Independent Churches as "post-Christian". In his view these movements are neither Christian nor traditional. Because of their ethnocentric features they cannot claim to be churches of Christ.[1] He apparently characterizes all prophetic churches — that is, the Zionist and Apostolic groups — and "messianic" movements as nativistic, as opposed to what he calls "Christian sects". The main characteristic of this post-Christian category is the upholding of the traditional cult rather than the Word of God.[2]

Beyerhaus, who also uses the term "post-Christian", is even more vehement in his rejection. According to him the "messianic" groups rely on a conscious, fallacious existential contradiction *(Widerspruch)* of the gospel.[3] He maintains that the Zionists are in a state of self-deception because they fail to realize that their concept of God is confined to the human dimension and bears no relation to the holy and mighty God.[4] All biblical concepts have been sacrificed and replaced with heathen ones. No Zionist rites can be regarded as a faithful rendering of Christian worship.[5]

Beyerhaus's sweeping criticism implies that when it comes to the Zionists and so-called messianic movements (such as those of Lekhanyane, Shembe, Mutendi and Kimbangu) there can be no question of *churches* with which one could possibly co-operate. All he finds there is confusion and distortion due to syncretism, rather than legitimate contextualization which may be developed and from which other churches could learn. Beyerhaus explicitly states that there is no possibility of serving these churches by

1   Oosthuizen, 1968(a), p. xiv
2   Ibid., p. 73-75
3   Beyerhaus, 1967, p. 510
4   Beyerhaus, 1969, p. 75
5   Ibid., p. 77

means of *theological training* and development from within owing to the lack of any spiritual basis on which to build. Since in his view the sole "spiritual base" of Messianism if evasion of the cross, any theological development could only lead to further confusion and syncretism.[6] The only theologically sound approach, he claims, would be confrontation through a new presentation of the *gospel of salvation:*

> In the nativistic group this gospel is not preached. Thus God himself is still unknown to them. The Bible, as we have literally seen on our visit to a worshipping Shembe group ... is a closed book even to their leaders. Let us go to them with the opened Bible ... It will shatter the fog of their dim impression of the 'unknown God' which is sensed only by way of legal prescriptions and as an impersonal life force.[7]

Beyerhaus even believes himself to be correct in Pauline terms when he evaluates the Black prophets as an extension of pagandom, possessed by demonic forces. He recommends that the demonic powers that enthrall these prophets be expelled through exorcism.[8] Here this theological systematizer pursues his line of a supposed process of degeneracy to its apparently logical conclusion: *demonic control.*

The somewhat arrogant way in which the Zionist leader is flatly condemned and reduced to an object of mission makes one wonder whether Beyerhaus ever took a serious look at the practical realities. His appraisal would appear to be based on a few sporadic observations. In all the Zionist churches without exception the Bible is by no means a *closed book,* but rather a *well-thumbed one* owing to constant use. It would seem that Beyerhaus's approach is based on an attitude of dissociation from the Independent Churches (at least as far as their religious experience is concerned), as if he is writing solely *for* the historical churches, as if these latter churches offer the only possible outlet for true Christian witness, and as if his judgements are based on a caricature rather than a balanced evaluation of empirical facts.

6 Ibid., p. 78
7 Ibid., p. 79
8 Ibid., p. 79

In her dissertation on Messianism in Africa Marie-Louise Martin concluded theologically that it is largely a case of *spurious* eschatology and a *false* Christology, pneumatology and ecclesiology.[9] As mentioned in chapter 5, her field study and eventual participation in the Kimbanguist church led her to change her mind and give this church her enthusiastic support. She admitted the limitations of her original approach which had been based mainly on a study of literary sources and in a fervent first article after her study maintains that the Kimbanguist church is *a true Christian church* representing the *whole* of Christian life.[10]

The striking shift in emphasis which follows an evaluation based on empirical study and consistent involvement with members of the church instead of a patchwork composed out of earlier literature leads to the inevitable conclusion that the *empirical infrastructure* certainly does not justify the sweepingly drastic theological evaluation of some of these observers. Part of the problem is a dearth of in-depth monographic studies, so that — despite an abundance of literature about the Independent Churches — such theologians get only a *fragmented overall image.* For this very reason one would expect them to be extremely cautious in their theological evaluations.

Representative empirical in-depth studies would have to include *analyses of sermons* (based on preaching in various contexts and by different leaders) so as to determine actual theological trends. It would also require prolonged *observation* of both the ceremonial and daily life of the church, as well as *interviewing* significant numbers of clergy and lay members to gauge the process of Christian concept formation. Only then would a fair theological exposition be at all feasible. But even then a theological evaluation would have to be extremely *cautious* and purely *provisional* in view of the dynamic and constant process of change in these churches.

Other factors that prompt caution are the enormous differences within a single church. Often the preaching of the paramount leader at church headquarters will differ vastly from those of office-bearers in outlying congregations, thus complicating gen-

9 Martin, 1964, p. 161
10 Martin, 1975, pp. vii-xi; Martin, 1968, p. 12

eralizations. In addition the researcher is confronted with the need to evaluate *people* — the ones with whom he identifies in the course of his study — and not simply a set of doctrinal statements on paper. The amazing thing is just this, for it is when the researcher is living among villagers belonging to the various churches that he discovers that the views and beliefs of individuals from historical and Independent Churches are not nearly as different as the ideological differences represented by the leaders would lead one to suppose. In a series of publications about an extensive study conducted in Soweto, Johannesburg, Moller shows that the differences in belief between individual members of the historical and Independent Churches are usually only ones of degree.[11] Among the Shona churches too I found that the individual members of the Reformed, Roman Catholic, "Ethiopian" and Zionist churches were usually in far greater agreement about such matters as the focal scriptural truths, the continuing role of spirits, sorcery and the like than their "official" viewpoints would lead one to believe.

This is not meant as a plea for a levelling of doctrinal differences. It is merely that a comparison and evaluation of churches based on the views and beliefs of individuals (rather than an ideal doctrinal image of the one, offset against the weaknesses of the other as observed in practice) result in different insights and prompt greater caution than is expressed, for instance, in Beyerhaus's radical condemnation.

In underscoring the *need for empirical research* for a fair theological evaluation one must point out that this presents missiology with a definite mandate. It is not enough simply to rely on inter-disciplinary co-operation, however important this may be, and then draw on sociological, anthropological or religio-phenomenological studies, as if these disciplines have a sort of monopoly on empirical field studies. Often the concern and inquiry of these sciences are such that their data are inadequate for meaningful theological reflection. *To my mind it is a task for theologians, and more specifically missiologists, to create facilities for empirical research in the field and to collect for themselves — by*

11 Moller, 1972

means of scientific sociological and anthropological fieldwork techniques — the data necessary for on-going reflection.

Since this study provides only general guidelines and, despite the focus on the Shona Independent Churches, does not afford sufficient data for a detailed evaluation of any specific church, we cannot endeavour to formulate a searching, minute evaluation of this nature. What we can do is to try to single out some of the more important theological trends and point out their significance for a theological evaluation, as well as discuss the criteria essential for such an undertaking.

7.1 CHRISTIAN CHURCHES?

What criteria are used to arrive at even a tentative decision as to whether the Independent African Churches are actually Christian churches? Although the three Reformed *notae ecclesiae* (namely uncorrupted *proclamation of the Word,* use of the *sacraments* and exercise of *discipline)* do not cover all points, a useful theological perspective can be obtained by measuring the available data in terms of these essential criteria.

7.1.1 *Proclamation of the Word*

Christ's position in preaching is probably one of the supreme criteria when evaluating the Christian nature and uncorrupted character of proclamation of the Word. Together with this one must consider the role of the Father and the Holy Spirit. Since we shall be dealing with the Trinity in more detail below, we shall not dwell on the matter here. However, the following comments can be made about the proclamation of the Word in the Shona churches.

Scripture is focal and is accepted as the final authority. Fragmentary interpretation seldom results in wholesale misconceptions about soteriology, anthropology, sin or any major theological issues. At the same time there is a tendency to single out certain texts — such as those referring to Ethiopia or Zion — and apply them literally to the church in question out of a desire to identify directly with the first Christian communities. This can result in an exclusive manifesto for the church based on a mistaken "exegesis" of texts. Often this is more a desire for a biblically sanctioned identity arising from an imperfect knowledge of church history, than a deliberate distortion of scriptural truths.

In the course of a series of sermons during an afternoon service one may feel that too much attention is focused on the central figure of the leader (e.g. Mutendi), on events in the church or the witness of people who had been prophetically healed. But there are usually also pure evangelical messages accompanying this, such as those about Christ the vine (and we the branches), Christ the healer and Christ the Saviour. These restore the balance and mitigate one's theological reservations about the supposed one-sidedness. It is this tremendous diversity of approaches in the preaching which quite rules out one-sided categorical pronouncements. Besides, the multiplicity of "circumstancial" or contextualized sermons reflecting the experiences of the group is a reaction against a preaching of the gospel which has not taken the African's *holistic life-view* into account.

As Bosch has pointed out, the Western mentality is conditioned by a dichotomous, dualistic anthropology which divides man into two separable entities — "soul" and "body". This view concurs neither with Scripture not with the African's traditional conception. Both Pietism and the Social Gospel are products of this dualistic approach, resulting in the sick soul being treated in church and the sick body in hospital, without any real integration of the two.[12]

The Independent Churches followed the traditional and biblical view of man and the world, which is more intuitive and partly a reaction against the dualistic view as a piece of conscious systematization. In this way they arrived at a holistic approach. The prophet took over the whole range of activities of the traditional *n'anga* and combined them pastorally and medically in the context of the church. His task literally reveals a comprehensive approach embracing the entire spectrum of sin, disease, sorcery, evil spirits, agricultural and other economic activities. In this respect the prophets have a ministry which the historical churches would do well to note, mindful of J.V. Taylor's warning:

12 Bosch, 1973(a), p. 75

251

> For until Christians can bring to their own ministers their
> sicknesses and their feuds, the sterility of their wives and the
> rebellion of their sons, with a sure expectation of enlighten-
> ment and healing, they will continue to look elsewhere for
> help.[13]

It stands to reason that the holistic approach of the Independent Churches will crystallize in their preaching. This entails a
real risk that the proclamation of the Word will be affected and
pushed into the background, yet circumstantial and witness
preaching (about healing or deliverance from the danger of sorcery) often provides the perfect illustrations to clarify the Word.
To a Western theologian it will always be difficult to regard such
preaching as "pure", but at the same time it is all but impossible
to brand it false or unchristian.

Something that frequently emerges from sermons is the imperfect distinction between the Old and the New Testament. As we
have shown, this results in Old Testament legalism and polygamy
being as it were sanctioned biblically. In consequence their concept of salvation is not altogether devoid of traditional pragmatism, principles of reciprocity and the meritorious behaviour
of individuals. Yet despite that these sermons so often contain
an unmistakable appeal to conversion in Christ, an affirmation
of the comfort and protection available through the Holy Spirit,
that one cannot speak of a distortion of God's grace in any absolute sense.

The use of "canonical" church documents such as Mutendi's
"Church history" and Johane Maranke's "New revelation" is
also significant for an evaluation of these churches' proclamation
of the Word. Yet in both these churches the historical descriptions of the origins of that church and the experiences of its paramount leader are used not as a substitute for the Bible, but are
introduced occasionally as *additional sources of information,* sub-
stantiating Scripture rather than contradicting it. Of all the
"Ethiopian" and prophetic churches among the Shona, there is
to my knowledge only *one* which indisputably *replaces* Scripture
with another book, namely Mai Chaza's *Guta raJehovah* (City

13 Taylor, 1963, p. 152

252

of God) movement. Here a church manual was consciously introduced as a substitute for the Bible. It is used for preaching and includes a portrayal of the Trinity which is totally unscriptural, with Mai Chaza elevated to one of the three divine Persons who was present even during the creation. Here the Christian message has degenerated and been superseded to a point where one can no longer speak of a Christian church in the true sense of the word.

7.1.2   *Use of the sacraments and discipline*

As we have shown, the sacraments of baptism and communion are found in most Independent Churches. True, some prophetic churches use *baptism* as a purificatory rite and certain prophetic "witch-finding specialists" employ it as a sort of Christian technique to conduct witch hunts in afflicted village communities. One must acknowledge the distortion of the true meaning of baptism and the misconceptions to which this may give rise. At the same time one must not lose sight of the fact that the prophetic leaders are perfectly aware of the difference between true baptism, which initiates the believer into the church, and the "adapted baptism" that serves some other purpose. Not that such practices can be theologically condoned, but before condemning them out of hand their positive value to people in trouble must be considered, and particularly the introduction of Christian elements in an area which the historical churches frequently neglected. Another highly significant point is that the "adapted baptism" is fairly rare pro rata to true baptisms, so that there is no question of a heretical practice superseding the true concept of baptism to any extent. The way in which baptisms are solemnized is sufficient evidence that the biblical essence of a transition from the old life to a new fellowship, in the name of the Trinity, is fully realized, and is moreover in many respects depicted more beautifully than in some historical churches.

As for *communion* there is hardly any church that does not practise it, even though in some groups it may not be celebrated more than once a year during a great conference. The eucharist is sometimes called "Easter" or "Pentecost", but throughout there is a clear grasp of the true significance of the use of the bread and wine. The fact that some individuals attach magical significance to both baptism and communion indicates that the purging of certain culturally determined ideas is an on-going and never ending process. The same problem is encountered by the historical churches. Officially, however, most historical and Independent Churches uphold the tenet that the sacramental elements are no more than symbols *(zviratidzo)* and have no intrinsic efficacy of their own.

As I have indicated above the majority of Independent Churches are characterized by legalistic trends which derive both from customary law and Old Testament prohibitions. The ethical codes of churches, which to a great extent reflect their identity in society, are generally maintained through *strict disciplinary procedures*. The practical effectiveness of such procedures have been alluded to, in that enough time is spent in church court proceedings to do justice to the human factor by considering a wide range of circumstancial factors involved in each case, establishing common guilt in addition to that of the accused and applying the realistic disciplinary measures which stimulate behavioural improvement rather than alienation. The zealously guarded religious legalism is mostly counterbalanced by the traditional legal procedure of "setting matters right" *(kuenzanisa mhosva)*, which in the context of the church court manifests itself as a kind of indigenized pastoral care. Hence it is not only a matter of meting out punishment for misbehaviour but also of repairing the wrongs done in relationships through reconciliation, and facilitating response to the challenge of spiritual renewal. In this respect IC court procedures are an expression of Christian concern, comparable to if not more effective than those of many of the historical churches.

I can imagine that Western theologians will be inclined to seriously question the content of the IC ethical codes which, in some instances, virtually exclude clear guidelines on Christian marriage and in the majority of cases permit polygamy. I, too consider monogamy as the Christian ideal, emanating not only from Western culture but also from New Testament theology. Nevertheless, the question arises whether Christianity stands or falls on this issue and whether a distinction between religious ideal and practices (the latter reflecting imperfections with prospects of gradual change) could not be a step, on the part of the historic churches, towards eliminating the issue of polygamy as a stumbling block which prevents interchurch recognition and co-operation. In addition, it should be kept in mind that polygamy does not of necessity imply sexual licentiousness and that traditionally contracted unions between men and women in the Independent Churches invariably reveal the same religious features as those solemnized by a church ceremony.

These comments on the *notae ecclesiae* are too sketchy to permit any final, definitive conclusions. However, with reference to the Shona Independent Churches (with the exception of the *Mai Chaza* movement), the indications are sufficiently positive to allow us to speak of Christian churches. Owing to defects and forms of syncretism a partial *degeneracy* may be discerned, but this is not so pronounced as to warrant calling them "post-Christian" or "neo-pagan". If one evaluated the religious beliefs of individual members of the Shona mission churches, one could apply the same qualification. Besides, internal developments among the Shona Independent Churches, including such projects as *Fambidzano,* suggest that they are moving from the periphery to the heart of Christianity.

7.2   THE TRINITY

7.2.1   God the Father

There is very little difference in the approach to God the Father (Shona: *Mwari Baba)* in the historical and the Independent Churches. As Bosch points out, the emphasis is consistently on the monotheistic God of the Bible, who has either taken the place of or been identified with the traditional Supreme Being.[14] In a sense God the Father has remained the remote God who, although the ultimate origin of all things, has little direct contact with individuals. Consequently fellowship with him is an implicit fact rather than a prominent feature of worship. In this respect the Shona churches differ somewhat from churches elsewhere in Africa, for even their traditional Supreme Being cult had assigned

14 Bosch, 1973(b), pp. 3-21

Mwari greater eminence (as the God of rain and fertility) than happened elsewhere. Hence adapted rainmaking rites in the Independent Churches, based on both the Mwari cult and local rainmaking rites *(mukwerere)*, have meant that *Mwari Baba* (God the Father), *Wedenga* (the One from heaven) and *Wokumusoro* (the One from above) probably acquired greater significance in the individual's religious experience than they did in other African churches. By and large one could say that God himself has become a far more clearly defined concept in the Independent Churches than he ever did in the traditional faith.

7.2.2 *Christology*

The crucial question in a theological evaluation of any church is the part assigned to Christ. In this respect Peter Beyerhaus provided very useful criteria. In his view there are four major aspects that should be considered when evaluating the Independent Churches:

(1) Christ must be proclaimed as *Christus Victor*, the one who triumphs over evil forces (Col 2: 15);

(2) Christ must be proclaimed as the *Crucified One* who took the curse of our sins upon himself;

(3) Christ must be proclaimed as the One who is *present*, still working powerfully among his people and assisting them in their need, danger and temptation; and

(4) He must be proclaimed as the One *to come* who will appear at the full revelation of God's kingdom.[15]

Ernst Damman pointed out four possible conceptions of Christ in the Independent Churches:

(a) A view of Christ which basically agrees with that of the historical church from which the movement was born (e.g. the African Methodist Episcopal Church);

15 Beyerhaus, 1967

(b) Although Christ is given a place in credal pronouncements, in the realities of religious experience he is a background figure (e.g. the *Musama Disco Christo* Church in Ghana);

(c) Christ is wholly superseded even in credal pronouncements (e.g. the Nazareth Baptist Church of Shembe); and

(d) Messianic attributes of Christ are transferred to the group leader — the Black Messiah is totally identified with the biblical Messiah (e.g. Simon Kimbangu).[16]

Damman's evaluation of the churches of Shembe and Kimbangu differs markedly from those of Sundkler and Marie-Louise Martin respectively. This indicates once more the problem of subjectivity and the preconceptions of each researcher. What is significant in Damman's approach is the determination of the position of the prophetic leader in relation to Christ and to his followers. The Mindolo consultation in 1962 laid down quite rightly with regard to the identification of the church leader with Christ:

> It should be noted that when this identification becomes substitution, the group has ... moved outside the sphere of the Christian Church.[17]

Of course, this still begs the question of how one should distinguish the point in the transition when such identification amounts to substitution. Have such prophetic leaders as Shembe, Lekhanyane, Mutendi and Kimbangu really replaced the figure of Christ? And are the evaluation of these movements based on adequate data? In chapter 5 I showed that in the cases of Mutendi and Johane Maranke there is in fact a considerable degree of identification with Christ and that one can at most speak of semi-messianic tendencies. At the time it was pointed out that despite the "custodian of the gate" function, the mediatorship of Christ has not been superseded and his authority and kingship remain

16 Damman, 1965, pp. 1-21
17 Turner, 1967,(c), p. 31

unaffected. In fact, in the ZCC recognition of the kingship of Christ is the impetus for their annual country-wide missionary campaigns.

Two grave dangers beset Christology in the Independent Churches. One is that the enormous emphasis on the work of the Holy Spirit in the prophetic groups results in an impoverished Christology. Turner's observation of the Church of the Lord *(Aladura)* in West Africa applies equally to the Shona:

> It is not so much that he (Jesus Christ) is ignored, as that his divinity is taken for granted, and his humanity overlooked, so that he is readily absorbed in the term God, whose present manifestation in the Spirit is of more importance than his historical work in the flesh.[18]

Thus on the whole it would be more correct to speak of an implicit, partially superseded Christology rather than a misconstruction and conscious denial of Christ.

The second danger is that some Independent Churches show a tendency to underrate the *cross,* or to see it as a stumbling block. In the struggle against disease, want and injustice there is need for a King and Sovereign, not a suffering Messiah in whose followers the strength in weakness is consummated. Hence it is very easy for the *Christus Victor* to overshadow the *crucified* Christ and for the *theologia gloriae* to outweigh the *theologia crucis.* Here it should be noted that these tendencies *rarely predominate in any absolute sense.* In certain circumstances an implicit Christology is transformed so convincingly into a totally involved Christ that any rigid conclusion would be difficult to maintain.

In the Zion Sabbath Church, whose prophetic activities are also based on the work of the Holy Spirit, it may happen that in the course of a faith-healing ceremony Christ would be thrust dramatically and deliberately into the foreground. Thus towards the end of a conference Bishop Gotore stood in the light of the setting sun, pressing his Bible against the belly of a pregnant woman and prayed: "You are Jesus who existed yesterday.

18 Turner, 1967(b), p. 344

You are the One about whom we preached today, the alpha and the omega, the beginning and the end. You are the One who changes all things. We who are in distress call to you for help, you the keeper and protector of flesh and blood, you who said that the pregnant young woman who has difficulty in giving birth normally will rejoice with her child and forget her pains. Bless this young woman, Lord Jesus. We commit her to you with this sunset, so that you can preserve her throughout her life. We ask that you will remind her to remember the things of heaven. Heal her womb, in the name of Jesus Christ, for evermore. Amen! "

Here Christ is present directly and focally, not a peripheral figure merely mentioned in passing. Indeed, in the heart throb of Zionism we find him as healer and Saviour. Committing a young woman who carries the promise of life in her womb to him with the sunset is one of the most poignant ways of expressing total dependence on him, the beginning and end of all things.

When the interrelationship between the inspiring, healing Spirit of God and the living Christ is so vividly manifested we have every reason to refrain from one-sided theological criticism and to proceed with circumspection in our evaluation. In my view it is the very fact that God's Word occupies such a central position in the Zionist movements that causes the Word to act as a corrective, so that the focus on the Holy Spirit is continually interspersed with and amplified by clear-sighted visions of Jesus Christ.

7.2.3   *Pneumatology*

The work of the Holy Spirit in the prophetic churches — particularly the Zionist and "messianic" movements — has preoccupied researchers and proved an extremely complex subject. Oosthuizen devotes an entire chapter to the "misinterpretation of the Holy Spirit" in the Independent Churches.[19] As pointed out earlier,

19 Oosthuizen, 1968(a), pp. 119-142

his chief objection is the confusion of the Holy Spirit with the ancestors. In his view this is one of the greatest theological problems in Africa, one which directly relates to the belief that the deceased prophet or messianic leader returns to influence his followers, just as an ancestral spirit remains involved with the weal and woe of his living descendants.[20] By superseding Christ and accentuating *uMoya* (the Spirit) the "Black Messiah" leads his followers back to the ancestors, the "blood and soil" of the tribe.[21] We have shown that Sundkler, Beyerhaus and Martin have noted a similar confusion and/or identification of Holy Spirit with ancestral spirits. Oosthuizen maintains that the prominence given to ancestor worship and the transfer of the ancestors' functions to the Spirit not only led to the usurpation of Christ's role, but also to the *total exclusion of the connection between the Holy Spirit and Scripture.*[22]

Observers have mentioned yet another form of conceptual fallacy in the prophetic movements, namely the syncretist distortion of the personal Spirit of God to an *impersonal, manipulated force.* Beyerhaus claims that the primordial desire of human beings for syncretism — that is, equating and identifying all supernatural forces and revelations — causes a depersonalization of God, and changes the sovereign Spirit to an impersonal force — an "it" — which man can control.[23] In her description of a spurious pneumatology Martin writes:

> In prophetic and messianic movements the prophets and messiahs 'possess' the 'Spirit' like an impersonal power they get hold of in their own way, and the 'Spirit' must give utterance in a visible and audible way (glossolaly, trembling, leaps) and not in the hidden manner of the new life in Christ which is the fruit of the Spirit (Gal. 5: 22f).[24]

Oosthuizen concurs with this when he says about the Ngunza Khaki "church" that the Spirit becomes the monopoly of the paramount leader.[25] In such an extension of traditional magic

20 Ibid., p. 120
21 Ibid., p. 120
22 Ibid., pp. 126, 129, 132
23 Beyerhaus, 1969, p. 75
24 Martin, 1964, p. 161
25 Oosthuizen, 1968(a), p. 124

and fetishism the prophetic leader has the duty of "giving" the "Spirit" to his followers.[26] Obviously such a transformation of the Holy Spirit into a manipulable force that can be used by people in their own and their group's interests must render the biblical doctrine of the Holy Spirit unrecognizable. This would be yet another sign of the *theologia gloriae* being stressed at the expense of the *theologia crucis*.

However, the Shona churches present a different picture. Contrary to assertions that the Spirit is confused with the ancestral spirits, resulting in a return to ancestor domination in that the Spirit as an angel (according to Sundkler) in fact prescribes ancestor worship, *the activities of Shona prophets among the Zionists and Apostles in fact point to confrontation and change.* This is nowhere more apparent than in prophetic faith healing where the prophet, inspired by the Holy Spirit, diagnoses the disease or problems of his patients and either applies or prescribes therapy. As mentioned in the preceding chapter, there is a clear parallel between the diagnoses of prophets and the traditional doctor *(n'anga)* inasmuch as the cause of the problem is traced to ancestral, alien or vengeful spirits or sorcery. This orientation to the traditional world-view could create the impression that the prophet's motive is to preserve the old mentality. That this is not the case is evident from the fact that the spirit is branded a demon, its claims on the patient — especially if these involve ancestor worship — are rejected and the spirit is exorcised. *Here the Holy Spirit and the ancestor spirit are usally diametrically opposed and it is a matter of confrontation rather that identification.* Hence it is not a question of an *uMoya* who is an extension of traditional spirit possession, as Beyerhaus maintains about the prophetic movements, or a Spirit who sanctions or prescribes the demands of the ancestral spirits (Sundkler and Oosthuizen). The Spirit's activity is rather an extension of Scripture which continues to be the key criterion, despite occasional misinterpretations. The result is that prophets who prescribed traditional religious rites are placed under discipline by senior office-bearers in their congregations or, in extreme cases, relieved of their posts. To my mind the fact that Shona traditionalists — especially the

26 Ibid., p. 133

n'anga — have reacted far more vehemently against Zionist and Apostle prophetic activity than against the medical and evangelical work of the historical churches, confirms that we are dealing with a Christian Spirit-inspired confrontation that reaches into the traditional world-view at a far more existential level than was possible for the historical churches with their Western theological norms and doctrinal purity.

Assertions that the Holy Spirit is seen as an *impersonal force*[27] possessed by the Messiah figure and "given" to his followers at his pleasure simply do not hold water in the context of the Shona prophetic churches. Interviews with prophetic office-bearers have shown that inspiration or revelation through the Holy Spirit is attributed to God's initiative, and not to that of any human being. Prophets often declare that they only receive guidance from the Holy Spirit after fasting, prayer and seclusion. They moreover readily acknowledge that these actions are not causal factors but that the initiative remains with the Spirit. Laying on of hands does imply conferring spiritual blessing on the parties concerned, but not that the prophet has "given" the fullness of the Spirit to a subordinate member. It is an *act of faith,* with the additional consideration that the spiritual state of the novice and the choice of the Spirit himself are decisive factors when it comes to unusual gifts such as speaking in tongues or faith healing. Many Zionists and Apostles confess such gifts as spiritual growth or successful church leadership through the Spirit without laying any claim to the gifts of prophecy or speaking in tongues. Other prophets speak in tongues, but admit that they lack the gift of interpreting or seeing prophetic visions of the future. Usually they account for this by saying that the Spirit wants to use them in a limited way only, or that they have never been totally filled by the Spirit. Such an attitude implies acceptance that the initiative rests with God and lies beyond human control.

Neither Mutendi nor Johane ever pretended that they could give the spirit to their followers at their own discretion. In the various Zionist and Apostle congregations those whose lives manifest spiritual depth and fellowship with God were accepted as reliable channels through whom the Holy Spirit could transmit

27 Daneel, 1974, p. 347f

his authentic messages to his people. Hence a person is only ordained to the prophetic office at church headquarters after it has become clear within his local congregation that he has exceptional gifts and lives a life inspired by the Spirit in the service of the church. A striking feature at prophetic ordinations is in fact the relevance of such biblical norms as godliness, willingness to serve and love, and not merely some arbitrary decision of a prophetic leader or "messianic" figure. This illustrates the close connection between the work of the Holy Spirit and "moral guidance", which Oosthuizen claims to be lacking in nativistic movements. If one moreover considers how intensely Zionist and Apostle prophets are involved with the moral standards of the group, with communicants' confessions before partaking of the sacrament and in exercising discipline (a prophetic service supposedly based exclusively on the inspiration of the Holy Spirit), then the alleged moral uninvolvement of the Spirit becomes no more than a theological fiction.

One cannot deny that the widespread use of symbolic objects with divine healing power in the churches of Johane and Mutendi gives rise to misconceptions. As we have pointed out, many members definitely attach a *magical interpretation* to the holy water, strips of linen or sacred staffs that have been blessed by the hands of, for instance, Mutendi. Instead of possessing the intended symbolic value, the power of God is identified with the object to such an extent that one could speak of a manipulable impersonal force. The crucial point, however, is that the side-effects of a magically oriented life-view in the Shona churches do not necessarily result in a misinterpretation of the Holy Spirit as an impersonal force. There is every indication that the prophetic movements experience the Holy Spirit mainly as a personal, divine being and not as an impersonal, manipulable force.

To sum up then: as far as the Trinity is concerned, at both the conceptual and the ritual level, there is in the Independent Churches an interaction between God the Father (who has drawn far closer to the individual than in the pre-Christian cult), God the Son (who is implicit and sometimes partially superseded, but continually re-emerges in surprising ways as the crucified one and the Saviour) and God the Holy Spirit (who continues to probe as a personal force to the innermost core of the indigenous mentality, there to triumph over threatening forces).

7.3 ESCHATOLOGY

For various reasons one can argue that there is a tendency towards a one-sided *realized eschatology* among the Independent Churches, and particularly the prophetic movements.

Martin speaks of the intense yearning for an *intelligible revelation here and now,* a longing to be delivered from evil and to enjoy a new fellowship of joy and happiness.[28] This longing assumes perspective only against the background of the Black man's traditional concept of time which, as explained by Mbiti, is oriented mainly to the *present* and the *past* (*Sasa* and *Zamani* in Swahili terminology).[29] The *future* as conceived of by the Western linear mind, was virtually non-existent. It was to such a world-view that the Western missionary proclamation came with a soteriological message and an *apocalyptic* emphasis which projected salvation onto this, to the Black man, non-existent dimension of time. Inasmuch as salvation cannot be seen and experienced in the immediate present, it was meaningless. The disillusionment which attended the unfulfilled future promises, such as the delay in the second coming, and the apparent absence of salvation from the daily acculturative and political dilemma of the Black man could only intensify these longings. Hence joining prophetic and "messianic" movements represents, albeit sometimes unconsciously, a desire to experience the realization of the unfulfilled eschatological hopes now, in the present.

Viewed thus it is not surprising that the prophet or Black "Messiah" — in response to his people's needs — should establish a colony which, as "Zion City", "Moriah" or "Jerusalem", implies the realization of redemption and salvation in this life. In the midst of the fragmentation of tribal customs and social change with the attendant frustrations and insecurity, the paramount leader of the new community stands as a prophet, king, Messiah — even as God.[30] This is expressed in the sermons of John Galilee Shembe, successor to Isaiah Shembe:

> You, my people, were once told of a God who has neither arms nor legs, who cannot see, who has neither love nor pity.

28 Martin, 1964, p. 135
29 Mbiti, 1969, pp. 15-28
30 Martin, 1964, p. 131

But Isaiah Shembe showed you a God who walks on feet and who heals with his hands and who can be known by men, a God who loves and who has compassion.

According to Sundkler the "God" referred to here is the Messiah, Isaiah Shembe himself.[31] Martin maintains that Edward Lekhanyane of the ZCC is worshipped in similar fashion. In prayer he is invoked as "our God, Lekhanyane". He is also a Moses figure, chief justice and healing Nazerene. Sometimes his followers mention neither Jesus Christ nor the second coming.

But this teaching seems for many to be of little importance, because they believe that in E. Lekhanyane their messiah is present. For them eschatology is realized.[32]

Some of the features of eschatology in messianic colonies which Martin considers to be "spurious" are the following. The eschatology is *materialistically* or *secularistically* distorted.

Oosthuizen finds that in all "nativistic" movements eschatology is secularized because it is interpreted in terms of the Black man's existential situation. He claims that in these movements it is explicitly stated that all enemies will be conquered so that the Black man will live in plenty in the new world that will be born of the old.[33] The accent is on *material affluence* — an Africanized utopia — in which Christ plays no part and where the Black Messiah sees to the health, fertility and material welfare of his followers.[34] Beyerhaus puts the question quite explicitly: are the messianic movements not a case of awareness of benefits that can be obtained from Western civilization, coinciding with a gospel message of God's imminent kingdom of peace, resulting in a discharge of the eschatological tension between the "already" and "not yet" of God's kingdom by means of a "secularist short circuit"?[35]

In a realized kingdom which is not merely *in* but also *of the* world, Christian salvation and redemption are narrowed down to healing, success, security and prosperity in this life. The deeply felt need for deliverance from physical and social suffering and

31 Sundkler, 1961, pp. 278f
32 Martin, op. cit., pp. 131-132
33 Oosthuizen, 1968(a), pp. 83-84
34 Ibid., p. 96
35 Beyerhaus, 1967, p. 516

stress has meant that the message of future salvation has become a stumbling block. Full salvation must be available *now*. Consequently the quest is for healing instead of salvation.[36] Because of this concentration on an Africanized salvation in the present the eschatological polarity between the "already" and "not yet" vanishes.[37] Because the future kingdom is as it were grabbed by force[38] (Martin and Oosthuizen refer to a "seizing" and a "snatching of the future"[39]), the perspective on eternal life and Christ's return disappears. Oosthuizen writes:

> In all their visions this snatching of the future is apparent. There is no idea of the tension between the present and the 'not yet', the Christian hope plays no part; here is the old natural man, freed from the cyclic concept of his religion to which he was so inexorably bound, but he has not found his feet in the new freedom. He has no central point on which these expectations are built . . .[40]

Martin stresses the *loss of true hope* which accompanies this snatching of the future:

> Whenever man takes it upon himself to strech out his hand to seize the future (i.e. the kingdom) and to take it by force, he has no real hope. What he has seized upon is always a hope of his own making, a messiah who is a false Christ, and sooner or later disappointment follows.[41]

All this creates the impression that prophetic and "messianic" eschatology in fact imply a complete elimination of biblical eschatology. It causes a stagnation in the cyclical time-conception so that there is no real future perspective.

Martin and Oosthuizen's assessment of a "realized eschatology" in the prophetic churches partly applies to the churches of Mutendi and Maranke as well. The realization of salvation and redemption in this life is extremely important. This is evident in all prophetic activities to protect man against disease and destruc-

---

36 Martin, 1964, p. 158
37 Ibid., 158; see also Oosthuizen, 1968(a), p. 97
38 Martin, 1964, p. 158
39 Ibid., p. 160; Oosthuizen, 1968(a), 97
40 Oosthuizen, 1968(a), p. 97
41 Martin, 1964, p. 160

tive forces. It is also apparent in the paramount leader's struggle against the White administration. Thus Mutendi's establishment of a Zion City was a partial breach of government policy as regards the structure of villages. To his followers his arrest and release confirmed the authorities' determination to rule in an absolute sense.[42] When he established his own school it symbolized a breakthrough of the White monopoly on education. The successful application of modern agricultural techniques was a sign of God's blessing on Zion. On the one hand Mutendi reminded them of the bygone glory of the Rozvi kings of the Mwenemutapa dynasty, on the other he acted as a Moses-like liberator in his relations with the administration.

However, it would be a mistake to decide, because of this emphasis on a kingdom of God here and now, that the future perspective has been totally eclipsed, that all hope of the coming salvation and return of Christ has been lost and that eschatology has been distorted in an absolutely materialistic and secularized sense. In the Shona Zionist and Apostle churches there is no "snatching of the future", no exclusive focus on prosperity in the present "Jerusalem" in the sense that the aforementioned observers would have it. The eschatological polarity between the "already" and "not yet" of God's kingdom is not a lost dimension, but clearly emerges in the preaching and praxis of the church. An analysis of a series of sermons by the Revd Ezekiah of the ZCC reveals a trend towards witnessing, which regularly depicts Mutendi as the "man of God" and the blessing of the Zionist Jerusalem, but in addition propagates the focal theme of God's judgement which is still to come. New Testament texts are quoted regularly to stress the need for repentance in the light of God's judgment. Frequently he falls back on the Old Testament prophets to illustrate the importance of change in the lives of individuals. To indicate the destructive power of God's judgment he referred either to the flood and disobedience to Noah's instructions, or the sword of Ezekiel 33, or the pit of fire *(gomba romwoto)*. This judgment can only be averted by taking refuge in God's kingdom. The Zionist missionary campaigns were declared to be campaigns to collect people in God's "granaries"

42 Daneel, 1971(a), p. 386f

(dura raMwari) where they will be safe. Ezekiah's image of the granary represented the partial and provisional nature of God's kingdom in the present order. For those who sought refuge in the granary, Zion City, there would be protection against racial discrimination, disease, sorcery and insecurity. On the other hand he repeatedly pointed out that suffering — for instance the suppression of Zionism — formed part of this life, quoting Hebrews 13: 14: "For we have no lasting city, but we seek the city which is to come." Ezekiah's consistent references to this text gave the kingdom of God a distinctly *futuristic orientation*. His preaching was marked by this orientation to the future, the "not yet" preponderating, so that he introduced a significant counterweight to the Zionist orientation on a salvation that is already achieved.[43]

If the Independent Churches' process of indigenization was no more than an integration into the old culture or a syncretist bridge back to pagandom, one could speak of stagnation in the cyclic concept of time. If the ancestors were still dominant, as some observers maintain, then the dominance of the *Sasa* and *Zamani* (present and distant past) would be clearly in evidence. But the striking thing of the adapted church rites of the Shona prophetic movement is in fact their transformation of the ancient rites through the introduction of a *markedly future-oriented element*. This is evident particularly in the aforementioned consolatory ceremonies *(runyaradzo)* which the Shona Zionists and Apostles introduced as a substitute for the *kugadzira* rite. The attention called to the deceased in the *runyaradzo,* although including the past — inasmuch as examples from the dead person's life are cited to strengthen the spiritual life of the congregation, — contains a very real promise of the immediate and distant future through the ceremony of "conducting" the deceased to heaven. Because of this futuristic element the distant ancestry of the deceased is not relevant. In fact, the breakthrough in the concept of time is illustrated in the *runyaradzo* sermon, which includes warnings against traditional rites and preoccupation with the ancestors. The transformation effected here is not necessarily perfect in every way, but any honest evaluator cannot afford to ignore such positive breakthroughs and their implications for eschatology in the Independent Churches.

43 Daneel, 1980, pp. 112-113

The Dutch missiologist Camps maintained that the Black man's cyclic concept of time — his orientation to the past and constant preoccupation with the ancestors — impedes the Western idea of progress. "What Africans need," he says, "is a new theology of time and of the ancestors so that they can wholeheartedly and from within accept progress."[44] In this regard the Shona Zionists and Apostles are making a *positive contribution*. By answering to the Black man's need to "live with the ancestors" through a rite that recognizes the direct link between the living and the dead, whilst at the same time placing the "living dead" in a new light — their future share in a life hereafter in heaven — new ideas of time and progress are introduced into the very core of their religion. In this way the process of *possession*[45] in the name of Christ crystallizes and the old approach acquires new meaning in the context of the church. This means that the dangers of a realized eschatology and distortion of Christian salvation into present security, wellbeing, health and the like are not necessarily affirmed. What we find are positive impulses helping to effect a balance in the polarity between the eschatological "already" and "not yet".

7.4   ECCLESIOLOGY

7.4.1   Tribal churches?

A variety of factors have contributed to the fact that the ecclesiology of the Independent Churches is somewhat superficial and restricted. The background of *Western denominationalism* created an image of dividedness and Protestant theology probably devoted insufficient attention to the doctrine of the church as the *one* body which transcends all barriers. Poor theological training did nothing to provide a clear historical perspective on the development of the church through the ages. Hence it was natural that the indigenous culture and social structure should have left their mark on the ecclesiology of the Independent Churches.

This background of a life regulated by innumerable taboos and kinship codes resulted in a legalistic approach, so that the

44 Camps, 1971, p. 7
45 Bavinck, 1954, p. 181

church was seen primarily as a new *tribal community* with new codes of conduct. Some church members saw church discipline as a new set of tribal sanctions. According to Martin the "messianic" movements in particular experienced the church as a new tribe or kingdom. As its "chief" or "king" the paramount leader represents the vitality of the tribe. Every blessing that befalls him reflects the vital energy and power of the tribe.[46] At an early stage Sundkler already referred to a growing tendency to turn religious groups into new "ecclesiastic tribes".[47] Oosthuizen too points out the widespread tendency in Africa to interpret the church as a new community functioning in the same way as a *traditional kinship group.*[48] Because of the concomitant ethnicity he arrives at a radical conclusion: "The whole tribe is the Church without any idea of personal decision. Its basis is purely ethnic, i.e. based on blood relationship."[49] If this verdict were to have general validity there could be no question of a Christian ecclesiology among the Zionist and "messianic" churches, and these movements would have degenerated into a modern version of tribal religion.

The traditional concept of time also adds to the poor ecclesiology. Bosch points out that the concentration on the present results in a sort of "de-historicizing" of salvation history. It means that the church is not the "holy apostolic church" of all ages, but simply a realizable actuality in the present, concrete religious community.[50] Thus it follows almost automatically that in terms of this "de-historicized" approach the church will be cast into the mould of the most obvious indigenous societal structures.

In the preceding chapters I have shown how the congregational structure of the Shona churches is based on kinship, the extended family and the rural village system. Even what was said about hereditary leadership and "ecumenical co-operation" between schismatic groups (reflecting the time-honoured solidarity of the *dunhu)* gives credence to the qualification of a "family" or "tribal" church.

46 Martin, 1964, p. 165
47 Sundkler, 1961, pp. 310-323
48 Oosthuizen, 1968(a), p. 82
49 Ibid., p. 84
50 Bosch, 1973(a), p. 79

At the same time this kind of definition is itself *misleading,* especially when it gives rise to such sweeping conclusions as Oosthuizen's, namely that the tribal concept is so dominant that there is no question of individual decisions. Such a verdict leaves out of account the *transformation of the traditional structure* in the context of the Independent Churches. It goes far beyond a mere integration into the former structure. To be sure, individual decision may be temporarily overlooked in some cases, as when a prophet baptizes an entire extended family unit. However, there is so much emphasis on individual conversion and moral choice — as is evident from such practices as the confession of sin — that what emerges is something *totally different* from the traditional corporate sense or tribal order. Even if kinship norms are reflected in the leadership hierarchy of the church, there is also the inversion of the principle of seniority, the new meaning imparted to reciprocal responsibilities, and affiliation to a central authority whose demands differ radically from those of the traditional chief.

Thus one cannot call it simply a return to the old order. The conciliatory integration of the sorcerer or witch into the new community, where such a person could in fact pose a threat, indicates a different approach by this "family", the church group. Even if the structure of the church manifests certain traits in common with tribal organization, for instance in the structuring and procedure of its courts, and even if the membership of some of the smaller groups is concentrated largely in a single tribal area, in experience and aim the difference, the *new identity* of the church group is so striking that one cannot dream of calling it a levelling process. In major movements, such as those of Lekhanyane, Mutendi, Maranke and Kimbangu, restrictive tribal loyalties are so consistently superseded by the expansion of the church across all territorial and national boundaries that one simply cannot speak of a "tribal" church any longer.

We do not deny that the old tribal system conditions and even subtly dominates in certain important areas within the church, but this does not justify unqualified generalizations which assume that adaptation and indigenization imply no more than a simplistic reversion to the old order.

271

7.4.2 *Corporate life*

In many respects the intimate corporate life of the Independent Churches is a corrective to the lack of *koinonia* in the historical churches. By contrast with the sober rationalism of the latter, the former express uninhibited emotional joy. Here the New Testament *agalliasis* (rejoicing, exuberant joy) is in evidence as it was at the feasts of the early church.

As Bosch points out, the need for warmth and fellowship is not only a spontaneous religious need among Africans, but expresses a yearning in the midst of the disruption and confusion of modern Africa. To many Africans joining an Independent Church is a step of desperation in the midst of change and uncertainty, an attempt at retrieving something of their lost security. In the alien environment of the modern city, and in the place of the crumbling extended family, the intimate church community provides a true "place to feel at home."[51] This new community is marked by mutual concern and voluntary service.[52]

The weekly church gatherings when members appear in festive mood in colourful garb, wearing distinctive insignia, aware of recognition and status within the group and all that, are par excellence occasions when the drabness, drudgery and problems of daily life can be forgotten. Here the great Easter conferences play an important part. On this occasion the *koinonia* is expressed in its fullest sense. As was shown in chapter 6, these feasts are a conglomeration of *every* religious activity: preaching, song, dance, prayer meetings, prophecy, confession, planning of church schedules, "court sessions" and so on, with, as the climax, the communion. As in the ZCC of Mutendi, this crescendo of communal experience is an incentive to mission, so that mutual service is turned outward to the world in preaching repentance. The interrelationship between fellowship, communion and missionary activity confronts the historical churches with certain questions that call for urgent attention. In view of the spiritual stagnation, and complacence that obscure fellowship in the historical churches, the example of the Indepenednt Churches presents a challenge to reflect anew on Christian *koinonia* in modern African life.

51 Welbourn & Ogot, **A place to feel at home, 1966**
52 Bosch, 1973(a), p. 76-77

7.4.3 *Liturgy and ritual*

In this sphere the Independent Churches manifest a variety, originality and flexibility that can teach the historical churches much. Their adaptation to the indigenous approach includes dramatic, emotional, repetitive and mobile dancing; a form of religious expression which is consistently spontaneous and hence authentic. As in the traditional cult, the ritual contains certain guidelines, but within this context there is plenty of scope for variation and improvisation. Sermons are based on the inspiration and insight of the moment rather than systematically developed ideas. *Proclamation is lived, danced, acted out with constant interaction between Bible reader, preacher and congregational response.* If necessary a sermon may turn into a debate and if a sermon continues too long, the congregation puts a stop to it. Preaching fluctuates between serious proclamation, sober teaching and sudden cries of joy. It flows into rhythmic dance and song in which everybody joins, then resumes like the waves of a tide when the dancing feet and fluttering robes are stilled.

Sermons are interspersed with prophecy, confession, testimonies to joy or grief, laying on of hands, faith healing and exorcism. Thus the need of the individual is shared and carried by the church. During exorcism the beleaguered soul is tied with sacred cords, and this symbolic act is accompanied by rhythmic song. The demon is then addressed, cursed and expelled by means of numerous symbolic acts. It is all deadly earnest, but if the exorcism should suddenly sound funny, people will laugh spontaneously and delight at the rebuking of the unwelcome spirit — without in any way marring the seriousness of the occasion.

To the Western mind such an indigenous expression of religious activity may appear disorderly. To the African it is the most meaningful response to God's Word.

7.5 *APPROACH OF TRADITIONAL RELIGION*

The basis for a theological evaluation of the Independent Churches' approach to traditional religion can be found in Romans 1: 18f, which in effect says that every facet of non-Christian religion is profoundly influenced by human sin and imperfection.

Hence there is no element that can be singled out as "good" and assimilated directly into the church. Naturally this is not meant as a rejection of anybody's human dignity and the need for mutual respect and dialogue. However, the adaptation of gospel proclamation to traditional views and structures in the process of indigenization is only theologically tenable if it embraces a *christianizing transformation.*

Bavinck's term *possessio* is apt, since the gospel cannot be arbitrarily slotted into heathen customs, but must instead take possesion of and transform them.[53] Personally I prefer to call it an *adapted transformation,* so that the emphasis will be on both the intelligibility of the gospel to the traditional worldview and the on-going christianizing process. The question is, is this process legitimately functioning in the adapted rites we have been discussing? To clarify this point, I shall confine myself to a brief exposition of the consolatory ceremony *(runyaradzo)*, substitute for the crucial traditional rite, the *kugadzira.*

7.5.1 *Mediatorship*

Recriprocal mediation as in the traditional cult is counter to Scripture, which says that there is but one Mediator, Jesus Christ (Ac 4: 12), and that it is only through faith in him that the sinner is saved (Heb 10: 19-22). If one accepts this, one must be critical of the measure of reciprocal mediation which still occurs in the *runyaradzo* ceremony, but in the process one must remember that the Zionists and Apostles do not see the church's task of "conducting" the deceased in any absolute light, as if Christ's mediatorship is bypassed and the dead person's place in heaven is assured. It is a positive transcending of the magical approach of the *kugadzira,* where the spirit is manipulated. The faithful departed's life *in Christ* and God's final judgment will decide his position in heaven. This is usually expressed in the sermon. Although the "conducting to heaven" is in fact a prophetic substitute for the traditional initiation of the spirit into the ancestral hierarchy, it has acquired a new meaning. Instead of automatic integration, "prophetic mediation" is mainly a projection of the

53 Bavinck, 1954, p. 181

274

church's responsibility onto the unknown realm where the deceased member is as it were introduced to God, just as an ordinary person has to be presented to an eminent personage. Hence this function is much the same as that which the "messianic" paramount leader is supposed to fulfil at the gates of heaven.

Similarly, the mediation of the departed believer does not assure the surviving members of the church of a place in heaven. God's judgment and their commitment to him remain the deciding factors. The typical case is not that of a rigidly circumscribed "task" of the deceased, but rather the very human hope of some form of reunion hereafter. Another point is that the involvement of the congregation transcends the more restricted loyalty between the deceased and the family. Hence the communion between the dead and the living now consolidates the church and not (merely) the kinship group.

The danger that Christ's mediatorship will be usurped is not imaginary. These adapted rites can nurture a dependence on the "Christian ancestors", which in actual fact will interfere with rather than strengthen fellowship with God (Ps 23: 4; 73: 28; Jn 14: 23; Hebr 13: 5).[54] Nonetheless the *runyaradzo* contains a very real possibility of completely transforming the traditional affiliation with and dependence on ancestral spirits.

7.5.2 Communication between the living and the dead

In his description of the "primal vision" J.V. Taylor suggests that the communication link between the living and the dead should be prayer:

> Surely the 'tender bridge' that joins the living and the dead in Christ is prayer ... To ask for the prayers of others in this life, and to know that they rely on mine, does not show any lack of faith in the all-sufficiency of God. Then in the same faith let me ask for their prayers still, and offer mine for them, even when death has divided us ... If death is what Christians believe it to be, direct address to the deceased should be natural and confident.[55]

54 Van der Merwe, 1967, p. 206
55 Taylor, 1963, p. 163

To some extent the approach of the Shona Zionists and Apostles is in agreement with Taylor's idea. Prayer to God on behalf of the dead and the expectation that the latter will act as intercessors form part of their religious activities, yet there is a significant difference: the Spirit-type churches shun direct communication with the dead. Because the prophetic leaders reject *kupira midzimu* (ancestor worship) as a sort of idolatry, they cannot possibly envisage communication with the dead as something natural, as Taylor suggests. This presupposes some sort of prayer that will be acceptable to them as Christians. At all events their approach is compatible with Scripture, which prohibits direct communication with the spirit world (Dt 18: 11). In this respect their approach is theologically even more acceptable than that of the Roman Catholic Church, which, in similar adapted rites among the Shona, include a direct addressing of various categories of ancestors.[56]

The distinction between heathen and Christian ancestors is also more definite in Zionist than in Catholic rites. The prophetic classification of heathen ancestors as demons indicate that the Zionists and Apostles are not prepared to equate the activities of these spirits with the work of Christ. Roman Catholic accommodation, which fails to uphold this distinction, exposes church members to (a) confusion about addressing the traditional *midzimu,* and (b) an incomplete view of God's judgment, which could give rise to the impression that all people will be admitted to the new community of God's kingdom.

Among the Shona both the Dutch Reformed and Ethiopian-type churches officially reject communication with the ancestors, but in practice inadequate confrontation with this cult — either by ignoring or covertly permitting it — results in continued participation in these rites by church members. Counter to orthodox scriptural doctrine, there is a syncretistic combination of the new and old in the lives of individual people.

7.5.3 *Commemoration*

The *runyaradzo* replaces *communication with* the deceased by a *discussion of* the departed. This modification is one of the most

56 Daneel, 1973, p. 60.

significant facets of transformation, since it strips the traditional rite of its *kupira* (veneration, worship) connotation and gives it the character of a positive commemoration of the deceased. Sermons at the *runyaradzo* usually contain countless references to the role the deceased had played in the church, his service to the community, exemplary traits and the like. In this way the traditional "living with the ancestors" is given a Christian focus, namely an awareness of and inspiration from the "cloud of witnesses" (Heb. 12: 1). The example is used to give the Christian fresh inspiration for his chosen way of life.

We have already mentioned the future-oriented element in the *runyaradzo,* an abrogation of the *sasa-zamani* (present and distant past) temporal concept. By concentrating on the immediate past and not on the whole hierarchy of ancestors stretching into the "distant past", *runyaradzo* proclamation escapes the quicksands of the *zamani.* Here the Spirit-type churches are more successful than the Roman Catholic Church, which overloads the church rite with traditional connotations by including virtually all ancestors. By contrast the prophetic leaders' conscious rejection of the *kugadzira* is an attempt of getting away from the focus on the *zamani.* The heavenly community towards which the deceased is "conducted" already exists, but must still be realized in the future. Hope of salvation and possible reunion with co-religionists in heaven reveal an eschatological prospect quite foreign to the traditional approach. Besides, this is not just an amorphous hope, for the summons to live according to the example of the dead person concerned and other deceased believers implies active participation in the work of the church planned for the future.

There is no doubt that all this holds out fascinating possibilities for scholars working on or thinking about a *theologia Africana.* An adapted liturgy could very well incorporate commemoration ceremonies, and elements of commemoration could be introduced into the sacrament. In this way the communion between the living and departed faithful could be embodied commemorating the "cloud of witnesses", the preaching could focus on the relationship between Christ and the departed, thus highlighting the significance of the *decensio Christi.* Both Taylor and Sundkler stress the significance of Christ's descent into death as a concept of reconciliation in the African church. Taylor maintains that Christ presents himself to Africans as "the Deliverer and Life-giver in the realm of the shades".[57] Sundkler quotes a Zulu student as summarizing the character of the good news as "forgiveness by Christ alone who died for all and went to the dead to show himself to the living ones".[58]

Note that the *runyaradzo* sermons of the prophetic churches do not take the *decensio Christi* as a basis for assertions about non-Christian forebears. Probably they believe that the recognition of Christ's kingship over the entire realm of death and his special attention to the living dead in heaven should be sufficient comfort for those who have problems about their heathen ancestors.

A theological evaluation of the Independent Churches' approach to the traditional cult should also take note of various other rites, such as the replacement of the Supreme Being cult, rain-making rites, exorcism of evil spirits and the role of fetishism and sorcery. However, all this cannot be accommodated in this study. I shall therefore conclude with two quotations from Bosch to give some indication of the theological problems concerning magic and witchcraft. With reference to the discarding of amulets and other fetishes at the insistence of church leaders, he writes:

> The question is whether in many cases one kind of magic is not merely exchanged for another. Do Christ, or the prophet, and all that pertains to him, not become new fetishes? This is probably one of the greatest questions confronting the church in Africa.[59]

Bosch also mentions the tendency to localize evil in the sorcerer and the implications this has for people's concept of sin:

> In regarding the combating of the evil sorcerer as one of their major tasks, the Independent Churches in fact do not deviate too much from the traditional faith. Here the great

57 Taylor, 1963, p. 165
58 Sundkler, 1962, p. 290
59 Bosch, 1973(a), p. 80; with reference to Haule, 1969

danger is that sin will be substantiated in the other person and not sought within one's own heart. Such an approach leaves no scope for repentance. Sin is never what one has done oneself, but rather what someone else (the sorcerer) has done to one.[60]

These problems must be faced. Among the Shona prophetic churches, however, it is a very promising phenomenon that the combating of witchcraft is in fact counterbalanced by a strong emphasis on individual confession of sin. They deal with both the besetting danger of *uroyi* which comes from without, and personal guilt which arises from within.

This chapter has demonstrated only too clearly that a theological evaluation of the Independent Churches is not a straightforward matter. Virtually every statement on any point demands a number of additional qualifications. My emphasis has been mainly on the Shona Independent Churches and it was not always possible to pursue the argument in respect of other African countries. Still, I suspect that continued research and reflection will show that the positive Christian elements which I have pointed out in the Shona churches will have their parallels elsewhere in Africa. The predominantly positive trends that can be discerned already, plus those that are still evolving, will probably lead to far wider recognition of the Independent movements by the Christian churches. This process is already under way, partly through growing interest in this phenomenon by means of research and increasing ecumenical contact.

As for relations between the historical and the Independent Churches, there is every reason to engage in dialogue, to reflect theologically on possibilities of co-operation, to become mutually involved in the theological training which the Independent Churches are increasingly requesting. This will result in more effective service and more profound *koinonia* in the life of the church. This does not mean that we are advocating a levelling of theologically questionable points. After all, we are speaking of Christian churches which, like every other church in this world

60 Bosch, 1973(a), p. 81

of ours, have their weaknesses on account of human corruption. But one point is certain, and that is that in the process of ecumenical co-operation the historical and Independent Churches can render service to one another. Because the church remains the "pillar of truth" the mission church with its historically based ecclesiology and insight into heresy can minister to the problem of truth among the Independent Churches. Conversely the prophetic leaders with their untrammelled enthusiasm can contribute to a new missionary vision and impetus in an often slow-moving church. But especially in the field of pastoral care the prophetic faith healers can make a very special contribution because they always occupy themselves with bringing the gospel message into the traditional spiritual and conceptual world. Even if this is not done consistently and systematically — a requirement which Western or Westernised White and Black theologians are inclined to set — and even if it is at the level of intuition and intuitive experience, its great value for the evolution of an authentic African theology is unquestionable and must be respected accordingly.

BIBLIOGRAPHY

Andersson, E. Messianic popular movements in the lower Congo. Studia Ethnographica Upsaliensis, XVI. London: 1958.

Aquina, M. Zionists in Rhodesia, in Africa, xxxix, 1969.

Baeta, C.G. Prophetism in Ghana. A study of some Spiritual Churches. London: 1962.

Balandier, G. Sociologie actuelle de l'Afrique noire. Paris: 1955

Barrett, D.B. Schism and renewal in Africa — an analysis of six thousand contemporary religious movements. London: 1968.

Barrett, D.B. Ad 2000:350 million Christians in Africa, in International Review of Missions, Jan. 1970.

Becken, Hans-Juergen. Theologie der Heilung — Das Heilen in den Afrikanischen Unabhaengigen Kirchen in Suedafrika. Hermannsburg: 1972.

Berglund, Axel Ivar. Church and culture change in a Zulu tribal community, in Bosch, D.J. Church and culture change in Africa (Lux Mundi 3). Pretoria: 1971.

Beyerhaus, P. Begegnungen mit messianischen Bewegungen in Afrika, in Zeitschrift fuer Theologie und Kirche, vol 64, 1967.

Beyerhaus, P. An approach to the African independent church movement, in Ministry, vol. 9, 1969.

Bosch, D.J. Onafhanklike kerklike bewegings. Studiegids: Sending en Godsdienswetenskap, BD III. Pretoria: UNISA, 1973(a).

Bosch, D.J. God in Africa — implications for the kerygma, in Missionalia 1(1), 1973 (b).

Buehlmann, P.W. Die christliche Terminologie als missionsmethodisches Problem. Schoneck-Beckenried, 1950.

Camps, A. Religion and change: some missiological implications, in Bulletin, Secretariatus pro non-Christianis 16, 1971.

Damman, E. Das Christusverstaendnis in den nachchristlichen Kirchen und Sekten Afrikas, in Benz, E. Messianische Kirche. Sekten und Bewegungen im heutigen Afrika. Leiden: 1965.

Daneel, M.L. The God of the Matopo hills — an essay on the Mwari cult in Rhodesia. The Hague: 1970 (a).

Daneel, M.L. Zionism and faith-healing in Rhodesia. The Hague: 1970(b).

Daneel, M.L. Old and New in Southern Shona Independent Churches, vol 1: Background and rise of the major movements. The Hague: 1971 (a). Vol. 2: Church growth — causative factors and recruitment techniques. The Hague: 1974.

Daneel, M.L. Shona Independent Churches and ancestor worship, in Barrett, D.B. (ed.) African initiatives in religion. Nairobi. 1971 (b).

Daneel, M.L. The Christian Gospel and the ancestor cult, in Missionalia, vol. 1, no. 2, 1973.

Daneel, M.L. Shona Independent Churches in a rural society, in Dachs, A.J. (ed.) **Christianity south of the Zambezi,** vol. I. Gwelo: 1975.

Daneel, M.L. The missionary outreach of African Independent Churches, in **Missionalia,** vol. 8, no. 3, 1980.

Daneel, M.L. Swart "Messianisme" — Verwording of kontekstualisasie. Intreerede, UNISA, 1982(a).

Daneel, M.L. Fission dynamics in African Independent Churches, in Vorster, W.S. **Denominatianalism. Its sources and implications.** Pretoria, UNISA, 1982 (b).

Hastings, A. **Mission and ministry.** London: 1971.

Haule, Cosmas. **Bantu "witchcraft" and Christian morality. The encounter of Bantu uchawi with Christian morality.** Schoneck — Beckenried. 1969.

Hess, M.M. Political systems and African church polity, in **Practical Anthropology,** iv (5), 1957.

Knoob, W. **Afrikanisch — christliche Bewegungen unter den Bantu. Koeln, 1961.**

Kuper, H. The Swazi reaction to missions, in **African Studies,** (v) 3, 1946.

Martin, Marie-Louise. **The biblical concept of messianism and messianism in Southern Africa.** Morija: 1964.

Martin, Marie-Louise. Prophetism, in the Congo — origin and development of an African Independent Church, in **Ministry: Theological Review for Africa,** vol. 8, no. 4. 1968.

Martin, Marie-Louise. **Kirche ohne Weisse.** Basel, 1971.

Martin, Marie-Louise. **Kimbangu — an African prophet and his church.** Oxford: 1975.

Mbiti, J.S. **African religions and philosophy.** London: 1969.

Moller, H.J. **Stedelike Bantoe en die kerk,** Deel 1-5. Pretoria: 1972-4.

Murphree, M.W. **Christianity and the Shona,** in Monographic Series on Social Anthropology, no. 36. London: 1964.

Ndiokwere, N.I. **Prophecy and revolution — the role of prophets in the African Independent Churches and in biblical tradition.** London: 1981.

Nida, E.A. New religions for old, in Bosch, D.J. (ed.) **Church and culture change in Africa** (Lux Mundi 3) Pretoria: 1971.

Oosthuizen, G.C. **Post-Christianity in Africa — A theological and anthropological study.** London, 1968 (a).

Oosthuizen G.C. Die konfrontasie met die onafhanklike kerklike bewegings ("separatiste") in Afrika in die jongste sendingteologie, in **Sendingwetenskap vandag — in terreinverkenning** (Lux Mandi 1). Pretoria: 1968 (b).

Pauw, B.A. **Religion in a Tswana chiefdom.** London: 1960.

Pretorius, H.L. **Kosmologie en Separatisme.** University of Pretoria, D.D. Thesis, 1972.

Religion in Africa, International African Seminar, Edinburgh, 1964.

Sundkler, B.G.M. Bantu prophets in South Africa. London: 1961.

Sundkler, B.G.M. The Christian ministry in Africa. London: 1962.

Sundkler, B.G.M. Zulu Zion and some Swazi Zionists. London: 1976.

Taylor, J.V. The primal vision — Christian presence amid African religion. London: 1963.

Turner, H.W. African Independent Church, Vol. 1: The Church of the Lord (Aladura). Oxford: 1967(a). Vol. 2: The life and faith of the Church of the Lord (Aladura). Oxford: 1967(b).

Turner, H.W. A typology for African religious movements, in Journal of Religion in Africa, (1)1, 1967(c).

Turner, H.W. African religious movements and Roman Catholicism, in Greschat, H.J. & Jungraithmayr, H. Wort und Religion: Kalini na Dini. Stuttgart: 1969.

Van der Merwe, W.J. Gesante om Christus wil. Kaapstad: 1967.

Welbourn, F.B. & Ogot, B.A. A place to feel at home. London: 1966.

West, M. Bishops and prophets in a Black city — African independent Churches in Soweto, Johannesburg. Cape Town: 1975.

Wishlade, R.L. Sectarianism in Southern Nyasaland. London: 1965.

APPENDIX

List of Publications on African Independent Churches

I General orientation

Barrett, D.B. Schism and renewal in Africa — An analysis of six thousand contemporary religious movements, Nairobi: Oxford University Press, 1968.

Barrett, D.B. (ed.) African initiative in religion. Nairobi East African Publishing House, 1971.

Hayward, V.E.W. (ed.) African Independent Church movements, IMC Research Pamphlet no. 11 London: Edinburgh House Press, 1963.

Oosterwal, G. Modern Messianic movements. Elkhart: Institute of Mennonite Studies, 1973.

II Regional studies

South Africa

Becken, H.J. Theologie der Heilung. Das Heilen in den afrikanischen unabhaengigen Kirchen in Suedafrika. Hermansburg: Missionsanstalt, 1972.

Becken, H.J. The African Independent Churches' understanding of the ministry, in Bosch, D.J. Ampsbediening in Afrika. Pretoria: N.G. Boekhandel, 1972 (Lux Mundi, 5).

Beyerhaus, P. An approach to the African Independent Church Movement, in Ministry, vol. 9, 1969.

Beyerhaus, P. Begegnungen mit messianischen Bewegungen. Zur Kennzeichnung der Missionswissenschaft als theologischer Disziplin in Zeitschrift fuer Theologie und Kirche, vol. 64, 1967

Dubb, A.A. The role of the church in an urban African society. Unpublished M.A. thesis, Rhodes University, Grahamstown 1962.

Dubb, A.A. Community of the saved — An African revivalist church in the East Cape. Johannesburg: Wits University Press, 1976.

Gerdener, G.B.A. Recent developments in the South African mission field, Part 2, Ch. 4: The trends of separatism and independence. Pretoria: N.G. Kerk-uitgewers, 1958.

Kamphausen, E. Anfaenge der kirchlichen Unabhaengigkeitsbewegung in Suedafrika. Geschichte und Theologie der Aethiopischen Bewegung 1872-1912. Bern: Herbert Lang, 1976.

Kiernan, J.P. The changing role of (Independent) African churches with particular reference to South Africa. Unpublished M.A. thesis, Manchester, 1967.

Kiernan, J.P. Where Zionists draw the line: A study of religious exclusiveness in an African township in African Studies, 33:2, 1974.

Kuper, H. The Swazi reaction to mission, in African Studies, 5:3, 1946.

Martin, M.-L. The church facing prophetic and Messianic movements, in Ministry, vol. 3, 1963.

Martin, M.-L. The biblical concept of Messianism and Messianism in Southern Africa. Morija, 1964.

Missiological Institute. Our approach to the Independent Church Movement in South Africa. Mapumulo: Lutheran Theological College, 1965.

Oosthuizen, G.C. Post- Christianity in Africa — A theological and anthropological study. London: 1968.

Pauw, B.A. Religion in a Tswana chiefdom. London: Oxford University Press, 1960.

Pauw, B.A. Christianity and Xhosa tradition. Cape Town. Oxford University Press, 1975.

Schlosser, K. Eingeborenenkirchen in Sued und Suedwest Afrika. Ihre Geschichte und Sozialstruktur. Kiel: Muehlau, 1958.

Sundermeier, T. Wir aber suchten Gemeinschaft. Kirchwerdung und Kirchtrennung in Suedwestafrika. Erlangen: Verlag der Ev. Luth. Mission, 1973.

Sundkler, B.G.M. Bantu Messiah and White Christ, in Frontier, I. 1960.

Sundkler, B.G.M. The concept of Christianity in the African Independent Churches, in African Studies, 20:4, 1961.

Sundkler, B.G.M. Bantu prophets in South Africa, 2nd edition. London: Oxford University Press, 1961.

Sundkler, B.G.M. Zulu Zion and some Swazi Zionists. Lund: Gleerup, 1976.

West, M.E. Bishops and prophets in a Black city — African Independent Churches in Soweto Johannesburg. Cape Town: David Phillip, 1975.

West, M.E. The shades come to town: Ancestors and urban Independent Churches, in Whisson, M.G. & West, M.E. (eds.) Religion and social change in Southern Africa — Anthropological essays in honour of Monica Wilson. Cape Town, 1975.

Sundkler's publications remain among the most significant for an introductory general study of the Independent Churches in South Africa. His research and interpretation of new perspectives over a period of some thirty years reflect the dynamically changing nature of these churches. Thus his recent Zulu Zion gives a far more flexible and positive evaluation of syncretist deviations in Zionism and the so-called messianic leadership of some prophets than does his Bantu Prophets.

Whereas Pauw's publications on the Tswana and the Xhosa are products of prolonged fieldwork and therefore comprise a thorough anthropological interpretation of the empirical data, the studies by Beyerhaus, Martin and Oosthuizen concentrate on theological evaluation of these movements and are therefore based rather on incidental, sporadic observation of religious activity and secondary literary sources. Oosthuizen and Beyerhaus in particular, in their theological evaluation of the Zionist and so-called messianic movements, are so categorical and cursory that they refuse to accept these groups as Christian churches.

By contrast with the bulk of these studies, which concentrate on the Independent Churches as a rural phenomenon, those of Dubb, Kiernan and West are valuable for their focus on these churches in urban areas.

Zimbabwe

Aquina, Sr M. Christianity in a Rhodesian tribal trust land, in **African Social Research**, I. 1966.

Aquina, Sr M. People of the Spirit: An Independent Church in Rhodesia, in **Africa**, 37:2, 1967.

Aquina, Sr M. Zionists in Rhodesia, in **Africa**, 39:2, 1969.

Daneel, M.L. **Zionism and faith-healing in Rhodesia**. The Hague: Mouton, 1970.

Daneel, M.L. **Old and new in Southern Shona Independent Churches; vol. I: Background and rise of the major movements**. The Hague: Mouton, 1971. Vol. II: **Church Growth: Causative Factors and recruitment techniques**. The Hague: Mouton, 1974.

Daneel, M.L. Shona Indpendent Churches and ancestor worship, in Barrett, D. (ed.) **African initiatives in religion**. Nairobi: East African Publishing House, 1971.

Daneel, M.L. The Christian Gospel and the Ancestor cult, in **Missionalia**, vol. I no. 2, 1973.

Daneel, M.L. Shona Independent Churches in a rural society, in Dachs, A.J. (ed.) **Christianity south of the Zambezi**, vol. I. Gwelo: Mambo Press, 1975.

Daneel, M.L. The growth and significance of Shona Independent Churches, in Bourdillon, M.F.C. (ed.) **Christianity South of the Zambezi**, vol. II. Gwelo: Mambo Press, 1977.

Daneel, M.L. Independent church leadership south of the Zambezi, in **African Perspectives: Religious Innovation in Modern African Society**. Leiden: Africa Study Centre, 1976/2.

Daneel, M.L. The missionary outreach of African Independent Churches, in **Missionalia**, vol. 8, no. 3, 1980.

Jules-Rosette, B. **African apostles. Ritual and conversion in the church of John Marange**. Ithaca, N.Y.: Cornell University Press, 1975.

Murphree, M. **Christianity and the Shona** (L.S.E. Monographs in Soc. Authrop. No. 36) London, 1969.

The bibliography on Shona Independent Churches is extensive because I am personally familiar with them and will be using them as a focal point for many illustrative examples in this study.

Zambia

Rotberg, R. The Lenshina Movement of Northern Rhodesia, in **The Rhodes-Livingstone Journal**, 29, 1961.
Taylor, J.V. & Lehmann, D.A. **Christians of the Copperbelt**. London: SCM Press, 1961.

Malawi

Shepperson, G. & Price, T. **Independent Africa: John Chilembwe and the origin, setting and significance of the Nyasaland Native rising of 1915**. Edinburgh University Press, 1958.
Wishlade, R. **Sectarianism in Southern Nyasaland**. London: 1965.

Zaire

Andersson, E. **Messianic popular movements in the Lower Congo**. London: Kegan Paul 1958.
Balandier, G. Messianismes et nationalismes en Afrique Noire, in **Cahiers Internationaux de sociologie**, Paris, 1953.
Balandier, G. Mouvements contraires, in **Afrique Ambigue**, Plon, Paris, 1957.
Fehderau, H.W. Prophetic Christianity in the Congo, in **Practical Anthropology**, 9, 1962.
Martin, M.-L. **Kimbangu. An African prophet and his church**, Oxford: Blackwell, 1975.

One is struck by the fact that Martin's interpretation and evaluation of the Kimbangu movement, written after many years of involvement with this church, is far more positive than the sharply critical approach of her earlier **The biblical concept of Messianism**... (see above) to what is known as "Messianism" in Africa. As in the case of Sundkler, here is another indication that continued study of empirical realities and identification with members of these churches result in greater respect and more cautious theological evaluation.

East Africa

Welbourn, F.B. **East African rebels** London: 1961.
Welbourn, F.B. & Ogot, B.A. **A place to feel at home**. London: 1966.

West Africa

Baeta, C.G. **Prophetism in Ghana: A study of some "Spiritual" churches** London: SCM Press, 1962.

Idowu, E.B. Selfhood of the church in Africa, in **International Review of Missions**, October 1964.

Parrinder, E.G. **Religion in an African City**. London: Oxford University Press, 1953.

Parrinder, E.G. Indigenous churches in Nigeria, in **West African Review**, xxxi, September 1960.

Peel, J.D.Y. **Aladura: A religious movement among the Yoruba**. Oxford: 1968.

Turner, H.W. **Profile through preaching. A study of sermon texts used in a West African Independent Church**, Research Pamphlet 13. London: 1965.

Turner, H.W. **African Independent Church, vol. I: History of an African Independent Church, the church of the Lord (Aladura). Vol. II: The life and faith of the church of the Lord (Aladura)**. Oxford: Clarendon Press, 1967.

Turner, H.W. **Religious innovation in Africa**. London: Oxford University Press. 1979.

Turner's study of the Aladura church is one of the most thorough and, in its theological interpretation, most balanced monographs in this field.

III Studies aimed at methodology, typology and comparative research

Guariglia, G. **Prophetismus und Heilserwartungsbewegungen als volkerkundliches und religionsgeschichtliches Problem**. Wenen: Berger, 1959.

Koebben, R.J.F. Prophetic movements as an expression of social protest, in International Archives of Ethnography, 49, 1, 1960.

Lanternari, V. **The religions of the oppressed — A study of modern Messianic cults**. London: Macgibbon & Kee, 1963.

Linton, R. Nativistic movements, in **American Anthropologist**, XLV, 1943.

Mair, L. Independent religious movements in three continents in **Comparative Studies in Society and History I**, 1959.

Turner, H.W.A. Typology for African religious movements, in **Journal of Religion in Africa, I**, 1968.

Turner, H.W. The place of independent religious movements in the modernization of Africa, in **Journal of Religion in Africa, 2**, 1969.

ibution of land; Location of Mission Stations and
eyed Independent Church Headquarters (before 1980).

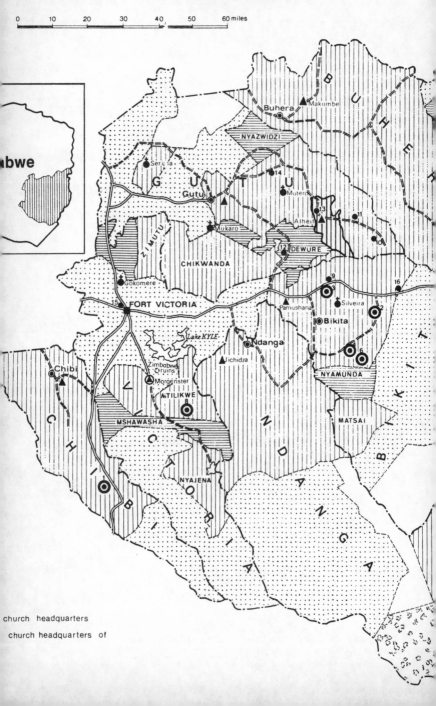

church headquarters

church headquarters of

INDEXES

1. Author Index

2. Index of Churches and Church Associations

Postori, Apostles, 39, 56, 99, 109, 114-5, 119, 130, 146, 151, 153, 158, 161-2, 164, 167, 175, 178, 189, 192, 204, 207, 225

Presbyterian Church, 50, 216-7

Reformed Independent Churches Association (RICA), 33, 210

Rhodesia Christian Conference, 33, 212

Rhodesia Christian Council; see Zimbabwe Christian Council

Roman Catholic Church; also RC Missions and Catholicism, 61-3, 82-3, 86, 88-99, 107, 112, 169, 190, 192, 237, 249, 276-7

Ruwadzano (Women's Association), 147, 154, 218, 244

Seventh Day Adventists, 85

Shaka Zulu Church, 50

Shinga Postora (Courageous Apostles), 205, 206, 208

Shonganiso (African Reformed Church), 52, 103, 114-5, 140, 153, 159, 162, 167-8, 176, 217, 219, 223

Spirit-type Churches, 21, 39-42, 48, 53, 56, 59, 80, 99, 102, 110, 119, 121, 129, 132, 144, 146, 148, 150, 153, 158, 210, 217-8, 221, 227, 229, 240, 276-7

St. John's Apostolic Faith Church, 59

Tembu National Church, 48, 50

Topia (FEC), 53, 147, 153, 161-2, 176

Turban Cult, 37

United National Church of Africa, 209

Watch Tower, 128

World Council of Churches, 53, 244

Zimbabwe Christian Council, 33, 212

Zion Apostolic Church, 54, 151, 172, 198, 200, 212

Zion Apostolic Church of Jesus Christ, 55, 199

Zion Apostolic Church of South Africa, 54-5

Zion Apostolic Faith Mission (ZAFM), 55, 127, 151, 159

Zion Protestant Church, 55, 198

Zion Sabbath Church, 55, 147, 198, 203-4, 206-8, 258

Zion Christian Church (ZCC), 34, 40, 44-6, 55-6, 59, 82-3, 114-5, 122-3, 141, 146, 150-1, 153-6, 161, 165-7, 172, 175-80, 183-6, 189-90, 226, 258, 265, 267

Zionists/Zionism; see also **Ndaza** Zionists, 34, 39-40, 54-6, 98, 103 108-11, 114-5, 118-9, 121-2, 127, 129, 135, 139, 143, 149, 158, 161 -2, 168-9, 180, 184-5, 189-90, 193, 202-3, 209-11, 231, 233, 235-6, 239, 241, 246, 249, 261-3, 267-9, 274, 276

Zulu Congregational Church, 52

3. Index of Church Leaders, Names and Places

215, 220, 227, 244, 246, 248, 257, 271

296

Rhodesia, Northern, 128

Rozvi, 52, 55, 122, 124, 126, 267

Rozvi dynasty/monarchy, 55, 122, 141, 267

Rufura, 130

Ruwana, Moses, ACC minister, 52

Rwanda, 73

Sao Salvador, 46-7

Selly Oaks, 34

Sengwayo, President ACC, 52, 98, 116, 122, 159, 162, 173, 178

Sharara, Willi, Zionist Bishop, 172, 200

Shembe, Isaiah, founder Nazarene Baptist Church, 59-60, 102, 127-8, 138, 180-4, 187-8, 215, 225, 246, 257, 264-5

Shembe, John Galilee, 264

Shoko, Andreas, Bishop ZAFM, 55, 127, 151, 159

Sibambo, ARC minister, 52, 168

Simon Mushati, 57-9, 142, 170, 172, 200

Sithole, Ndabaningi, 130

Sotho, 51

South Africa, 19, 25, 28, 33, 36, 38, 40, 43, 44-5, 47-50, 52-5, 59, 73, 81, 83-4, 98, 102-3, 118, 127-8, 163, 165, 173, 177, 180, 182, 209, 211, 215 225

South West Africa, 36, 48

Soweto, 133-4, 136-7, 142-3, 249

Swaziland, 69

Tambaram, 28

Tanzania, 73

Taung district, 88

Tanzania, 73

Third World, 29

Tile, Nehemiah, 48-50

Torera, Apostolic healer, 171

Transkei, 48

Transvaal, 48, 51, 55, 58

Triangle district, 179

Tswana, 87-8, 232

Tuebingen, 182

Uganda, 86

Umtali (Mutare), 54, 56, 59, 98, 103, 119, 132

uMvelingqangi (Zulu deity), 183

Van Loggerenberg, N., 210

4. Index of Themes

301

302

sacrament(s), 31, 57, 66, 72, 100, 143, 176, 222, 225-9, 243, 250, 253-4, 263

sacrifice, 145-7, 179, 184, 232, 239

salvation, 22, 26, 38, 40, 48, 64, 71, 77-8, 181-2, 189, 192, 221-2, 224-6, 242, 247, 252, 264-6, 269-70, 277

sanctity/sanctification, 48, 108, 110, 144, 221, 228

sasa (the present); see time-concept, 264, 268, 277

satan/satanic powers, 240

Saviour, 77, 183, 185, 188, 194, 219, 251, 259, 263

schools, 21, 51, 53, 56, 62, 64, 78, 84, 99, 104, 106, 111-6, 147, 162, 244, 267

school-leaving, 21, 113

schisms, 20, 29, 44, 48-9, 52-4, 58, 72-7, 82-4, 87-9, 92, 97-8, 106, 138, 153-5, 170, 172-3, 177, 195-203, 206-8, 212-3, 215, 270

Scripture(s): scriptural truth, 26, 31, 161, 249, 251; instruction in, 116, 162; interpretation of, 68, 72, 74-5, 84-6, 90, 111, 148, 180, 183-4, 250-2, 260-1, 274, 276

secession, 87-9, 138, 151, 175, 177

secretary, 151-2

sects/sectarian developments, 17, 30, 33, 88, 182, 245, 246

secularism, 79-80, 265, 267

sekuru (maternal uncle), 156

separatists/separatism, 17, 27-8, 30, 69-70, 75, 92, 98, 166, 174, 177, 209

sermons, see: preaching

sin, 78, 92, 146, 149, 193, 206, 221-2, 224, 227-8, 235, 251, 256, 271, 273, 279

singing/song(s), 63, 78, 105, 131, 165, 206, 219, 224, 226, 229, 272-3

social/sociological factors, 18, 35, 70, 73, 79, 106, 134-5, 241, 249-50, 264; socio-economic factors, 20, 68; socio-political factors, 21, 29-30, 39, 69, 195, 207

sorcery, see witchcraft

speaking-in-tongues, 39, 58, 141, 156, 158-9, 168, 221, 229, 262

Spirit: of God, 37, 40, 57, 100, 110, 126, 135, 147, 158, 220, 224, 226; Spirit inspiration, 72, 158, 263

spirit-world, 95-6, 135, 161, 234-6, 238-40, 249, 261, 274, 276

spirit medium, 94, 124, 146

spirit possession, 46, 121, 133, 226, 232, 247, 261

spirituality/spiritual leadership, renewal, care, power, etc: of ICs, 25,

308